First World War
and Army of Occupation
War Diary
France, Belgium and Germany

14 DIVISION
41 Infantry Brigade
Rifle Brigade (The Prince Consort's Own)
7th Battalion
20 May 1915 - 31 May 1918

WO95/1896/1

The Naval & Military Press Ltd
www.nmarchive.com
Published in association with The National Archives

Published by

The Naval & Military Press Ltd

Unit 10 Ridgewood Industrial Park,

Uckfield, East Sussex,

TN22 5QE England

Tel: +44 (0) 1825 749494

www.naval-military-press.com

www.nmarchive.com

This diary has been reprinted in facsimile from the original. Any imperfections are inevitably reproduced and the quality may fall short of modern type and cartographic standards.

© Crown Copyright
Images reproduced by permission of The National Archives, London, England, 2015.

Contents

Document type	Place/Title	Date From	Date To
Heading	1896/1		
Heading	14th Division 41st Infy. Bde. 7th Bn Rifle Bde May 1915- May 1918		
Heading	War Diary Of 7th Bn Rifle Brigade 14th Division From 20/5/15 To 31/5/15 (Volume I)		
War Diary	Boulogne	20/05/1915	20/05/1915
War Diary	Millain	21/05/1915	26/05/1915
War Diary	Zootpeene	26/05/1915	27/05/1915
War Diary	Fletre	27/05/1915	28/05/1915
War Diary	Dranoutre	28/05/1915	31/05/1915
Heading	14th Division 7th Rifle Brigade Vol. II 1-30.6.15		
War Diary	Dranoutre	01/06/1915	06/06/1915
War Diary	La Clytte (Rozenhill Muts)	06/06/1915	06/06/1915
War Diary	La Clytte (Rozenhill Muts) M. 6. A.	07/06/1915	07/06/1915
War Diary	Pioneer Fm H. 33. D.	08/06/1915	10/06/1915
War Diary	Brasserie S.E. Corner Of N. 5 B.	11/06/1915	13/06/1915
War Diary	Rozenhill	14/06/1915	14/06/1915
War Diary	Poperinghe	14/06/1915	15/06/1915
War Diary	Vlamertinghe	15/06/1915	16/06/1915
War Diary	Ypres I. 13. C.	17/06/1915	18/06/1915
War Diary	Vlamertinghe	18/06/1915	20/06/1915
War Diary	Vlamertinghe H.9.a.	21/06/1915	29/06/1915
War Diary	Hooge	30/06/1915	30/06/1915
Heading	14th Division 7th Rifle Brigade Vol. IV From 1-31.8.15		
War Diary	Near Hazebrouck	01/08/1915	02/08/1915
War Diary	Near Hazebrouck (G.5.d.)	02/08/1915	10/08/1915
War Diary	Watteau	11/08/1915	13/08/1915
War Diary	Potijze	13/08/1915	24/08/1915
War Diary	N. Ypres	25/08/1915	31/08/1915
Heading	14th Division 7th Rifle Brigade Vol 5 Sept. 15		
War Diary	Trenches S. Of Potijze	01/09/1915	13/09/1915
War Diary	Poperinghe 1 Mile East Of	14/09/1915	25/09/1915
War Diary	Vlamertinghe Huts West of	26/09/1915	28/09/1915
War Diary	Railway Wood	28/09/1915	30/09/1915
Heading	14th Division 7th Rifle Bde. Vol 6 Oct. 15		
War Diary	Railway Wood	01/10/1915	06/10/1915
War Diary	Ypres	07/10/1915	08/10/1915
War Diary	H. 2. C.	09/10/1915	11/10/1915
War Diary	I. 10.	12/10/1915	13/10/1915
War Diary	H. 11 B. 9.4. (Seminaire)	14/10/1915	18/10/1915
War Diary	I. 10.	19/10/1915	19/10/1915
War Diary	Railway Wood I. 11. B.	20/10/1915	21/10/1915
War Diary	Coppernollyhoek A. 9. b.	22/10/1915	31/10/1915
Heading	14th Division 7th Rifle Bde Vol 7 Nov. 15		
War Diary	Coppernollyhoek	01/11/1915	03/11/1915
War Diary	Elverdinghe Chateau	04/11/1915	11/11/1915
War Diary	Sheet 27. F. 27. a. Poperingh	12/11/1915	19/11/1915
War Diary	Ypres Canal Bank Sh. 28. C. 25. D.	20/11/1915	22/11/1915
War Diary	Trenches	22/11/1915	26/11/1915
War Diary	Huts. K. I. D. 8.8. (Vlamertinghe)	27/11/1915	30/11/1915

Heading	14th Div. 7th Rifle Bde. Vol 8		
Heading	War Diary Of 7th Battalion Rifle Brigade From 1-12-15 To 31-12-15 (Volume VIII)		
War Diary	Sheet 28 C. 21. a. and C. 15. C.	01/12/1915	04/12/1915
War Diary	Canal Bank C. 25. D.	05/12/1915	08/12/1915
War Diary	Sheet 28 C. 21. a. & C. 15. C.	09/12/1915	12/12/1915
War Diary	Vlamertinghe Huts. H. I. D. 3.8.	13/12/1915	28/12/1915
War Diary	Lancashire Fm C. 14. C. O. 2.	29/12/1915	31/12/1915
Miscellaneous	7th Bn. Rifle Brigade Casualty State	21/12/1915	21/12/1915
Miscellaneous	7th Battn. Rifle Bde. Roll Of Officers		
Miscellaneous	7th Battn Rifle Brigade Nominal Roll		
Miscellaneous	7th Bn. Rifle Brigade		
Heading	7th Rifle Brigade Vol 9 Jan.		
Heading	14th Div. 7th Bn. Rifle Bde. Vol. 10		
Heading	War Diary of 7th Bn. Rifle Brigade From 1-4-16 to 30-4-16 (Volume XII)		
Heading	War Diary of 7th Battn. Rifle Brigade From 1-3-16 to 31-3-16 (Volume XI) 7 Rifle Bde Vol 11		
War Diary	Huts. A. 16 C. Sheet 28.	01/01/1916	03/01/1916
War Diary	C. 13. B. Trenches	04/01/1916	08/01/1916
War Diary	Poperinghe	09/01/1916	12/01/1916
War Diary	C. 14. C. Trenches	12/01/1916	16/01/1916
War Diary	Camp. A. 16. C. Sheet 28	17/01/1916	20/01/1916
War Diary	C. 14. C. Trenches	21/01/1916	24/01/1916
War Diary	Poperinghe	25/01/1916	31/01/1916
Heading	War Diary Of 7th Battn. Rifle Brigade From 1st February 1916 To 29th February 1916 (Volume X)		
War Diary	Poperinghe	01/02/1916	01/02/1916
War Diary	Trenches Lancashire Fm	02/02/1916	07/02/1916
War Diary	Camp. A. 16. C. Sheet 28.	08/02/1916	11/02/1916
War Diary	Winnizeele	12/02/1916	15/02/1916
War Diary	Oudezeele	16/02/1916	21/02/1916
War Diary	Naours	22/02/1916	24/02/1916
War Diary	Doullens	25/02/1916	25/02/1916
War Diary	Warluzel	26/02/1916	29/02/1916
War Diary	Arras	01/03/1916	05/03/1916
War Diary	Simencourt	06/03/1916	12/03/1916
War Diary	Trenches Arras St. Sauveur Sector	12/03/1916	19/03/1916
War Diary	Arras	20/03/1916	25/03/1916
War Diary	Trenches Arras St. Sauveur Sector	26/03/1916	31/03/1916
War Diary	Simencourt	01/04/1916	06/04/1916
War Diary	Trenches Arras St. Sauveur Sector	07/04/1916	12/04/1916
War Diary	Arras	13/04/1916	18/04/1916
War Diary	Trenches Arras St. Sauveur Sector	19/04/1916	24/04/1916
War Diary	Wanquetin	25/04/1916	30/04/1916
Heading	War Diary Of 7th Battn. Rifle Brigade From 1-5-16 To 31-5-16 (Volume XIII)		
War Diary	Trenches Arras St. Sauveur Sector	01/05/1916	04/05/1916
War Diary	Wanquetin	05/05/1916	09/05/1916
War Diary	Chelers	10/05/1916	16/05/1916
War Diary	Neuville St. Vaast Sheet 51. C. F. 6. And F. 12	17/05/1916	22/05/1916
War Diary	Neuville St. Vaast	22/05/1916	24/05/1916
War Diary	St. Eloy. Sheet 51. C. F. 1 & 2.	25/05/1916	31/05/1916
Miscellaneous	Appendix III N. S. V. Casualties		
Heading	14 7th K.R.R.C. Vol 9		

War Diary	War Diary Of 7th Battn. Rifle Brigade From 1/6/16 To 30/6/16 (Volume XIv)		
War Diary	St. Eloy. Sheet 51. C. F. 1 & 2.	01/06/1916	02/06/1916
War Diary	Maroueil	03/06/1916	10/06/1916
War Diary	Ecoivres	11/06/1916	20/06/1916
War Diary	Arras	21/06/1916	21/06/1916
War Diary	Trenches (K.I.) Roclincourt	22/06/1916	27/06/1916
War Diary	Duisans L.8.C.	28/06/1916	30/06/1916
Heading	War Diary Of 7th Battn. Rifle Brigade From 1-7-16 To 31-7-16 (Volume XIV)		
War Diary	Duisans L.8.C.	01/07/1916	03/07/1916
War Diary	Roclincourt Trenches K. 1 Sector	04/07/1916	09/07/1916
War Diary	St. Nicholas (Arras)	10/07/1916	15/07/1916
War Diary	Roclincourt Trenches K 1 Sector	15/07/1916	21/07/1916
War Diary	Duisans L. 8. C.	22/07/1916	29/07/1916
War Diary	Wanquetin	30/07/1916	30/07/1916
War Diary	Beudricourt	31/07/1916	31/07/1916
Heading	41st Brigade 14th Division. 1/7th Battalion Rifle Brigade August 1916		
Heading	War Diary Of 7th Bn. Rifle Brigade From 1-8-16-31-8-16 (Volume XVI)		
War Diary	Mezerolles	01/08/1916	01/08/1916
War Diary	Gezaincourt	02/08/1916	07/08/1916
War Diary	Deraincourt (Albert)	08/08/1916	11/08/1916
War Diary	Montaubon. S. 26. d.	12/08/1916	12/08/1916
War Diary	W of Delville Wood S. 11. D	13/08/1916	14/08/1916
War Diary	Montauban S. 26. d.	15/08/1916	17/08/1916
War Diary	W of Delville Wood S. 11. d.	18/08/1916	19/08/1916
War Diary	Montauban. A. 8. a.	20/08/1916	25/08/1916
War Diary	S.22.d. 9.4.	26/08/1916	27/08/1916
War Diary	Dernancourt	28/08/1916	30/08/1916
War Diary	Warlus (Amiens)	31/08/1916	31/08/1916
Miscellaneous	Appendix 1	31/08/1916	31/08/1916
Miscellaneous	Casualty-Report 12th Bn. K.R.R. Corps. attached 7th Bn. Rifle Bde.	31/08/1916	31/08/1916
Miscellaneous	Casualty-Report 16th Bn. K.R.R. Corps. attached 7th Bn. Rifle Bde.	31/08/1916	31/08/1916
Miscellaneous	7th Bn. Rifle Brigade Casualty Return	31/08/1916	31/08/1916
Heading	War Diary of 7th Battn. Rifle Brigade From 1-9-16 To 30-9-16 (Volume XVII)		
War Diary	Warlus (Amiens)	01/09/1916	07/09/1916
War Diary	Dernancourt	08/09/1916	09/09/1916
War Diary	Becordel	09/09/1916	11/09/1916
War Diary	Montauban	12/09/1916	14/09/1916
War Diary	In Action	15/09/1916	15/09/1916
War Diary	Account of action fought on this date	15/09/1916	16/09/1916
War Diary	Dernancourt	17/09/1916	21/09/1916
War Diary	Lucheux	22/09/1916	26/09/1916
War Diary	Wailly Trenches F 1 Sector	27/09/1916	30/09/1916
Miscellaneous	Appendix W.L.4. 7th Battn. The Rifle Brigade	30/09/1916	30/09/1916
Miscellaneous	Casualties-Officers		
Heading	War Diary of 7th Battn. The Rifle Brigade From 1-10-16 To 31-10-16 Volume XVIII		
War Diary	Wailly Trenches F 1 Sector	01/10/1916	09/10/1916
War Diary	Riviere	10/10/1916	14/10/1916
War Diary	F 2 Sector	15/10/1916	25/10/1916

War Diary	Beaumetz	25/10/1916	25/10/1916
War Diary	Sombrin	26/10/1916	31/10/1916
Heading	War Diary of 7th Battalion The Rifle Brigade. From 1.11.16. To 30.11.16. (Volume XIX)		
War Diary	Sombrin	01/11/1916	30/11/1916
Heading	War Diary of 7th Battn. The Rifle Brigade From 1-12-16 To 31-12-16 (Volume XX)		
War Diary	Sombrin	01/12/1916	13/12/1916
War Diary	Gouy	14/12/1916	14/12/1916
War Diary	Riviere	15/12/1916	21/12/1916
War Diary	Trenches F2 Sector	22/12/1916	28/12/1916
War Diary	Beaumetz	28/12/1916	31/12/1916
Heading	War Diary of 7th Battn. The Rifle Brigade From 1-1-17 To 31-1-17 (Volume XXI)		
War Diary	Beaumetz	01/01/1917	02/01/1917
War Diary	Trenches F2 Sector	03/01/1917	08/01/1917
War Diary	Riviere	09/01/1917	14/01/1917
War Diary	Trenches F2 Sector	15/01/1917	20/01/1917
War Diary	Simencourt	21/01/1917	26/01/1917
War Diary	Trenches F2	27/01/1917	31/01/1917
Heading	War Diary of 7th Battn. The Rifle Bde. From 1-2-17 To 28-2-17 (Volume XXII)		
War Diary	Trenches F2 Sector	01/02/1917	03/02/1917
War Diary	Simencourt	04/02/1917	04/02/1917
War Diary	Sombrin	05/02/1917	28/02/1917
War Diary	War Diary of 7th Battn. The Rifle Brigade From 1-3-1917 To 31-3-1917 (Volume XXIII)		
War Diary	Sombrin	01/03/1917	02/03/1917
War Diary	Dainville	03/03/1917	17/03/1917
War Diary	Gouy	18/03/1917	21/03/1917
War Diary	Dainville	22/03/1917	23/03/1917
War Diary	Arras (Ronville)	24/03/1917	27/03/1917
War Diary	In Trenches Hz Sector (Old German Line)	28/03/1917	31/03/1917
Heading	War Diary of 7th Battn The Rifle Brigade From 1-4-17 To 30-4-17 (Volume XXIV)		
War Diary	Ronville (Arras) Caves	01/04/1917	08/04/1917
War Diary	Battle of Arras	09/04/1917	13/04/1917
War Diary	Monchiet	14/04/1917	14/04/1917
War Diary	Sombrin	15/04/1917	23/04/1917
War Diary	On March to Wancourt	24/04/1917	27/04/1917
War Diary	Wancourt	28/04/1917	30/04/1917
Miscellaneous	7th Battn. The Rifle Brigade. Casualty Return Appendix 73 (a)		
Heading	War Diary of 7th Battn. The Rifle Brigade From 1st May, 1917 To 31st May, 1917 (Volume XXIV)		
War Diary	Wancourt	01/05/1917	14/05/1917
War Diary	Wancourt Trenches	15/05/1917	19/05/1917
War Diary	Wancourt	20/05/1917	24/05/1917
War Diary	Beaurains	25/05/1917	31/05/1917
Miscellaneous	7th Battn. The Rifle Brigade. List Of Casualties For Action Of 3/4th May. "Appendix IX 77a"	03/05/1917	03/05/1917
War Diary	War Diary Of 7th Battn. The Rifle Brigade From 1-6-17 To 30-6-17 (Volume XXVI)		
War Diary	Beaurains M 10 02	01/06/1917	03/06/1917
War Diary	Neuville Vitasse	04/06/1917	09/06/1917
War Diary	Beaurains	10/06/1917	10/06/1917

War Diary	Monchiet	11/06/1917	11/06/1917
War Diary	Saulty	12/06/1917	12/06/1917
War Diary	Bertrancourt	13/06/1917	30/06/1917
Heading	War Diary of 7th Battn. The Rifle Brigade 1-7-1917 31-7-1917 (Volume XXVII)		
War Diary	Bertrancourt	01/07/1917	09/07/1917
War Diary	Berwal	10/07/1917	11/07/1917
War Diary	Clare Camp Croix de Poperinghe	12/07/1917	29/07/1917
War Diary	Frontier Camp	30/07/1917	31/07/1917
Heading	War Diary Of 7th Bn The Rifle Brigade From 1/8/17 To 31/8/17 (Volume XXVIII)		
War Diary	Frontier Camp.	01/08/1917	05/08/1917
War Diary	Hazewinde	06/08/1917	15/08/1917
War Diary	Dickebusch	15/08/1917	15/08/1917
War Diary	Chateau Segard	16/08/1917	16/08/1917
War Diary	Front Line Stirling Castle	17/08/1917	19/08/1917
War Diary	Dickebusch	20/08/1917	21/08/1917
War Diary	Chateau Segard	22/08/1917	22/08/1917
War Diary	Dickebusch	23/08/1917	23/08/1917
War Diary	Front Line Stirling Castle	24/08/1917	26/08/1917
War Diary	Dickebusch	27/08/1917	28/08/1917
War Diary	Meteren	29/08/1917	31/08/1917
Miscellaneous	7th Bn. The Rifle Brigade. Casualty Return		
Miscellaneous	1. Operation Of 26th August, 1917	25/08/1917	25/08/1917
Miscellaneous	H.Q. 41st Inf. Bde.	27/08/1917	27/08/1917
Miscellaneous	Headquarters, 41st Infantry Brigade.	29/08/1917	29/08/1917
Miscellaneous	41st Infantry Brigade Daily Summary of Information received up to 12 noon 27/8/17	27/08/1917	27/08/1917
Miscellaneous	7th Battn. The Rifle Brigade. Casualty Return	31/08/1917	31/08/1917
Miscellaneous	Extract from II Corps Summary of Information No. 72 received up to 6 p.m. 28th August, 1917	28/08/1917	28/08/1917
Heading	War Diary Of 7th Battalion The Rifle Brigade for September, 1917 (Volume XXIX)		
War Diary	Meteren	01/09/1917	01/09/1917
War Diary	Celtic Camp	02/09/1917	08/09/1917
War Diary	Shankill Camp Neuve Eglise	09/09/1917	09/09/1917
War Diary	Bristol Castle Messines	10/09/1917	16/09/1917
War Diary	Front Line Right Sector	16/09/1917	20/09/1917
War Diary	Shankill Camp	21/09/1917	30/09/1917
Operation(al) Order(s)	41st Infantry Brigade Operation Order No. 169	18/09/1917	18/09/1917
Miscellaneous	Report On Raid	21/09/1917	21/09/1917
Miscellaneous	7th Battn. The Rifle Brigade List of Casualties for month of September		
Miscellaneous	7th Battn. The Rifle Brigade List of Honors etc. for September, 1917	00/09/1917	00/09/1917
Heading	War Diary of 7th Battn. The Rifle Brigade for October 1917 (Volume XXX)		
War Diary	Shankill Camp.	01/10/1917	05/10/1917
War Diary	Wood Camp	06/10/1917	08/10/1917
War Diary	Dickebusch	09/10/1917	09/10/1917
War Diary	Front Line	10/10/1917	16/10/1917
War Diary	Ridge Wood Camp	17/10/1917	21/10/1917
War Diary	Murrumbidgee Camp	22/10/1917	22/10/1917
War Diary	Meteren	23/10/1917	31/10/1917
Miscellaneous	7th Battn. The Rifle Brigade. List of Casualties.		

Heading	War Diary of 7th Battn. The Rifle Brigade Period November 1917 (Volume XXXI)		
War Diary	Meteren	01/11/1917	10/11/1917
War Diary	St. Martin Au Laert	11/11/1917	29/11/1917
War Diary	Red Rose Camp. Vlamertinghe	30/11/1917	30/11/1917
Heading	War Diary Of 7th Battn. The Rifle Brigade From 1/12/17 To 31/12/17 (Volume XXXI)		
War Diary	Red Rose Camp Vlamertinghe	01/12/1917	01/12/1917
War Diary	Capricorn Camp.	02/12/1917	04/12/1917
War Diary	Front Line Passchendaele	05/12/1917	08/12/1917
War Diary	Red Rose Camp	09/12/1917	18/12/1917
War Diary	Hasler Camp	19/12/1917	21/12/1917
War Diary	Front Line Passchendaele	22/12/1917	26/12/1917
War Diary	Setques	27/12/1917	31/12/1917
Miscellaneous	List of Casualties 1-8th Dec. 1917 Appendix A.	08/12/1917	08/12/1917
War Diary	List Of Casualties 22-26/12/1917 Appendix B	26/12/1917	26/12/1917
Heading	War Diary of 7th Bn. The Rifle Brigade From 1-1-18 To 31-1-18 (Volume XXXII)		
War Diary	Setques	01/01/1918	02/01/1918
War Diary	Cerisy	03/01/1918	21/01/1918
War Diary	Beaucourt	22/01/1918	22/01/1918
War Diary	Lignieres	23/01/1918	23/01/1918
War Diary	Crissolles	24/01/1918	24/01/1918
War Diary	Jussy	25/01/1918	31/01/1918
Heading	War Diary of 7th Bn. The Rifle Bde. From 1/2/18 to 28/2/18 (Volume XXXIII)		
War Diary	Jussy	01/02/1918	01/02/1918
War Diary	Clastres	02/02/1918	03/02/1918
War Diary	Front Line Urvillers	03/02/1918	15/02/1918
War Diary	Clastres	16/02/1918	16/02/1918
War Diary	Urvillers	17/02/1918	20/02/1918
War Diary	Front Line Urvillers	21/02/1918	28/02/1918
Heading	14th Division 41st Brigade. 7th Battalion The Rifle Brigade March 1918		
Heading	War Diary of 7th Bn. The Rifle Brigade From 1-3-18 To 31-3-18 (Volume XXXIV)		
War Diary	Front Line Urvillers	01/03/1918	12/03/1918
War Diary	Clastres	12/03/1918	12/03/1918
War Diary	Rly. Cutting Essigny & La Sabliere	12/03/1918	21/03/1918
Miscellaneous	7th Rifle Brigade		
War Diary	Clastres	21/03/1918	21/03/1918
War Diary	Jussy Canal	21/03/1918	21/03/1918
War Diary	Beaumont-En-Beine	22/03/1918	22/03/1918
War Diary	Flavy Le Martel	23/03/1918	24/03/1918
War Diary	Beines	24/03/1918	24/03/1918
War Diary	Porouericourt	25/03/1918	26/03/1918
War Diary	Thiescourt	26/03/1918	26/03/1918
War Diary	Thiescourt Elincourt	26/03/1918	26/03/1918
War Diary	Rouvillers	27/03/1918	28/03/1918
War Diary	Cinqueux	28/03/1918	29/03/1918
War Diary	Nogent-Sur-L'Oise Ebbicourt	29/03/1918	30/03/1918
War Diary	Bacouel	30/03/1918	31/03/1918
Heading	41st Inf. Bde. 14th Div. War Diary 7th Battn. The Rifle Brigade April 1918		
Heading	War Diary of 7th Battn. The Rifle Brigade From 1-4-18 To 30-4-18 (Volume XXXV)		

War Diary	Bacouel	01/04/1918	01/04/1918
War Diary	Dormart Sector	02/04/1918	04/04/1918
War Diary	Vaire Wood Vicinity	04/04/1918	09/04/1918
War Diary	St. Fuscien	10/04/1918	28/04/1918
War Diary	Lisbourg	29/04/1918	29/04/1918
War Diary	Fressin	30/04/1918	30/04/1918
Heading	War Diary of & 7th Bn. The Rifle Brigade From 1-5-18 To 31-5-18 (Volume XXXVI)		
War Diary	Fressin	01/05/1918	01/05/1918
War Diary	Embry	02/05/1918	15/05/1918
War Diary	Boeseghem	16/05/1918	17/05/1918
War Diary	Les Ciseaux	18/05/1918	31/05/1918

(198)

13TH DIVISION
41ST INFY BDE

7TH BN RIFLE BDE
MAY 1915 – MAY 1918

Returned to UK with Div
16 & 18 / absorbed Coy
/3 BN London Re....

4/14

13/5513

CONFIDENTIAL

WAR DIARY
OF
7th Bn. RIFLE BRIGADE
14th Division

(VOLUME I)

Not

from 20/5/15 to 31/5/15

May '15

Army Form C. 2118.

WAR DIARY
or
INTELLIGENCE SUMMARY.
(Erase heading not required.)

Instructions regarding War Diaries and Intelligence Summaries are contained in F.S. Regs., Part II. and the Staff Manual respectively. Title pages will be prepared in manuscript.

Hour, Date, Place		Summary of Events and Information	Remarks and references to Appendices
BOULOGNE.	20.5.15. 1 a.m.	Entered "Rest Camp from England. Crossed in S.S. QUEEN. Strength. 30 Officers. 907 R & F. (3 Officers and 101 with Reg'l Baggage crossed via HAVRE and rejoined Batt'n at BOULOGNE at 10 p.m.) Battalion entrained at 10 p.m.	Special orders as regards detraining were handed to me just as the Train was starting, so that there were no means of preparing the fatigue parties required for detraining until arrival; this caused delay which might have been avoided had more orders been given.
MILLAIN	21.5. 4 a.m.	Battalion arrived and went into Billets. Determined at WATTEN. D Coy billeted at WATTEN. B Coy at LES CLITRES. A.C. & HQrs at MILLAIN	
"	22.5.	Brigade exercises. Fine and very warm.	
"	23.5.	Sunday.	
"	24.5.	Brigade exercises. Maj. R.A. Lupton to hospital here. Sick.	2 Coln German Howitzers.
"	25.5.	Batt'n exercises.	
"	26.5. 9 a.m.	Batt'n marched to ZOUTPEENE. Very hot day. Several fell out in spite of great care being exercised. Blankets were returned to Ordnance.	
ZOUTPEENE	" 1 p.m.	Batt'n billeted at ZOUTPEENE. — There was a sudden cloud-burst, which did not reach us till 6 p.m.	

Army Form C. 2118.

WAR DIARY
or
INTELLIGENCE SUMMARY.
(Erase heading not required.)

Instructions regarding War Diaries and Intelligence Summaries are contained in F. S. Regs., Part II and the Staff Manual respectively. Title pages will be prepared in manuscript.

Hour, Date, Place		Summary of Events and Information	Remarks and references to Appendices
ZOUTPEENE. 27.5.	7. a.m.	Battⁿ. marched to FLETRE. 11M. N wind + cloudy. Much cooler. Billeted	
FLETRE. 27.5.	noon.	Billeted	
28.5.	9 a.m.	Battⁿ. marched to DRANOUTRE. Brigade distributed among 46 Div for instruction in trench warfare. Battⁿ attached to 138ᵗʰ Infy Bde.	
DRANOUTRE "	noon	Billeted.	
"	5 p.m.	A + B Coys distributed 1 platoon to each Coy of 5ᵗʰ Lincs & 4ᵗʰ Leicesters in trenches for instruction	
29.5.	8 p.m.	H.Q. & Bⁿ. Cadre moved both sections during evening	
30.5.		Sunday. Ch Parade for O+B Coys at 6.30 p.m.	
		- No 306 Rfn. WARDEL. J. (A Coy) wounded.	
31.5.		- No 2. Rfn. NORTH. A. (A Coy) wounded.	
"	8 p.m.	C + D Coys relieves A + B Coys for instruction in trenches.	Fighting strength 31 hvy 28 Officers 892 R + F.

121/5935

14th Division

7th Rifle Brigade

Vol: II — 30.6.15.

(3)

(VOLUME II)

Army Form C. 2118.

WAR DIARY
or
INTELLIGENCE SUMMARY.
(Erase heading not required.)

Instructions regarding War Diaries and Intelligence Summaries are contained in F.S. Regs., Part II. and the Staff Manual respectively. Title pages will be prepared in manuscript.

1915	Hour, Date, Place	Summary of Events and Information	Remarks and references to Appendices
DRANOUTRE. 1 June.		C + D Coys in Trenches. N.E. Wind. Very fine. No 2 Rfn. NORTH. A. (A Coy) Died of wounds at Bruern at On-Tre Farm dressing Station.	That the following were wounded about 10th on 31st May and are on duty. No 295. Rfn. COLEMAN. J. A Coy " 246. " REEVES. J. A " 2431. " PROSSER. W. B "
" 2 June.		Heavy firing from direction of LA BASSEE all day. Very fine, hot sun. Mild N.E. Wind.	
	8 p.m.	A + B to Trenches for instruction in platoon. C + D returned to billets.	
" 3 June.	8 p.m.	C + D to Trenches for instruction in platoon. A + B returned to billets. No 7320 Rfn CANTERFORD. H.Q. D Coy wounded 403 " WIFFEN. C. A Coy "	
" 4 June.	8 p.m.	C and D remained in trenches for instruction as companies. A + B absent to " " "	
" 5 June.	11 p.m.	All Companies arrived at respective billets.	
" 6 June.	8 a.m.	Battn. left DRANOUTRE and marched to ROZENHILL HUTS near LA CLYTTE. S.W. Wind.	
LA CLYTTE. (ROZENHILL HUTS)	11 a.m.	Battn. arrived. Very hot day. S.W. Wind.	

Army Form C. 2118.

WAR DIARY
or
INTELLIGENCE SUMMARY.
(Erase heading not required.)

1915

Hour, Date, Place	Summary of Events and Information	Remarks and references to Appendices
LA CLYTTE ROZENHILL HUTS. M.G.A. 7 June.		Ref. Map. Belgium & France B Series Sheet 28. Bivvies at farm on Spoil hr. G. 36. c.
12.30 p.m.	Battn altogether in temporary hts. v. hot. Slight W wind. No. 5083 Rfn BURNER (A Cy) accidentally shot himself with a Browning Pistol which he had in his possession, he died almost at once. He also wounded No. 6 Rfn MANSELL S.H. (A Cy) in the arm with the same bullet.	
8 p.m.	Brigade taking over trenches N.s. O.s. and P.s. Battn in Bde Reserve, moved to PIONEER Fm (H. 33. d) arrived PIONEER Fm & bivouacked under tarps.	MH
10 p.m.	Battn in Bde Reserve. No move. very hot. Thunderstorm passed from S to N by W of us.	MH
PIONEER Fm H.33.d. 8 June	Battn in Bde Reserve. Carps constructing shelter against shell fire at Reserve bivouacs. 40 Officers & N.C.O.s and 660 men employed as carrying parties to Battalion in Trenches.	MH
" 9 June.		
" 10 June.	Fatigue parties returned at various hours in a.m. Heavy Thunder storm. Fair by 8.a.m.	MH
6.a.m.		

WAR DIARY
or
INTELLIGENCE SUMMARY.
(Erase heading not required.)

Army Form C. 2118.

Instructions regarding War Diaries and Intelligence Summaries are contained in F.S. Regs., Part II and the Staff Manual respectively. Title pages will be prepared in manuscript.

(5)

Hour, Date, Place	Summary of Events and Information	Remarks and references to Appendices
PIONEER F". H.33.d. 10 June. 8 p.m.	Battalion relieved 8 B". R.B. in O. & P. Trenches. B" H.Q". at the BRASSERIE. A, C, & D Coys in adv. Trenches — A Coy in support.	
BRASSERIE. 11 June. S-E Corner of N.5.b. 8 p.m. 8 p.m.	Situation unaltered — — No activity on front of enemy. Return brought up by 8"A" R.B. Situation as yesterday.	NIL NIL
" 12 June. 1 a.m.	No activity on front of enemy. 2 M.Guns of 8" A. have M.G. Battery arrived 1.a.m. and position in O.B. Casualties Killed No. 7173 Rfn. T. JACKSON B. Coy. " No. 7773 Rfn. DAVIES. C. Coy. " No. 3458 " F. PERRY C. Coy. Wounded No.1294 " N. JACKSON B. Coy (self inflicted) " No. 2436 — J. TAYLOR B. Coy. " No. 7067 a/cpl E. WATTS. B. Coy.	NIL
" 13 June 4 a.m. 6 a.m.	Relieved by Suffolk Regt. and Northumberland Fus. of 84th Inf. Bde. Wounded No. 3387 Rfn. R. COSTELLO. Battalion Collected and bivouacked at ROZENHILL.	} bivouacs at the BRASSERIE

Army Form C. 2118.

WAR DIARY
or
INTELLIGENCE SUMMARY.
(Erase heading not required.)

Instructions regarding War Diaries and Intelligence Summaries are contained in F.S. Regs., Part II and the Staff Manual respectively. Title pages will be prepared in manuscript.

Hour, Date, Place		Summary of Events and Information	Remarks and references to Appendices
ROZENHILL. 14 Jun.	7.a.m.	Battalion moved.	
POPERINGHE. "	11 a.m.	Battn. arrived and bivouacked 3 Miles W. (5th Corps) in Corps Reserve.	
" 15 Jun.	8 a.m.	C.O. sent to reconnoitre position S of YPRES.	
"		B"s in readiness to move at any moment.	
"	9.15 p.m.	Battalion moved.	
VLAMERTINGHE "	11.30 p.m.	Battalion arrived at huts in H.14.a. Battn in Corps Reserve.	
" 16 Jun.	2.45 a.m.	Bombardment & assault on BELLEWAARDE Farm	
"	10.30 a.m.	Battn moved to S of YPRES 4 Miles and took shelter along S.W. bank of Rly in I.13.c. still in Reserve. Fine.	
YPRES. I.13.c. 17 Jun.		Still along Rly embankment in reserve. Fine. N.E.wind.	Bivvies I.13.c. (23) 150 yds West of Railway and Junc N of stream.
" 18 Jun.	10.45 a.m.	No. B. 1508 Rfn. F. LESTER, B. Coy. accidentally killed by another gun who was cleaning his Rifle.	
"	8.30 p.m.	Battalion returned to huts in H.14.a. arrived 10 p.m. Fine.	
VLAMERTINGHE. 19 Jun.		Resting.	
" 20 "	11 a.m.	Sunday. Left huts in H.14.a. and moved to huts in H.9.a.7A. Found them in filthy condition & spent rest of day in cleaning them and bivouacs. Fine.	

Army Form C. 2118.

WAR DIARY
or
INTELLIGENCE SUMMARY.
(Erase heading not required.)

Instructions regarding War Diaries and Intelligence Summaries are contained in F.S. Regs., Part II and the Staff Manual respectively. Title pages will be prepared in manuscript.

Hour, Date, Place		Summary of Events and Information	Remarks and references to Appendices
VLAMERTINGHE. H.Q.a.			
"	21/June. 7 a.m. 10.30 "	German aeroplane overhead. 4 p.m. Some H.E. Shells. No casualties. German aeroplane overhead.	17th 17th
"	22/June. 7.30 p.m.	Guns all round commenced a bombardment.	
"	23/June. 6.30 a.m.	Working party of 200 men under Capt. Milward left for KUISTRAAT.	
"	3.50 p.m.	Camp shelled. 8 shells. No 1743 Rifn C. Pugh. D. Coy. slightly wounded. (at duty.)	17th
"	24/June. 9.50 a.m. 4.30 p.m. 7.30 p.m.	Camp shelled. 10 shells. No 5213 Sgt E. CAKE. B. Coy (Sgt. Instr. Musk) slightly wounded (at duty) — CAKE " " 5 " Rest left to dig communication trenches East of YPRES.	17th 17th
"	25/June. 12-15 p.m. 3 a.m. 10.30 a.m. 5.30 p.m.	5 shells over camp. No casualties. Returned from digging. Heavy rain in evening. 10 Shells over camp. Draft of 1 N.C.O. and 47 Riflemen arrived. Quiet day. Coy Officers down trenches in Salient.	17th 17th
"	26/June. 27 " noon 1.10 p.m.	Sunday. Camp shelled. 6 shells " " 6 " C.O. & adjt. reconnoitred trenches at HOOGE & Salient. All companies digging communication trenches in Salient. Returned 3 a.m. 28th No 2828 Rifn H. READING. D. Coy wounded.	17th 17th
"	8 p.m.		17th

(8)

Army Form C. 2118.

WAR DIARY
or
INTELLIGENCE SUMMARY
(Erase heading not required.)

Instructions regarding War Diaries and Intelligence Summaries are contained in F.S. Regs., Part II. and the Staff Manual respectively. Title pages will be prepared in manuscript.

Hour, Date, Place		Summary of Events and Information	Remarks and references to Appendices
VLAMERTINGE. H.Q.a. June 28th	9 a.m.	Camp shells to shells.	
	1 a.m.	C.O. met 2nd Army Commander at 8th Divn H.Q. S.W. wind. Damp & cool. 87°h.	
" June 29th		Camp shells. 8 shells.	
	1 p.m.	Bttn marched to The Menin Trenches from	
	7 p.m.	D.H.Q. at Hq Bn between HOOGE and BELVAARD Fm	Stacey Dh
		A. Coy at I. 12. c. B Coy. N. W. corner of I. 18. a.	with trenches
		C. Coy in support along S. of I. 18. a.	Offs. 26.
		D. Coy in support along E. of I. 18. c. 87°h	other ranks 842.
HOOGE. June 30th	2 a.m.	Relief carried out. Battalion carried 16000 sandbags into the trenches. Handed in KRUISTAAT and SALLY PORT.	
		B. Coy. No 1450 Rfn CLEGG } wounded slightly, remained at duty.	
		C. Coy. No 1584 " NICHOLAS }	
		Found trenches in bad condition, a great deal of work	
		Following casualties during the day	
		No 3417 Rfn E. SPARROW. C. Coy. Killed	Batch buried in Square
		No 11771 " SYMES C. Coy Killed	I. 16. B. 1. 4.

(73989) W4141—463. 400,000. 9/14. H.&J.Ltd. Forms/C. 2118/10.

WAR DIARY
or
INTELLIGENCE SUMMARY.
(Erase heading not required.)

Army Form C. 2118.

Hour, Date, Place	Summary of Events and Information	Remarks and references to Appendices
1915 HOOGE. 30 June.	No 7339 Rfn BOLLARD. A Coy. Killed. No 3452 Sgt TONDEUR. C<s>h</s> Coy. Wounds. 3433 Rfn HARDY. C<s>h</s>. Coy. " 2907 " TOFT C " 3420 A/Cpl PEARCE C " 3456 Rfn DERYCK C " 11660 " COOK A " 162 " GRIGGS A " 7832 " QUARLEY. A " Casualties all incurred in ordinary trench duty, mostly from shell fire, of which there was a great deal all day, especially between 7 & 8 p.m. KMc	Buried in Sq. I 12.c. Fighting Strength on 30 June 27 officers 901 R+F

121/6607

14th Division.

7th Rifle Brigade
Vol: IV

From 1 - 31. 8. 15

Army Form C. 2118.

WAR DIARY
or
INTELLIGENCE SUMMARY
(Erase heading not required.)

Instructions regarding War Diaries and Intelligence Summaries are contained in F.S. Regs., Part II and the Staff Manual respectively. Title pages will be prepared in manuscript.

Hour, Date, Place	Summary of Events and Information	Remarks and references to Appendices
HAZEBROUCK. Aug 1.	Sunday Resting and sorting Battn. in	
" Aug 2.	Battalion inspected by Sir John French. Corps Commander. 4 Platoons and 4 officers lent to 8th Bn KRR for duty in trenches N. of MENIN ROAD.	Casualties 2nd – 6th Aug while in trenches N. of Menin Rd with 8th Bn K.R.R. Wounded 6 5644 Rfn HURLEY C.E. A.Cs 3026 Cpl JAMES. C. " 3240 Rfn GILBERT. J. " 525 A/Cpl PRESTED. A. " 11740 Rfn MOXON. S. " 3393 Rfn BROOKER. W. D.C. 11764 Rfn SMITH. A " Missing 500 Rfn GEDGE. M. A.Cs Self wounded – 8375 Rfn FISHER. A. "
" Aug 3.	" Little doing.	
" Aug 4.	"	
" Aug 5.	"	
" Aug 6.	"	
" Aug 7.	2 Platoons returned from trenches with 8th K.R.R. Some wicker on to relief of other two completed then to bivouacs. other 2 platoons rejoined at 12.30 a.m.	Casualties on 30 July see attached note.
" Aug 8.	"	
" Aug 9.	Sunday Resting	
" " 10	6 p.m. Left G.S.A. and marched to a river west below I.M S.E of WATTEAU bivouacs there after dark.	

Army Form C. 2118.

WAR DIARY
or
INTELLIGENCE SUMMARY.
(Erase heading not required.)

Instructions regarding War Diaries and Intelligence Summaries are contained in F.S. Regs., Part II and the Staff Manual respectively. Title pages will be prepared in manuscript.

Hour, Date, Place		Summary of Events and Information	Remarks and references to Appendices
WATTEAU.	11 August	The following officers joined the Battalion on posting —	
		Temp. Lt R.C. CUMBERBATCH 2nd Lt R.G. BARNES	
		" 2Lt G.H.R. COMBE " 2Lt A.E. LAWSON	
		" 2Lt F.R. SALTER " 2Lt R.W. EYTON	
		" 2Lt J.S. GREENWAY " 2Lt C. CLARK	
	12 Aug	C.O and by Convoy visited Trenches at POTIJZE	1/8/15
	13 Aug	" " " " " " " Relieved the	1/8/15
5 p.m.		Bn. left in motor busses for " ". 1st Bn. Lincoln Rgt. Complete at 1.50 p.m.	
		320 men from 8th R.E.R.B. attached to us to make up numbers.	
		No. 1677 Rfn STANTON. E. D. Coy wounded (A7 and A8)	
POTIJZE		A.&D. Coys to fire trenches. (x 4 x 5)	
		B.&C. " Support " " wounded	1/8/15
	14 Aug	No 7482 Rfn PIPPETT. R.G. A Coy. wounded	1/8/15
	15 Aug	Sentry Duft of 50 Jews Baths	
		No 5686 B/c EDGAR. J " wounded A Coy	1/8/15
		" 2/8 Rfn PLATTEN. A " " A Coy	
	16 Aug	" 1164 " BROWN. W. " " D Coy	1/8/15
		2 Lieut SALTER. F.R " " A Coy	
		No 108 Rfn TENNANT A " " A Coy	

Army Form C. 2118.

WAR DIARY
or
INTELLIGENCE SUMMARY.
(Erase heading not required.)

Instructions regarding War Diaries and Intelligence Summaries are contained in F.S. Regs., Part II and the Staff Manual respectively. Title pages will be prepared in manuscript.

Hour, Date, Place	Summary of Events and Information	Remarks and references to Appendices
POTIJZE		
7 Aug.	Tried to join B.Oh. in trenches but owing under the influence of fire shells from YPRES asylum — they fired and Sgt. Wounded, and were unable to proceed so than we went out back to transport lines.	
18.	Bn. arrived tea 16 at ... with suffering from lost any kit effects.	Buried at T. 4. a. 10.
	Casualties in Trenches	
	10429 Pte ALLEN. H. Killed A Coy	
	" ROBERTSON F.C. Wounded C Coy	
	9533 " BROWN A " "	
	9383 " MCKENS F.J. " "	
19.	8441 R.E. STEVENS J. Killed A Coy	Buried at T. 4. a. vi.
	11/38 " WALKER W.J. " A Coy	
	5 Germans were captured in dugout with telephone & rifles and 3 more shortly after — no guns... ... between ... ... they were fired at ... over... ... 200 -	
20.	4872 Pte MCMANUS J. C. Coy Wounded (slight injuries)	
	10213 " SAGE R.J. A Coy Wounded	
	1813 " GALLAGHER J. A Coy "	
	4872 " ~~Sergt~~ " " (8" R.How.)	
	3095 Off WRIGHT A D.Coy "	

WAR DIARY
or
INTELLIGENCE SUMMARY
(Erase heading not required.)

Army Form C. 2118.

Hour, Date, Place		Summary of Events and Information	Remarks and references to Appendices
POTIJZE	Aug 21st	No 6159 Rfn HOWES W. B Coy wounded	
"		8462 " SEAVE S. C - " accident. self inflicted	
"		6054 " MARSHALL E. A - "	
"		1990 " TILBURY H. D - "	
"		8685 " ORGAN E. A - "	
"		3144 " POWELL A. " - "	
"		2166 A/Cpl PALMER A. " - "	
"		5246 Rfn BEARD A.E. " - "	
"	Aug 22.	7234 Rfn FIELD .R. "	
"	Aug 23.	Relieved by 1st N'lds & 2nd'ly Rgt	
"	Aug 24.	Arrived Canal Bank N of BRIELEN R'd at 3 a.m.	
		moved however to (?) on Coy D. to KAMIE Salient	
N of YPRES	Aug 25.	HeadQrs moved to BRIELEN HOUSES.	
"	Aug 26.	Instructions to (?)	
"		" "	
"	27	Reinforcements of 14 (?) Bussen (?)	
"	28	Sunday	
"	29	Lts Trenton, Sgt POTIJZE. B & C Coy to post line	
"	30	C to 2D into Reserve line. Relief completed at 10-30p.m.	
		in KAMIE SALIENT.	
"	31.	No S9546 Rfn WISE .E. C. Coy Killed. Burial at I.4.a.1.0.	Fighting Strength
		B.2279 " HYDE F. " wounded	18 Officers
			737 O.R.

121/7050

4/14th Division

7th Rifle Brigade
Vol 5.

Sept. 15

Army Form C. 2118.

WAR DIARY
or
INTELLIGENCE SUMMARY.
(Erase heading not required.)

Instructions regarding War Diaries and Intelligence Summaries are contained in F.S. Regs., Part II and the Staff Manual respectively. Title pages will be prepared in manuscript.

Hour, Date, Place	Summary of Events and Information	Remarks and references to Appendices
Tuesday S.G POTIJZE 1 Sept.	No 5209 Cpl CARTER. J. C. Coy. wounded (31 Aug.) bullet	
	457 L/Cpl FORBES. H. B " wounded "	
	1687 Rfn BEECHEY. C. A " wounded shell	
	4997 Cpl BURROWS. E. D " wounded bullet	
	1561 Rfn HIGGINSON. N. D " wounded "	
2 Sept.	Transport found	
3 Sept.	7562 Sgt FLAGG. A. B. B. Coy accidental with Very Pistol	
4 Sept	1634 Rfn HOPKINS. H. B. Coy wounded } Shell	
	11358 " WARDLE. G. A Coy wounded	
	11216 " FOSTER. W. B " wounded	
	512.3 L/Cpl PHILLIPS. P.J. A " wounded	
5 Sept	3424 Rfn GIBBS. R.J. C " Killed bullet	Buried at Cemetery POTIJZE
6 Sept	406 Rfn BURTON. H. A Coy Killed shell	" "
	1754 " O'HARA R. D " Killed bullet	" "
	Reinforcement of 40 N.C.O.s + Rfn joined B.n in Trenches	
7 Sept	9579 B/m HERRMAN. J.T. C Coy wounded bullet	
	11220 " HASKINS. H. B " wounded shell	Buried at Cemetery POTIJZE
	6221 " HARRISON. C. B " killed shell	" "
8 Sept	7709 " PARSONS. M.M. A " killed bullet	
	1262 " CASH. A. B " wounded shell	
9 Sept	703 " APPLETON. C. B " wounded shell	
	11238 " DENN. R. A " wounded "	
	9640 " JONES D. R " wounded "	
	401 " LYONS H. A " wounded "	

WAR DIARY
or
INTELLIGENCE SUMMARY.

(Erase heading not required.)

Army Form C. 2118.

Hour, Date, Place	Summary of Events and Information	Remarks and references to Appendices
Trenches S. of POTIJZE Sept 10th	Fine. Work continued on restoration of parapets, wiring etc.	No casualties
Sept 11th	Bombardment of 49 N.C.O.s & Riflemen arrived at Frezenberg Camp. YPRES SALIENT heavily bombarded.	
	R.110433 Rfn PIRGER F. D Coy Killed Shell	Buried in YPRES between the Prison & the Water-Tower in square C.7.D.2.5.
	" 2064 " FIELDER. R " Wounded "	
	" 9433 " TALBOT. A " Wounded "	
Sept 12th	Lt. Col. J. R. H. Smithland D.S.O. assumed command of the Brigade in the departure of Brigadier-General O. NUGENT. C.B. to another command.	
Sept 13th	Lieut. HUNTER. H.J.E. wounded	
	Batt'n relieved in trenches at 9 P.M. by 1st Bn K.R.R.C. and marched to rest camp. B.5181. Regt. HARRINGTON. Cpl. B.Coy. Wounded by shell	
POPERINGHE Sept 14th 1 mile EAST of Sept 15th	13th Battalion refitted with clothing	
Sept 16th	Companies marched into POPERINGHE to 14th Division's huts. Transport inspected by Lt. General Sir John Keir K.C.B. Commanding 6th Corps.	
	Battalion practised for military position with musketry with near YPRES each party of the Officers & 100 Rank & File each visiting the rail head with 8 Sgts & Battn to comport at extra hour.	No casualties
Sept 17th	Men parcel to YPRES	No casualties
	Working parties in Ypres	

WAR DIARY or INTELLIGENCE SUMMARY

Army Form C. 2118.

(Erase heading not required.)

Hour, Date, Place	Summary of Events and Information	Remarks and references to Appendices
POPERINGHE Sept 19th	Working parties to Ypres.	No casualties
In aide Huts of Sept 20th	Reinforcement of 110 N.C.O's & Men from Wiltshire incest camp. 3 working parties furnished: out of 1 Officer & 110 Rank & file	MAC
	No. 9384 Pte. FOSTER. L. — Killed	Buried in Cemetery POPERINGHE at APC 51
	No. 10869 A/Cpl. BOND. A. — Wounded	
	" 295 Cpl. COLEMAN. J. — Wounded	Three casualties resulted while the
	" 12062 Pte. MASH. W. — Wounded	men were on a trek from Poperinghe MAC
	" 11739 " MARSHALL. P. — Wounded	Also wounded on railway branch YPRES.
	" 994 " HOLTON. J. — Wounded	HAC
	" 2685 " CUNNINGHAM. P. — Wounded	
	" 9434 " TOMLIN. T. — Wounded	
	" 1095 " SANDERS. F. — Wounded	Shell. All men of "A" Coy
		MAC
Sept 21st	The rest of the Brigade crabs out of the trenches into camps EAST of POPERINGHE	No casualties
	Two working parties of 1 Officer & 100 men.	MAC
Sept 22nd	Three working parties of 1 Officer & 100 men each	MAC
Sept 23rd	Battalion carried for route march	MAC
Sept 24th	Reinforcement of seven Music N.C.O.'s in morning	
Sept 25th	Reinforcement of three Officers arrived	
	Battalion in Divisional reserve for combined attack by 14th & 3rd Divisions on BELLEWAARDE FARM — HOOGE position. Battalion not engaged & moves in afternoon into huts just WEST of VLAMERTINGHE	MAC
VLAMERTINGHE Sept 28th	Sunday. Battalion Resting. 1 Officer joins.	MAC

(27)

Army Form C. 2118.

WAR DIARY
or
INTELLIGENCE SUMMARY.
(Erase heading not required.)

Hour, Date, Place	Summary of Events and Information	Remarks and references to Appendices
YPRES-MARTINAHE. Sept 27th Halt west of	Reinforcement of 40 R.C.O. & men all men who had been wounded at HOOGE on 30th July. Orders received to take over trenches near RAILWAY WOOD on 28th. Company H.Q. Ypres Ramparts Trenches.	
Sept 28th	Battalion takes over trenches from 1/4th Somersetshire Light Infantry. H.Q.	Fighting Strength. 28 officers 900 O.R.
RAILWAY WOOD. Sept 29.	A. Coy. 2/Lt. J.D.V. MAITLAND received wounds in the Battalion. 87 a/Cpl LEONARD. T.W. ⎫ 8 Rfn BEATTIE. H. ⎬ A. Coy wounded. Shell 6 " MANSELL. G. ⎭ 1978 " HORTON " 2267 " WOOD. W. C. Coy " 2848 " WILSON. G.W. D. Coy " 1690 " SULLIVAN G.J. A. Coy " Killed. Bullet 11787 " WELLDON A. A. Coy " Killed. Shell	KIB KIB
Sept 30.	Heavy firing all afternoon S. of MENIN Rd.	

121/7594

14th Hussars

7th Rifle Bde.
Vol. 6

Oct 15

Army Form C. 2118.

WAR DIARY
or
INTELLIGENCE SUMMARY.
(Erase heading not required.)

Instructions regarding War Diaries and Intelligence Summaries are contained in F.S. Regs., Part II and the Staff Manual respectively. Title pages will be prepared in manuscript.

Hour, Date, Place		Summary of Events and Information		Remarks and references to Appendices
RAILWAY WOOD.	1 Oct.	Quiet day. No Casualties.	Fine	S.No.785 Rfn PEDDER. W. B.Cy ⎫ wounded S. 11776 " SMITH. A. A.Cy ⎬ B. 3373 A/Cpl NOYCE. P.J. -(died) 3 Oct. B. 270 Rfn VENNER. E. ⎭ B. 172 Sgt EDWARDS. H. D.Cy
" "	2 Oct.	" "	"	ttt
" "	3 Oct.	Sunday " "		ttt
" "	4 Oct.	Draft of 2 officers and 79 O.R. joined at Transport lines.		
		No. 2591 Rfn NICHOLAS. A.W. D.Cy wounded - still 2592 A/Cpl WHITE. E. " " "		
		No. 3429 A/Cpl COWLEY. E.F. C.Cy. Killed Shell.⎫ Buried in cemetery 2907 Rfn TOFT. J. " Killed " ⎬ behind Rly WOOD 12066 " STONES. F. " Killed " ⎭ I.11.B.3.5. 5940 A/Cpl SANTER. F. " Wounded " 7160 Rfn AYLING. T. " " " 7169 " MILLS. C. A.Cy. " " 6110 " CROWDER. A. " " " 7710 " POWELL. L. C. " "		ttt ttt ttt ttt ttt ttt ttt
" "	5 Oct.	Quiet day. No Casualties.	Fine	
" "	6 Oct.	" " Relieved by 8th 65 K.R.R.C.		
YPRES.	7 Oct.	2 Cuy. at KAAIE SALIENT. 2 Cuy & H.Q° at H.11.b.q.4.		ttt ttt
"	8 Oct.			ttt
H.2.c.	9 Oct.	Battalion moved and collected in Huts at H.2.c.		ttt
H.2.c.	10 Oct.	Sunday no change. Baths at POPERINGH. Resting.		ttt ttt
" "	11 Oct.	Relieved 8th Bt R.B. in G.H.Q. line (1-10)		ttt
" "	12 Oct.	Very heavy German Bombardment about 6 p.m. against YPRES Carrying parties delayed. No Casualties.		ttt
1.10.	13 Oct.	YPRES again bombarded. Baton Relieved by Shropshire L.Inf. No. 3392 Rfn BROOKER. A. D.Cy. wounded - Shell. No. 7317 " YOUNG. H. B. " No. 1786 Cpl. MASON. J.W. B. "		ttt

Army Form C. 2118.

WAR DIARY
or
INTELLIGENCE SUMMARY.
(Erase heading not required.)

Instructions regarding War Diaries and Intelligence Summaries are contained in F.S. Regs., Part II. and the Staff Manual respectively. Title pages will be prepared in manuscript.

Hour, Date, Place	Summary of Events and Information	Remarks and references to Appendices
H.Q. B. 9.4. (Séminaire)		
14 Oct.	Battn. occupied billets at 1 a.m. at following:- H.Q. & A.Y.B. Coy. at H.U.B. C.+D. Coy. attached to 42nd Inf. Bde. in Bde. Reserve.	
15 Oct.	Battn. attached to 42nd Inf. Bde in Bde. Reserve.	
"	Quiet day. Carrying parties to trenches at night.	407467 Rifn. CURRY. A. C.Coy wounded on 18th died of wounds on 17th. Buried at Mil. Cemetery RENINGHELST — POPERINGHE (near POPERINGHE) MAS
16 "	" " " " " " "	One Casualty
17 "	Sunday. 6.20 a.m. Ordered to stand to in front of Rly Wood.	No. 2905 Rifn. SHEPPARD. F. C.Coy wounded on 19th slightly. MAS
18 "	Battn. moved to T.10. (G.H.Q. line) 6 p.m. moved to RAILWAY WOOD. 6 p.m.	No. 470 Rifn. SHELLEY. A.C. A.Coy wounded 20th slightly (at duty). MAS
19 "		
1.10.		
RAILWAY WOOD 1-11-B.		
20 "	Quiet day.	MAS
21 "	Relieved by 2nd Battn. Y+L Regt. Battn. to COPPERNOLLYHOEK & rest. Relieved O+P Buch in trenches. MAS	MAS
COPPERNOLLYHOEK. A.9.b.		
22 "	Arrived about 1 a.m. MAS	
23 "	— — MAS	
24 "	Sunday — — MAS	
25 "	— — MAS MAS	
26 "	— — MAS	
27 "	H.M. the King inspected representatives of Battn. and Bde. MAS Found all day. MAS	
28 "	Fine. MAS	
29 "	Corps Commander inspected Corps at Training. MAS	
30 "	Sunday. Fine. MAS	Fighting Strength. 31 Oct. 30 Offs. 909 O.R.
31 "		

14th Division

7th Rifle Bde.
Tot. 7
12/
7624

Nov. 15

WAR DIARY
or
INTELLIGENCE SUMMARY.

(Erase heading not required.)

Army Form C. 2118.

Instructions regarding War Diaries and Intelligence Summaries are contained in F.S. Regs., Part II and the Staff Manual respectively. Title pages will be prepared in manuscript.

Hour, Date, Place		Summary of Events and Information	Remarks and references to Appendices
COPPERNOLLYHOEK.	1 Nov.	W.J. Resting.	
"	2 Nov.	W.J.	
"	3 "	Bn. marched to ELVERDINGH CHATEAU.	W.J.
ELVERDINGH CHATEAU. A.	4 "	trenches on Reserve Bn. One of their Bn. having got wet in trenches.	W.J.
"	5 "	About ½ Bn. employed working in trenches & back trenches for 147th AB.	W.J.
"	6 "	Do.	W.J.
"	7 " (Sunday)	Ditto. Rfn. YOULDEN. T. D-Coy wounded. Shell by "K" visit	W.J. W.J.
"	8 "	No. 7896 Rfn. NAPIER. W. B. Coy " "	W.J.
"	9 "	" 13224 " HERDEN. J. " " "	W.J.
"	10 "	" 12761 " HUNT. F. " " "	W.J.
"	11 "	Relieved by Som: L.I. of 43rd Inf. Bde. Battalion marched by route march to Camp A. Sheet 27. F.27.a.	W.J.
Sheet 27. POPERINGH. F.27.a.	12 "	Very Stormy & wet. Mud everywhere.	W.J.
"	13 "	Do. Do. Nothing to report.	W.J.
"	14 "	Sunday. - -	W.J.
"	15 "	- -	W.J.
"	16 "	Officers reconnoitring Canal Bank trenches view to move.	W.J.
"	17 "	Nothing to report.	W.J.
"	18 "	- -	W.J.
"	19 "	Bn. from POPERINGH to YPRES. Taken up position on Canal Bank in support of 1st Lin. N. of WIELTJE.	W.J.

Army Form C. 2118.

WAR DIARY
or
INTELLIGENCE SUMMARY.
(Erase heading not required.)

Instructions regarding War Diaries and Intelligence Summaries are contained in F.S. Regs., Part II and the Staff Manual respectively. Title pages will be prepared in manuscript.

(31)

Hour, Date, Place	Summary of Events and Information	Remarks and references to Appendices
YPRES. Canal Bank. C.25.D. Sh.28. Nov 20th	In support to trenches B.14 to D.12 (C.21.B & C.15.c. Sh.u. 28) working parties at night.	
" 21st	Sunday do. do.	
" 22	Battn relieved 8th KRRC in trenches. Victor Trench B Co. HQ. 9.2 B.16.17 Dir (C.21 & C.15.c) 8th R.B. on our right. W.Yorks & 49th Suss on our left.	
Trenches 23	No. 12843 Rfn. CURD. H.C. B. Coy. killed. 1853 " MYALL. W. C. Coy. No. 17. Cn. U.Ir on 23.11.15 buried there) No. 3369 Rfn. SIBLEY H.J. C. Coy. killed.	buried ESSEX FARM C.25.d. 3.2 buried in LA BRIQUE cemetery
" 24	Rfn. CHANNEL. S.A. C. Coy. killed. " COLE. N. C. Coy. " " JAMES W C. " died from wds. 10679 " JAMES W C. dies. 26 Nr. 10 at 9.47 C.C. St. wounded. 3463 " JACOBS J C killed. 11296 " MITTEN A Buried. 11290 " COOPER. W. A killed.	buried " " buried " " buried " "
" 25		
" 26	Battn relieved by 8th KRRC. & returned to huts H.1.D.8.8. The trenches are in a non existent state it is impossible to visit them by day as shelter any kind is non existent. They are badly knocked about any attempt by parties to work on them in daylight results in immediate retaliation. The enemy still & but here send over occasional minor and distant no work was done working parties.	

Army Form C. 2118.

WAR DIARY
or
INTELLIGENCE SUMMARY.
(Erase heading not required.)

Hour, Date, Place		Summary of Events and Information	Remarks and references to Appendices
H.Q. N.I.D 8.8 (VLAMERTINGHE)	Nov 27	Routine Inspection	
"	28	Sunday " "	
	29	Nothing to report	
	30	Battn. returns to Trenches Trenches (C.21.B to C.15.C. Sh. 28) 1st K.R.R. Strength of 38 Junior B. Soldiers	Fighting Strength 27 Offrs 956 O.R.

7th Rifle Bde.
Vol: 8

14th Div.
4/ Bde

CONFIDENTIAL.

War Diary of

7th Battalion Rifle Brigade

From. 1-12-15   To   31-12-15

(Volume VIII)

WAR DIARY
or
INTELLIGENCE SUMMARY.
(Erase heading not required.)

Army Form C. 2118.

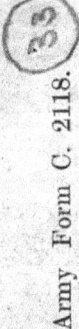

Hour, Date, Place	Summary of Events and Information	Remarks and references to Appendices
Sheet 28 Dec 1st C.21.a and C.15.c.	No 6426 A/Cpl. LAWS. W.H. A Coy wounded night of 30 Nov. Bullet.	Buried ESSEX F.m C. 25. a. 3.9.
	13173 Rfn. BUTT. F. D Coy ditto ditto on 1st	
	9596 " MICKLINS. E. " " " slightly on duty	
	9504 " FORRESTER F. " " "	
	5098 " MANDERSON. R. " " "	
	360 A/Cpl JOHNSON B " " " Killed	Buried LA BRIQUE Cemetery
	2272 Rfn. SMEE F. " " " wounded	
	2 Lieut. KIRKPATRICK T.W. whilst standing on back side.	
Dec 2nd	a very disturbed day.	
	No 12814 Rfn. BROWN. G. D Coy Killed. Shell	Buried LA BRIQUE Cemetery
	1891 - AINLEY A " " wounded. "	
Dec 3rd	No 6015 " POINTING A C Coy Killed. "	"
	8172 " FEATHERSTON. R/C Coy " "	"
	5556 " EARLE. J. C Coy " "	"
Dec 4th	No Casualties but plenty of shelling.	
	Relieved by 3rd K.R.R.C.	
Dec 5th Sunday	1 Bn Reserve. Canal Bank. Shelled in evening	
CANAL BANK C. 26. D.	Capt. MILWARD. P.H. wounded. Shell	
Dec 6th	No 10662 Rfn. MATTHEWS. T wounded at 10 Coy. H.Q.	
	Capt MILWARD died of wounds. Shell	Buried at 1st Cav CLg.St. ABEELE.
	No 01 Rfn. LYONS. H. A Coy " slightly "	
	2771 " BEESON H. D.Coy "	
	13021 " JOHNSON G. A.Coy " Bullet. finger.	
Dec 7.	1835 A/Cpl COWLEY G. D.Coy ⎫ Killed. Shell whilst attached to 8 KRR	Buried LA BRIQUE Cemetery.
	11176 Rfn. BURKE J. B.Coy ⎬ on Machine Guns.	
	1102 " BAILEY. A. D. ⎭	

Army Form C. 2118.

34

WAR DIARY
or
INTELLIGENCE SUMMARY.
(Erase heading not required.)

Instructions regarding War Diaries and Intelligence Summaries are contained in F.S. Regs., Part II. and the Staff Manual respectively. Title pages will be prepared in manuscript.

Hour, Date, Place	Summary of Events and Information	Remarks and references to Appendices
Canal Bank. C.15.D.	Dec 8. Returned to trenches. Sheet 28 C.21.a. and C.15.c. relieved 8 Bt KRRC.	
Sheet 28. C.21.a. & C.15.c.	Dec 9. No 3392 Rft BROOKER D.Coy wounded. slight.	
	Dec 10. 2nd Lieut BAKER. E.C.A. wounded. severe.	
	No 3442 A/Sgt ROBERTS. G.E. Coy. still slight.	
	5473. Cpl MARGETTS. F. Coy " "	
	1756. A/Cpl DAVIES. H. " " trivial	
	2604 Rif PETT A. C " slight	
	2125 " BENJAMIN. W. C " Serious	
	1191 " HALL. R. C " slight	
	11364 " GIBSON J. C "	
	8852 " TALLYDAY S. C " Bullet	
	11779 " WELLS G. A " Shell died on 11th. No 17 C.C.S. ABELE	
	343 " HANTON L A " wounded. buried La Brique la Brique cemetery.	
	2468. " THOMPSON A "	
	Dec 11. No casualties.	
Sunday	Dec 12. No 1447 Cpl METCALFE. B. Coy wounded shell	
	621 Rif BLOOMBORG B " shell "	
	1359 " WARD B " shell " died on 12th. buried LA BRIQUE.	
	5185 Cpl BARKER B "	
	3377 Rif WHEATLEY T.W. C "	
	Relieved by 8 KRRC.	
"	13 Lt. P.B. MERRIAM and A Coy to Hut Camp A. nr VLAMERTINGHE. B.J.Coy. ??	
VLAMERTINGHE. H.Q. H.1.D.39.	Lt E.F. PURDON with M.G. section of Battn. The Guns joined with the Bn. on the day after the arrival of the Bn.	
	[?] 8. K.R.R.C. in the rest billets in this Area.	
	14 Short route march.	
	15 No 3473 Cpl Haydn ?? died of wounds. buried at Liverpool Merchants hotel km ETAPLES.	

Army. Form C. 2118.

WAR DIARY
or
INTELLIGENCE SUMMARY.
(*Erase heading not required.*)

Instructions regarding War Diaries and Intelligence Summaries are contained in F.S. Regs., Part II and the Staff Manual respectively. Title pages will be prepared in manuscript.

Hour, Date, Place	Summary of Events and Information	Remarks and references to Appendices
VLAMERTINGHE Huts. H.1.D.3.8. Dec 16.	Nothing to report	MH3
17.	Officers reconnoitred R.14 C. Trench. Alarm position for R3rd in case of attack.	MH3
18.	Nothing	MH3
Sunday 19. 5 a.m. 5.30 a.m.	Very heavy bombardment. Previous 8 p.m. distinctly [heard] - 2 (two?) terrific [reliefs?] (whole Batt. been called out) Bn. warned to stand by in case of emergency. Buses ordered to move up to front line at 11 a.m. — ...	
	All day — news from the field very meagre in which orders came in. Battn. stood ready to move at short notice at 2 p.m.	
20.	Nothing to report.	MH3
21.	" "	MH3
22.	" "	MH3
23.	" "	MH3
24.	Sent 1 Cpl. 2 Offrs. 47 Rifles around	MH3
25.	Xmas Day. Nothing to report.	MH3
26.	Sunday " " C.O. reconnoitred Trenches C.14.c.	MH3
27.	" "	MH3
28.	1 C. Trenches C.14.C. 8th R.B. on left B & C. Coy. in front line. Relieved 4th A. Y. & L. Regt. 49th Div. A & D in reserve on Canal Bank	MH3
29.	9007632 Cpl. SCUDDER J. C. Coy killed	
	10418 Rfn. MIGNOT J. " shell	} two buried at LANCASHIRE Fm. C.14.C.0.2 Sheet 23
	11782 " SPRINGETT R. "	
	1747 A/Cpl. NORRIS H. W. " died of wounds	
	21H. GOSNEY. H. W. " (Same date)	
	1620 Cpl. VALENTINE A. C. Coy " Slight	
	6117 Rfn. DEARMAN. G. " "	2833 A/Cpl HICKS W. Coy Burned in dugout 6441 Rfn. DEARSLEY B Coy. Shell shock 9300 " CROWE W.L.C Shell in. dugout
	2149 " CLARKE. A. B. Coy. " Slight	
	2569 Cpl. HOARE C. " Severe	
	3008 " MURPHY G. A. Coy. "	
	759 Rfn. IZZARD W.A. D. Coy. "	
	2509 " ALLCOM. C. " Bullet Wnd. Surg. injuries	MH3
30.	Relieved by 8th KRRC. Bn. moved to huts at A.16.C. where	MH3
31.	...	MH3
LANCASHIRE Fm. C.14.C.0.2		Fighting strength 23 officers 923 O.R.

(73989) W4141—463. 400,000. 9/14. H.&J.Ltd. Forms/C. 2118/10.

7th Bn. Rifle Brigade
Casualty State

No	Rank & Name	Coy		Folio on Roll	Remarks
S/9522	Rfn. ✓Bean	W.	C.	31	From Hospital
S/1044	" ✓Panting	D.	"	37	To Hospital
S/12846	" ✓Garnham	H.	B.	21	From Hospital
S/5045	" ✓Sharp	J.	C.	38	Evacuated
S/11795	" ✓Williams	C.	A.	14	Evacuated
S/8608	" ✓Shrosbree	G.	C.	38	Evacuated
B/3435	" ✓Ashmore	H.	C.	31	Evacuated

21/12/15.

[signature]
Capt. & Adjt.
7th Bn. Rifle Brigade

7th Battn. Rifle Bde

Roll of Officers

Rank	Name		Remarks
Lt Col	Maitland	J.A.H., D.S.O	
Major	Ross	A.D.	
Capt.	Stewart	W.R.	Adjutant
"	Scott	P.A.	Town Major, YPRES.
"	Maxwell	J	
"	Shuttleworth	Hon E.J	
"	Norbury	C.G. Kay	
"	Shaw	H.E.	Sick
Lieut	Winter	C.E.	Transport Officer
"	Merriam	L.P.B.	
"	Fraser	W.N.	14th Div. Mining Section.
"	Cumberbatch	R.C.	
"	Maude	A.P.	
"	Barnes	Hon R.G.	Signalling Officer
"	Brown	R.C.	Bombing Officer
2nd Lt	Clark	C	Sick (This officer in England)
"	Lawson	A.C.	
"	Combe	G.N.R.	
"	Eyton	R.W.	
"	Grenway	J.D.	
"	Moline	E.N.	
"	Stuart	C.R.	
"	Shoobert	W.N	
"	Hall	J.S.	

RANK & NAME			REMARKS
2nd Lt	Oakey	J M	
"	Gosney	H W	
"	Warren	C N	
Lieut	Coonts	A S	Quartermaster
Capt	Dunlop	W A L	Medical Officer

7th Battn Rifle Brigade.

'A' Coy   Nominal Roll.

No.	Rank & Name		Remarks
5258	QMS	Roberts J	Gazetted 2nd Lt. to date from 2/11/15
B/157	C.S.M.	Smith A.J	
1903	CQMS	Price A.	
B/350	Sgt	Hall A.	
B/25	"	Jones H.	
B/583	"	Needham G.N.	
B/105	"	Needs W.	
S/6113	"	Rogers H.	
B/213	"	Rumbelow A.	
B/104	"	Shields G.W.	Orderly Room Clerk
B/392	"	White A.S.	
8253	"	Williams A.	
B/72	A/Sgt	Lee T.	Divisional Train
B/103	"	Pearce T.	
B/133	Cpl.	Beech G.	
A/3	"	Blake W.	
1710	"	Hardy W.	
S/4821	"	McKechnie H.	

'A' Coy (contd)

No	Rank & Name		Remarks
B/3027	Cpl.	Munt A.J	
B/2274	"	Sears E.J	
B/2920	"	Stone C.E	
B/585	A/c	Edgar W.	
B/416	"	Foweraker A.	Hospital
S/2132	"	Gregory 7.	
S/7584	"	Holland W.	
B/3025	"	Jarvis E	
S/11765	"	Shire C	
B/23	"	Caygill A.	
B/244	"	Duddridge J	
S/8196	"	Gallia M.	
S/1391	"	Harris C.	
B/399	-	Holland A.	Clerk 41st Inf Bde
B/87	-	Leonard G.	
B/6	-	Mansell G.	
B/3020	-	Peach W	
B/299	-	Wicker G.	
S/5123	-	Phillips P.	

36

"A" Coy (contd.)

No	Rank & Name	Remarks
B/132	Pte. Archard H	
S/12055	" Armett A	
S/5618	" Annetts R	
P/2585	" Appesley G	Hospital
S/4301	" Barrett S	
S/9993	" Bate G	Hospital
S/11329	" Beach H	
B/1744	" Bailey A	
B/8	" Beattie H	
B/1680	" Beaver J	Hospital
S/10144	" Bennett J	
S/7642	" Bennett A	
S/9494	" Betts S	
S/13147	" Best J	
S/10869	" Bond A	Hospital
B/444	" Bonter L	
S/5058	" Cardy R	
S/6160	" Carter G	
S/10258	" Chinnery G	
R/3030	" Chenrells G	
S/11281	" Christmas J	Hospital
B/80	" Clarke A H	
S/9573	" Clarke A	Hospital
S/6178	" Clarke S	
B/2054	" Clarke R	
B/136	" Coles A E	YPRES Police
B/2164	" Collis A	

57

"A" Coy (cont'd)   4

No.	Rank & Name	Remarks
B/~~2169~~		
B/75	Rfn. Cox H	
B/295	" Coleman J	Hospital
4416	" Cousins P	
B/2684	" Condrow J	
S/11660	" Cook A	
B/398	" Cunniss G	
B/2685	" Cunningham P	Hospital
S/6110	" Crowder A	Hospital
1753	" Cowen G	
Z/370	" Calcott W	
S/11086	– Bailey E	
Z/367	Rfn. Dale T	
S/9822	" Davis C	
S/13136	" Day W	
B/2797	" Dawson G	
S/4976	" Dean W	

'A' Coy. (contd.)

No.	Rank & Name		Remarks
S/1898	Rfn	Dennick H	
S/13211	"	Dennis T	
Z/480	"	Debney C	
B/346	"	Dunton G	
B/347	"	Dunton J	
B/634	"	Dodd J	
B/169	Rfn	Edwards F	
S/9334	"	Edwards A	
B/58	"	Elmer W	
B/9	"	Elliott E.W.	
S/1983	"	Entwistle A	
S/11213	"	Ewington G	
B/			

"A" Coy (contd.)

No	Rank	Name	Remarks
9606	Rfn	Hackert J	
280	"	Halford H.	
2/7392	"	Harris L	
B/241	"	Harrison T.	
3/12056	"	Harrison T.	
5969	"	Haylock F.	
S/2131	"	Hickson S	
S/5948	"	Higgins P.	
13298	"	Hilliard W	
3/5945	"	Hinton A	Hospital
S/7238	"	Hickmott C	
S/6660	"	Hallett C	
13/542	"	Hodges E	
S/8741	"	Hollington D.	
9994	"	Holton J	Hospital
R/27	"	Howell S	
S/5649	"	Hurley C.E	
S/15124	"	Hammet W.	

"A" Coy (contd.)   6.

No	Rank & Name	Remarks
B/2513	Rfn. Field W.	
B/310	" Findon J.	
z/277	" Forshaw a.	
S/4395	" Foot a S	
S/10273	" Ford G.	
B/188	" Forman S.	
S/11262	" Foster J.	
Z/2550	" Foulshaw W.	
5114	" Frencew S	
Z/1149	Rfn. Gallagher M.	
596	" Gilby J.	
Z/1119	" Glenn a.	
B/261	" Gordon H.	
B/2504	" Gubbins a.	
S/9641	" Gudley W.	Hosptl.
S/9110	" Gunning J.	

97

"A" Coy (contd).

No.	Rank	Name	Remarks
S/5172	Rfn.	Mack T.	
S/12062	"	Mash W.	Hospl
S/11729	"	Marshall P.	Hospital
R/6054	"	Marshall B.	
S/5593	"	Matthews W.	
476	"	Mills J.	
S/5907	"	Mills E.	
S/12059	"	Mills A.	
B/21	"	Miller W.	
S/11296	"	Mitten W.	
S/13182	"	Mogford E.	
S/11740	"	Moxon G.J.	
S/9713	"	Morgan H.	
6015	"	McBain C.	
S/11295	"	Munslow J.	
2681	"	Mummery T.	
S/11734	"	Monk A.R.	
S/11941	"	Neale W.	
B/3373	"	Noyce P.	Hospital
S/495	"	Langstone J.	
S/12060	"	Monery G.	

156

"A" Coy (contd)   8

No	Rank & Name	Remarks
8/2915	Rfn. Imbet A	
Z/795	" Izzard W	
8/110	" Jackson B.	
8/450	" Jackson A	
8/3211	" Jackson G	
S/5006	" Jeffery A	
8/187	" Jenkins J	
8/1986	" Jones J.	
S/9640	" Jones D.	
S/13031	" Johnson G	
8/3361	" Jordan J	
S/461	" Joseph A.J	
8/1853	" Kass G	
S/304	" King C.J.	
4735	" Key H.	
S/13304	" Kelleher J	
A/55	" Knight T	
S/13183	" Knight H	
S/11123	" Kelly A	
S/5074	" La Fontaine F.	Clerk 41st Inf Bde
S/5196	" Leffley A.J	
8493	" Lucas J	
S/11069	" Little A	Hospl
S/10145	" Lloyd J.	
8009	" Lukes T.C	
A/341	" Lyons W	
B/1101	" Lyons H	Hospl. off strength

138

"A" Coy (contd.)

No	Rank & Name		Remarks
S/7406	Rfn	Olsen J.	
S/3685	"	Organ E.	
S/379	"	Parry T.	
S/11354	"	Parry T.	
6600	"	Parker C.	
B/530	"	Parkis R.	
P/2156	"	Palmer A.	
B/3070			
4104	"	Pearce T.	
S/9238	"	Pearce H.	
5451	"	Peters S.	
S/6042	"	Perkins G.	
S/9309	"	Parkinson A.	
S/6041	"	Postlethwaite G.	
S/344	"	Powell A.	
S/10842	"	Pullen S.G.	
B/2130	"	Pimlott E.	
B/342	"	Pyke A.	
S/9497	"	Pye E.	

'A' boy (contd)   11

No.	Rank & Name	Remarks
B/402	Rfm Quiney W	
B/352	" Rogers W.G	
B/1840	" Rogerson C	
S/9193	" Rostron C	
B/263	" Russell G.H	
B/60	" Ryans M.J	
S/9305	" Read A	
S/9245	" Robertson J	
S/10222	" Rudkin W	
B/166	" Ruffell B	
S/11302	" Ruckhuss H	
S/11309	Rfm Styles R	
S/8350	" Smith C	
S/12067	" Scott H	
B/309	" Sharples J	
B/170	" Shelley A.C	
B/2115	" Sands T	

'A' Coy (contd)   12.

No.	RANK & NAME		REMARKS
B/1075	Rfn. Sanders	F.	
B/246	" Stoner	A.E.	
B/309	" Searle	W.	
S/3116	Rfn. Thomas	F.	
S/300	" Taylor	H.	
S/11313	" Thorpe	T.	
S/12069	" Thorne	A.B.	
S/6122	" Trebble	G.	
S/9434	" Tomlins	T.	Hospital
S/11777	" Tucker	T.	
S/	" ~~Thompson~~	A.	~~Hospital~~
S/429	" Turner	C.	

A. Coy (contd.)   13

No.	Rank	Name	Remarks
3/348	Rfn	Upson C.	
S/11361	"	Vanies W.	
S/8430	"	Vaughan F.	
270	"	Venour E.	
S/11268	"	Vaughan J.	
S/11068	Rfn	Walker A.	
B/83	"	Walsh M.	
B/84	"	Walsh J.J.	
S/19711	"	Webber H.	
298	"	Wallis P.	
S/242	"	Wallace A.E.	
S/396	"	Wade L.	
S/569	"	Waters S.	
Z/580	"	Warboys F.	
S/6173	"	Waymark W.	
S/11786	"	Webb L.	
S/11787	"	Weldon A.	
S/9306	"	Wheatcroft W.	
Z/2337	"	Wilson J.	
S/11784	"	Wilson L.	
B/297	"	White A.J.	

A Coy. (contd).   14

No.	Rank & Name		Remarks
3/9333	Rfn	White E.	
3/471	"	Willis E.	
3/10852	"	Williams J.	
3/11798	"	Wheeler J.	
3/354	"	Winter E.	
3/7322	"	Woodmer E.	
3/249	"	Wright E.	
3/90	"	Wright E.	
3/82	"	Wyatt J.	
B/1	"	Whitcher H.	
11793	"	Williams E.	
3/11083	"	Walker J.	
3/463	Rfn	Young E.	
2/1205	"	Young J.	
3/291	"	Yorke H.	

217

7th Bn Rifle Brigade

15

No	Rank & Name	Coy	Remarks
3052	C.S.M. Borne J	B	
S/7471	C.Q.M.S. Butcher W.H	"	
S/9770	Sgt Higgs J	"	
5038	" Green J	"	
818	" Bonham J.W.	"	
B/712	" Bonham A	"	
B/53	" Beckingham A	"	
1260	" Hopkins A	"	Signalling Sergeant
B/1669	" Kenchatt J	"	
S/9023	" Martin J	"	
B/4767	" Fairhead E	"	
B/1435	A/Sgt Tomkinson G	"	Bombing
B/1439	" Robinson J	"	Machine Gun
1912	Cpl Young A.	"	
B/1440	Cpl Bowler J	"	
S/1529	" Burness W.	"	Machine Gun
2741	" Dillon A	"	
3160	" Elsey A	"	
S/1368	" Nash J	"	
B/1306	" Pember W.	"	
B/1364	" Stephens R.	"	Hospital
B/709	" Tovey G.	"	Signalling Corporal
B/1444	" Walker J	"	

22

No	Rank and Name	Coy	Remarks
S/5196	A/Cpl Bryant A	B	
2682	" Burton S.	"	
S/10652	" Davies E	"	
S/7333	" Green H	"	
0/457	" Forbes H	"	
4771	" Harrison J	"	
X/8935	" Hadley J.	"	
B/1529	" Moore A	"	
B/3100	" Green A. R.	"	
B/2053	" Allen J.	"	
S/9254	" Evans A	"	
B/77	" Milward J	"	
4219	" Bean R.	"	
1711	" Boardman J	"	
S/7305	" Harrison W.	"	
B/0184	" Moffatt G. H	"	
S/12064	" Rogers C	"	
B/629	" Silver L	"	

40

No	Rank and Name	Coy	Remarks
B/1374	Rfn. Allen L. H.	B	
B/704	" Angel E	"	
S/10211	" Argent H	"	
S/10455	" Armstrong G	"	
B/609	" Ballard J	"	
B/780	" Bates W	"	
B/2646	" Barry T	"	
B/1432	" Bentley A	"	
1516	" Bransby T	"	
Z/2342	" Bridge W. J.	"	
B/1456	" Brown G. L	"	
B/613	— Butler G.	+	
B/1352	" Binks W	"	
S/8154	" Burns T	"	
S/10491	" Bundock E. G	"	
S/10495	" Bushy G. H	"	
B/819	" Bird T	"	
S/12864	" Bailey A	"	
S/9398	" Bedson L	"	
S/5559	" Biggs A. E.	"	

No	Rank	& Name	Coy	Remarks
3/7320	Rfn	Canterford W.	B	
B/698	"	Connolly G.	"	
B/739	"	Chapman W.	"	
B/755	"	Conley H	"	
B/745	"	Clarke H.M.	"	
S/6052	"	Cox A	"	
B/818	"	Clark W.	"	
S/6116	"	Cohen B	"	Hospital
S/9980	"	Crane J	"	
S/11177	"	Crookes H	"	
B/858	"	Curtis L.	"	
S/9536	"	Cooper W.	"	
S/9825	"	Coyne P.	"	
Z/1262	"	Cash A	"	
6/513	"	Carter C.	"	
Z/1427	"	Carpenter L.	"	
Z/2365	"	Clougher J	"	

76

No	Rank & Name	Coy	Remarks
B/784	Rfn Daniels W.	B	
3726	" Davis W	"	
1789	" ~~Darlington P.~~	"	Evacuated
P/757	" Dudley J.	"	
B/1582	" Dutton	"	
B/1366	" Devenport J	"	
6116	" Dombraine S.	"	
S/8156	" Durham J	"	
~~S/7326~~	~~" Deverell~~	~~"~~	
S/7326	" Deverell J	"	

No.	Rank and Name	Coy	Remarks
S/7512	Rfn Edema E.	B	
S/11326	" Eltringham M	"	
S/5235	" Eagles V.	"	Hospital
S/9387	Rfn Farnham W.	B	
S/5092	" Fathing H.G.	"	
S/9302	" Fyles J	"	
2389	" Fisher J	"	
D/861	" Flwin J	"	
S/7336	" Franks E.	"	
B/505	" Frost J.	"	
S/1298	" Foster J	"	
D/707	" Fincham C.	"	
S/2687	" Fowler C.	"	
B/93	" Fox C	"	

No	Rank and Name		Coy	Remarks
S/10992	Rfn	Gilbert E.	B	
B/2437	"	Green E.	"	
S/9455	"	Goulding J.	"	
S/12837	"	Giles C.	"	
S/12846	"	Garnham J.	"	Hospital
S/5642	"	Griffen A.	"	
B/1659	"	Griffiths T.	"	
B/3105	"	Hawley J.	"	
S/6033	"	Hanks A.	"	
B/2356	"	Harper S. J.	"	
Z/2004	"	Hoy J.	"	
B/1292	"	Harris J.	"	
B/711	"	Hanbury E.	"	
S/11184	"	Hilton J.	"	
B/740	"	Holloway S.	"	
S/5090	"	Hulley J.	"	
C/9278	"	Houghton W.	"	
B/606	"	Hicks G. A.	"	
B/1288	"	Higgins A.	"	
S/9986	"	Higgins A.	"	
S/11340	"	Helm J.	B	

No	Rank	Name	Coy	Remarks
2/5181	Pte	Hannington G.	B	
2/11693	"	Hitchcock T	"	
13/1510	"	Hanson W.	"	
2/11221	"	Herbert J.	"	
S/12055	"	Hodges C	"	
2/9608	"	Henley W	"	Hospital
2/10625	"	Harvey A	"	
S/12057	"	Hayward R.	"	
2/6188	"	Hayes T. P	"	
13/554	"	Lyyard G	"	
S/12748	"	James V. W.	"	
13/703	"	Jenkins T	"	
13/1519	"	Jones J. G.	"	
13/1295	"	Jones G.	"	
2/7341	"	Jones E. G.	"	

23

No	Rank & Name	Coy	Remarks
S/10618	Rfn Keefe H	B	
B/742	" Kopp A	"	
S/4182	" Keightley	"	
S/6190	" Kelleway W.	"	
3715	" Leslie M.	"	
B/443	" List G	"	
B/835	" Liston W. P.	"	
S/9669	" ~~Lyons~~ Lynch J	"	
S/5062	" Lyons H.	"	
S/8737	" Liddiard W	"	
S/12070	" Mather A. J.	"	
S/12061	" Matthews R	"	
Z/1947	" McMahon J	"	
S/11741	" McKinley A. G	"	
767	" Millen G	"	
O/2438	" Murphy P. J.	"	
Z/214	" Murphy J	"	
S/11349	" Moody H.	"	
S/11171	" Mitchell E.	"	

150

24

No	Rank & Name	Coy	Remarks
~~S/5771~~	~~Rfn~~ ~~Mitchell E.~~	~~B~~	
S/5771	" Merry J.	"	
Z/1131	" Metcalf J.	"	
B/822	" Nally J.	"	
B/630	" Noble H.	"	
B/1529	" North J.	"	
B/2412	" Nicholls W	"	
S/13221	" Newton J.	"	Hospital
S/9809	" Ost W.	"	
S/11266	" O'Connor P	"	
S/5154	" Palmer W	"	
B/785	" Pedder W.	"	
S/7513	" Pate W	"	
638	" Pattison J	"	
B/1520	" Poynter J	"	
Z/1923	" Pierse H	"	
S/9568	" Parsons J	"	

165

No	Rank & Name		Coy	Remarks
S/8642	Rfn	Palmer S	B	
S/6035	"	Porter A. V.	"	
S/9241	Rfn	Richards R	"	
S/863	"	Rickard J	"	
Z/863	"	Roberts J	"	
B/716	"	Ridley J	"	
S/5163	"	Russell G.A.	"	
S/11773	"	Sale C	"	
B/472	"	Searle W	"	
B/1296	"	Smith C	"	
B/707	"	Styles A	"	
Z/1926	"	Smith W	"	
Z/1815	"	Stephenson J	"	
B/1449	"	Smith C. E	"	
B/1984	"	Smith A	"	
		~~Spencer~~	—	?
3/10506	"	Stone B.	"	
3/10268	"	Spearing V	"	
S/12071	"	Summers J	"	

26

No	Rank & Name			Remarks
S/12840	Rfn	Spurgeon F S	B	
S/11762	"	Stowe A. S.	"	
Z/150	"	Sherratt J	"	
S/8932	"	Smith N. W.	"	
S/6835	"	Stead H	"	
B/2984	"	Scading E	"	
P/440	"	Tappin J. H	"	
6/237	"	Taylor C	"	
S/5162	"	Taylor S	"	
S/8719	"	Till H	"	
S/5089	"	Toms C	"	
S/8120	"	Thom J	"	
S/259	"	Thompson F. A	"	
B/1446	"	Townsend J	"	
S/9262	"	Turner H	"	
S/1509	"	Thomas H	"	
B/647	"	Tweed B	"	
S/11585	"	Teague E	"	
S/8788	"	Tebble E	"	
Z/1358	"	Tucker D	"	

203

27

No	Rank & Name	Coy	Remarks
S/6120	Rfn Upston N. G.	B	
B/1361	" Voice C. J.	"	
S/11258	" Vickers J.	"	
S/6576	" Walton E.	"	
B/1979	" Walker J	"	
S/6023	" Winfield H	"	
B/220	" Wilson H	"	
S/9354	" Wilkes J.	"	
S/6124	" Williams A. J	"	
S/9572	" Whitehouse B	"	
B/749	" Woodford P	"	
Y/11317	" Whittle G	"	
B/1365	" Wall W.	"	
S/11131	" Welford L. A.	"	
S/654	" ~~Weston H~~	"	
S/9121	" Waters B	"	
S/6220	" Wooster H	"	

219

No	Rank and Name	Coy	Remarks
B/1287	Rfn Worthington J	B	
S/11798	" Wisbey E. W	"	
S/7527	" Young H	"	

222

7th Bn. Rifle Brigade 29

No	Rank & Names		Coy	Remarks
7473	C.S.M.	Charlton A	C	
1043	"	Love A	C	✓
1892	C.Q.M.S.	Lyall J	"	
B/3447	Sgt	Binet F	"	✓
B/3459	"	Blunt C	"	✓
B/3412	"	Chumbly J	"	✓
8303	"	Cooke J	"	✓
3749	"	Franks J	"	✓
9921	"	Hine H	"	✓
B/3747	"	Morrison J	"	✓
2225	"	Riddell J	"	✓
B/325	"	Rous J	"	✓
B/3416	"	Sparrow G	"	✓
B/3481	"	Whiteley J	"	✓
B/351	A/Sgt	Hall H	"	✓
B/2113	"	Jones E	"	✓
S/5886	"	Parmanter D	"	
B/3225	"	Williams R	"	✓
Z/1501	Cpl	Carter W	"	✓
B/616	"	Every W	"	✓
S/6429	"	Lelean H	"	✓
B/1997	"	McBirnie A	"	✓
B/1597	"	O'Kell C	"	✓
B/3517	"	Robotham A	"	✓

30

No	Rank and Name		Coy	Remarks
B/1994	Cpl	Sims E	C	✓
B/1620	"	Valentine A	"	✓
" 1533	"	Westlake M	"	✓
		Brocker A	"	
8793	L/Cpl	~~Andrews~~ #	"	✓
B/3458	"	Day H	"	✓ ✗
2005	"	Grace M	"	✓
S/11192	"	Harle G	"	✓
G/2833	"	Hicks W	"	✓
B/3371	"	Hope J	"	✓ ?
S/6583	"	Jefferys W	"	?
B/3482	"	Jones E J	"	✓
B/3411	"	Matthews C	"	✓
B/1747	"	Norris W	"	✓
3179	"	Parker D	"	✓
S/8382	"	Parslow G	"	✓
B/2665	"	Perry J C	"	
B/2324	"	Russell G	"	✓
C/3376	"	Slack J G	"	✓
B/3205	"	Saxby J G	"	
B/3851	"	Wilson J R	"	✓
4833	"	Yarrow R	"	✓

45

31

No	Rank and Name		Coy	Remarks
B/3437	Rfn	Alldridge S	C	✓
S/8972	"	Allison J	"	✓
B/3518	"	Ashford C	"	✓
B/3935	"	Ashmore H	"	? Hospital
S/5942	"	Attwood F	"	✓
S/9133	"	Barker F	"	✓
S/11599	"	Baldwin D	"	✓
S/10360	"	Barton G	"	✓
S/11084	"	Batt C	"	✓
B/635	"	Balderstone W	"	✓
S/12627	"	Bennett A	"	✓ Hospital
B/1681	"	Beattie R	"	✓
S/9522	"	Bean W	"	✓ Hospital
S/7175	"	Bishop H	"	✓
B/3457	"	Bissett J	"	✓ ?
B/1656	"	Bird H	"	✓
B/2777	"	Blackwell Q	"	✓
S/12752	"	Blake a	"	✓
S/8531	"	Bliss J	"	?
S/9975	"	Blyde J	"	✓ Hospital

No	Rank & Name		Coy	Remarks
B/3480	Rfn	Blakoe V	C	✓
S/8214	"	Bouchet J	"	✓
S/11263	"	Bonner G	"	✓
S/10458	"	Briggs H	"	✓
B/2846	"	Brooks A	"	✓
1897	"	Buckner W	"	✓ Hospital
S/11586	"	Burgess C	"	✓
B/3233	"	Brewer G	"	✓
S/6022	"	Capon G	"	✓
S/3160	"	Chambers R	"	✓ Hospital
S/12759	"	Church W	"	✓
S/12697	"	Clarke H	"	✓
S/5003	"	Clarke S	"	✓
B/1517	"	Clarke H	"	✓
D/2852	"	Cookson J	"	✓
D/453	"	Condon J	"	✓
S/6157	"	Craig E	"	✓
S/9830	"	Crowe W	"	✓
D/3475	"	Curtis J	"	✓

No	Rank + Name		Coy	Remarks
S/261	Rfn	Davis H	C	✓
S/6160	"	Day W	"	✓
B/3470	"	Dearman W	"	✓
S/6170	"	Dearman G	"	✓
B/3456	"	Deryck A	"	✓
S/13449	"	Dennett J	"	✓
B/2119	"	Dixon J	"	✓
B/3437	"	~~Dolphin~~ Duncan H	"	
B/786	"	Dunn L	"	
S/12858	"	Dudley J	"	
1863	"	Dowsett H	"	Hospital
B/3031	"	Edwards W	"	
S/5166	"	Estall Y	"	
S/9194	"	Evans D	"	
S/5056	"	Evans R	"	
Z/1039	"	Eyles W	"	
S/7261	"	Fallover Y	"	
S/11240	"	Farman S	"	
D/3032	"	Ferris D	"	
B/2342	"	Finlayson B	"	
B/558	"	Forrester F	"	
S/8812	"	Frost E	"	

Tot 99

34

No	Rank	Name	Coy		Remarks
13/4409	Rfn	Freer	J	C	
429	"	Fuller	J	"	
5/6070	"	Gubbins	G	C	
3/11471	"	Goddard	J	"	
5/5360	"	Garrett	W	"	
6/616	"	Graves	E	"	Hospital
2/1191	"	Hall	R	"	
6/1662	"	Handley	J	"	
5/7171	"	Haines	W	"	
13/451	"	Harvey	W	C	
5/10232	"	Hayward	A	"	
5/12054	"	Harman	P	"	
2/2261	"	Haslam	H	"	
5/10391	"	Henson	G	"	
5/10342	"	Horst	E	"	Hospital
2/879	"	Howe	F	"	
2/1085	"	Holland	J	"	
13/1670	"	Hunt	P	"	Hospital
2/1665	"	Hilton	J	"	

bd 115

No	Rank & Name		Coy	Remarks
S/9288	Rfn	James W	C	
B/2134	"	Jeffery G	"	
S/5889	"	Jaffrey E	"	
B/2767	"	Jenner F	"	
B/2516	"	Jones W	"	
S/9524	"	Johnson J	"	
S/12747	"	Johnson A	"	
4051	"	Jones C	"	
B/2851	"	Kilburn G	"	
S/11749	"	Lane C	"	
B/9128	"	Lawrence C	"	
S/7172	"	Leach J	"	
B/1671	"	Livings J	"	
S/10137	"	Lockhart J	"	
B/2831	"	Lillystone J	"	

No	Rank and Name		Coy	Remarks
3383	Rfn	Mahon Y	C	
Z/324	"	Maidment H	"	
B/1586	"	Martin E	"	
S/10602	"	Maslin W	"	
S/9712	"	Maynard A	"	
S/12063	"	May W	"	
S/7534	"	Matthews J	"	
S/9576	"	Melling J	"	
S/10418	"	Mignot J	"	
S/10128	"	Miles A	"	
B/2515	"	Moore B	"	
S/5033	"	Money N	"	
S/8699	"	Morgan R	"	
A/2768	"	Moreland J	"	
S/8592	"	Mears G	"	
S/10511	"	Nowell J	"	
B/3282	"	Noyce J	"	

No	Rank and Name		Coy	Remarks
2/906	Rfn	Oldham 7	C	
P/864	"	Oliver 7	"	
S/1685	"	Orton S	"	
P/2027	"	Owen 9	"	
S/11176	"	Osborne a 9/7	"	
P/2968	"	Oldfield y 7	"	
2/1044	"	Panting D	"	
S/10298	"	Parr H	"	Hospital
2/2042	"	Pansey D	"	
S/11129	"	Parry a	"	
P/2160	"	Pearce 9 y	"	
B/2210	"	Payton y	"	
S/12739	"	Powell a	"	
9/1996	"	Plumbridge 7 y	"	
B/2055	"	Pugh y	"	

38

No	Rank & Name		Coy	Remarks
B/555	Rfn	Radford J	C	
S/12065	"	Reeves J	"	
S/11969	"	Ridout J	"	
S/10274	"	Riley V	"	
S/4146	"	Roberts E	"	
S/6983	"	Rogers A	"	
S/10204	"	Rogers L	"	
S/8596	"	Rock A	"	
S/509	"	Rout A	"	
B/1658	"	Ryan R	"	
Z/1636	"	Roberts J	"	
S/10612	"	Rogers J	"	Hospital
S/5927	"	Sargeant A	"	
S/9140	"	Scothern H	"	
S/10607	"	Shaile J	"	
S/5045	"	Sharp J	"	Hospital
B/2965	"	Shepherd A	"	
S/6633	"	Shurton G	"	
S/6608	"	Shrosbree O	"	
S/8823	"	Seabright M	"	
S/10472	"	Singer W	"	
S/6027	"	Smart S	"	
B/1822	"	Smith J	"	Hospital

No	Rank & Name		Coy	Remarks
B/2775	Rfn	Smith R	C	
4252	"	Smith W	"	
S/6709	"	Smith L	"	
S/10221	"	Smith W	"	
S/10339	"	Smith R	"	
B/2669	"	Southeran W	"	
8066	"	Sparkes W	"	
B/2112	"	Spencer C	"	
S/11762	"	Springett R	"	
B/637	"	Stevens W	"	
S/7167	"	Steptoe A	"	
S/13607	"	Street D	"	
S/5891	"	Strudwick H	"	
S/12742	"	Stocks W	"	
8/3448	"	Stocken Y	"	
S/12857	"	Surey W	"	
S/5790	"	Sykes N	"	Hospital
B/2123	"	Symons F	"	
S/9916	"	Smith J	"	

Tot 199

No	Rank & Name		Coy	Remarks
S/6125	Rfn	Tache P	C	
S/12741	"	Taylor A	"	
B/2429	"	Thomas A	"	
S/8869	"	Thomas J	"	
B/3391	"	Thomas a	"	Hospital
S/13055	"	Thompson H	"	
S/6217	"	Thiel W	E	
S/10401	"	Turner E	"	
C/3231	"	Venning H.	"	
1764	"	Walker A	"	
S/11797	"	Walker G	"	
S/9388	"	Whitbread a	"	
B/3471	"	White J	"	Hospital
S/335	"	Willis g	"	
2/2113	"	Williams C	"	
S/11130	"	Windsor F	"	
S/11156	"	Wood P	"	
B/2267	"	Wood a	"	
B/3033	"	Wroe A	"	

= 216

41

No	Rank & Name	Coy	Remarks
B/3396	Rfn Wilkinson J	C	
1079	" Williams R	"	
B/1683	" Wyatt J	"	

30 219

'D' Coy   7th Bn Rifle Brigade

No	Rank	Name	Remarks
B/3505	S.M	Morgan C	
4513	C.S.M	Shearing H	
B/2671	C.Q.M.S	Wilkins H	
B/871	Sgt	Saunders P	M.G Sgt.
B/553	"	Willson R	Master book
B/3021	"	Scott a I	
B/2350	"	Wedge F	
B/1902	"	Hunt H	
S/961	"	Pope S	
6056	"	Hopwood a	
B/140	"	Herd I	
B/5047	A/Sgt	Hennessey F	
B/2692	"	Hilling F	
B/496	"	Howell G	
S/13195	Sgt	Macadam J	Sgt Shoemaker
B/10	A/Sgt	Wansborough R	
B/790	L/pl	Hopkins E	Hospital
S/1593	"	Hutton C	
B/2346	"	Anderson a	

18

"D" Coy (contd)   43.

No.	Rank & Name		Remarks
3/3019	Cpl	Wilkinson G.	
S/4575	"	Carroll D.	
S/6027	"	Lewin F.	
S/6028	"	Lewin H.	
3/3008	"	Murphy J.	
S/8394	"	Barrett H.	
Z/2569	"	Hoare C.	
1994	"	Read W.	
13/1972	A/C	Brindley J.	
3/2870	"	Campbell G.	
S/5103	"	Caughlin W.	
13/3223	"	Lee F.	
3/1895	"	Lee C.	
13/164	"	Parfitt H.	
S/1502	"	Gessey C.	
3/3222	"	Hodder W.	
3/3583	"	Mycock H.	
5902	"	Stoddard F.	

36

'D' Coy (cont'd)   44

No.	Rank	Name		Remarks
13/791	L/C	New	T.	
B/2587	"	Richardson	J	
B/2423	"	Welland	W.	
B/2510	"	Bone	G.	
S/8524	"	Bennett	T.	
S/2347	"	Pearce	J	
S/2416	"	Machin	W.	
T/3169	"	Edwards	K	Hospital
S/~~266~~	"	~~Johnson~~	~~B~~	~~Hospital~~
B/1600	"	State	A	
S/3097	"	McEvoy	G	
B/2502	"	Watts	W.	

B/2509	Rfm	Allcorn	E	
Z/~~1921~~	"	~~Airdrie~~	~~A~~	~~Hospital~~
B/1599	"	Archer	R	
S/3096	"	Arnold	R.	
B/2187	"	Astwood	A	
S/11601	"	Adams	J.	

51

D' Coy (contd)   45.

No.	Rank & Name		Remarks
S/10330	Rfn	Armstead E	
B/1905	Rfn	Baker A	
B/1755	"	Ball J	Hospital
S/1249	"	Barroughs A	
S/2415	"	Barnes W	
B/2189	"	Bargent H	
S/2072	"	Berry G	
S/4200	"	Brown C	
B/2693	"	Bishop J	
S/~~___~~	"	~~Butt___ 7~~	~~Hospital~~
Z/360	"	Blandy 7	
B/1664	"	Brown A	
S/12668	"	Bambridge 7	
S/5195	"	Braybrooke 7	
B/1916	"	Bradbury J	
S/3393	"	Brooks A	
S/3002	"	Burpitt R	
S/3600	"	Burns W	
S/2076	"	Burke J	
B/2850	"	Bayless A	

69

"D" Coy (cont'd.)   46.

No.	Rank & Name	Remarks
S/9707	Rfn. Brookes J.	
S/9511	" Burbridge G.	
S/9538	" Bathgate J.	
S/13303	" Bryant F.	Hospital
S/7476	" Booth W.	
S/6495	" Burke C.	
S/7106	" Burton H.	
S/3222	" Bryson J.	
S/13174	" Barber J.	
S/12745	" Bourgaize T.	
S/1595	" Brookes F.	
B/3113	Rfn. Cain R.	
B/1906	" Cheek F.	
B/2895	" Chilton T.	
S/12816	" Colverson A.	
S/2576	" Clarke S.	
B/1675	" Corrall H.	
S/6044	" Cox H.	
S/6219	" Collier E.	
S/9794	" Cutmore W.	Hospital

'D' boy. (cont'd)   47

No.	Rank & Name		Remarks
3/9434	Rfn. Childs	H	Hospital
3/9229	" Clarke	A	
Z/2990	" Clark	R	
3/12735	" Carr	J	
3/11066	" Charman	S	
3/13437	Rfn. Dacey	J	
B/2649	" Davies	J	
B/1766	" Davies	W	Hospital
B/3205	" Dewell	S	
3/13152	" Devey	A	
3/6130	" Dedier	E	
3/11667	" Dukes	E	Hospital
Z/164	" Davis	J	
3/5036	" Davey	A	

"D" Coy (cont'd)   48.

No.	Rank & Name	Remarks
B/1897	Rfn. Eaton T.	Hospital
B/2349	" Edmonstone C.	Hospital
B/2668	" Elms W.	
S/234	Rfn. Feld R.	
S/5160	" Farrell J.	
B/2595	" Fennessey G.	Hospital
B/2078	" Finbow T.	
S/242	" Fowler L.	
S/9426	" Forester H.	
S/6043	" Frost J.	
S/9324	" Fairman W.	
B/3215	Rfn. Garner H.	
B/1589	" Godson H.	
B/1752	" Gordon W.	
B/5101	" Goodhew C.	
S/3201	" Griffiths W.	Div. Train

'D' Coy (contd) — 49

No.	Rank & Name		Remarks
S/2362	Rfn	Grimes W.	
S/7251	"	Greaves S.	
S/7250	"	Graham T.	
S/9909	"	Gregory E.	
Z/148	Rfn	Hughes W.	
S/7245	"	Hills W.	
B/2074	"	Hogg G.	
S/13441	"	Helling J.	Hospital
S/792	"	Harris J.	
S/12317	"	Hemmings W.	
S/3216	"	Hawkens C.	
S/13157	"	Hindley J.	
S/7231	"	Haggetty M.	
S/5067	"	Hitchcock W.	
S/11697	"	Howard T.	
S/9876	"	Holmes A.	
S/9449	"	Hills C.	
S/11134	"	Howard J.	
S/5909	"	Holloway A.	Hospital

"D" Coy (contd)   50.

No	Rank + Name		Remarks
S/9658	Rfn. Jackson	H	Hospital
S/3105	" Jackson	T	Hospital
S/9731	" Jackson	W	
Z/408	" Johnson	H	
S/2586	" Jarod	C.	
B/543	" Kennett	J.	
S/1989	Rfn. Lefts	M	
Y/7572	" Lumings	W	
B/2273	" Leggett	C	
Z/751	" Liddington	T	Hospital
Z/1836	" Lea	T	
S/10368	" Miller	M	
S/3093	" Moss	T	
S/5128	" Mahoney	D.	
B/2196	" Matthews	C	
S/3107	" Mills	T.	
B/626	" Montgomery	P.	
B/446	" Montgomery	T	
B/3234	" Mosley	W	
Y/7331	" Medway	H	
S/6064	" McBean	R.	

"D" Coy (contd)   57

No.	RANK & NAME		REMARKS
3/6062	Rfn	Marvell J.	
2/9383	-	Moon A.	
9/24114	-	Matthews G.	Hospital
1/10486	-	Martin F.	
3/9289	-	Martin R.	Hospital
3/6220	-	Meade H.	
2/2981	-	Murphy C.	
2/1571	-	Miller F.	
13/40644	-	Mills B.	
9/2269	Rfn	Norton T.	
3/9596	-	Nickless E.	
3/9250	Rfn	Olney A.	
1/3053	-	Powell C.	
3/1472	-	Pemberton W.	
3/1841	-	Page J.	
3/2594	-	Parker S.	
3/10178	-	Parsons W.	
13/2636	-	Peak J.	

162

D. Coy. (cont'd.)   52

No	RANK & NAME	REMARKS
9/2663	Rfn. Pether J	
9/1921	" Phillips J	
9/2662	" Preston H	
9/1913	" Pugh G	
9/2478	" Pearson R	
9/5051	" Phillips J	
9/6045	" Payne H	
9/1590	" Pimley T	
9/1073	" Parker W	
9/10408	" Pateman G	
9/11753	Rfn. Rose R	Hospital
9/5121	" Redding G	Hospital
9/2014	" Roberts W	
9/345	" Randall G	
9/348	Rfn. Smith H	
9/1604	" Salt G	
9/2263	" Schofield A	

177

"D" Coy (contd)   53

No	Rank	Name	Remarks
8/5647	Rfn	Shaw J.	
8/2772	-	Smith T.	Nv. Trans
8/13154	-	Shaw H.	
8/2506	-	Sommerville J.	
8/1971	-	State B.	
8/1975	-	Standing T.	
8/2664	-	Stanley A.	
8/5151	-	Squires T.	
8/3218	-	Swinstead C.	
8/5038	-	Spiro W.	
8/9207	-	Smith C.	
8/9441	-	Stanley W.	
8/1079	-	Simmonds A.	
8/1666	-	Schofield A.	
8/~~272~~		~~Smith T~~	~~Hospital~~
8/4574	-	Smith W.	
8/6227	-	Stevens H.	
8/13281	-	Stephenson D.	
8/5024	-	Smith E.D.	
8/2687	-	Stennett W.S.	
8/11764	-	Smith A.	
8/8735	-	Stoakes A.	

198

D Coy (contd.) 54

No.	Rank & Name		Remarks
B/1903	Rfn	Toms G.	
S/5161	-	Thripp W.	
B/1750	-	Tristram T.	
B/7229	-	Tylyard H	
B/328	-	Thatcher A.	
B/1990	-	Tilbury H	
B/3104	-	Tophams J	Hospital
S/13139	-	Toms F.	

B/3326	Rfn	Underwood A	
S/2578	-	Veal R.	
S/12969	-	Weding J	
S/10452	-	Williams R.	
S/3114	-	Weston A	
B/2499	-	Willcocks G	
B/2770	-	Woodcock A	
B/1842	-	Woods A	
S/7244	-	Weine H	
S/7232	-	Warner J	
S/11321	-	Webb C.	
S/12807	-	Wymes J	
S/3151	-	Wren C H	
S/12744	-	Woodard F.	

'D' Coy (contd)   55

No	Rank & Name	Remarks
S/13106	Rfn. Whyley W	
S/9373	" Williamson G	
S/9454	" Weeks W	Hospital
S/9552	" Wyllie W	~~Hospital~~ Base 20/12/15
B/676	" Youlden T	

7th Rifle Brigade

1st G. Tan

4/ Bde

(14)

14th Div.
7th Bn. Rifle Bde.
Vol. 10.

CONFIDENTIAL

WAR DIARY

OF

7TH BN RIFLE BRIGADE

FROM 1-4-16   TO 30-4-16

(VOLUM XII)

[signature] LT COL
COMMDG 7TH BN RIFLE BRIGAE.

CONFIDENTIAL

WAR DIARY OF

7TH BATTN. RIFLE BRIGADE

FROM 1-3-1916   TO 31-3-16.

(VOLUME XI)

[signature] LT. COL
COMMDG 7TH BATTN. RIFLE BRIGADE

Army Form C. 2118.

WAR DIARY
or
INTELLIGENCE SUMMARY.
(Erase heading not required.)

Instructions regarding War Diaries and Intelligence Summaries are contained in F.S. Regs., Part II and the Staff Manual respectively. Title pages will be prepared in manuscript.

Place	Hour, Date	Summary of Events and Information		Remarks and references to Appendices
H.Q. A.16.c. sheet 28.	1916. Jan. 1.	Arrived. 2 a.m. from Trenches.		
	Jan. 2.	Sunday. Resting.		
	3	" "		
C.13.B. Trenches	4	L.T.R. Trenches. B.Coy to Canal Bank in sup. to Batt.		
"	5	No 13639 Rfn BAXTER. J. A.Coy AT.D. in front line. 8 R.B on right 41st R? on [left?]	Wds	No 2156 Rfn HARPER.T. A Coy wounded 23 min [illeg]
		No 9302 Rfn FYLES. Y. B - " seagnified. Bullet	Wds	
		11258 " VICKERS.T. B - " wounded. Bullet	Wds	
		13151 " WREN. E. D.Coy " Rifles	Wds	Buried at Elinger Cottage C.13.B.3.3. sheet 23.
	6	11321 " WEBB. C. D.Coy " "	Wds	
		11133 " CROOKS. H. B.Coy " Shell	Wds	
		9869 " LYNCH. J. B " "	Wds	
		11317 " WHITTALL. G. B " "	Wds	
	7	6833 " YARROW. R. C " "	Wds	
		2145 " SANDS. T. A " Killed. Bullet	Kd	do
	8	11123 " KELLY. A. A " " Shell	Kd	
		Relieved partially by 7 K.R.R. partly by 5th K.R.S.L.L. who were very late & above but [illeg]ly to the Canal Bank.		
		We got away at midnight and reached Billets in POPERINGHE by train from ASYLUM at 4 a.m.		
POPERINGHE	9	Sunday. arrived 4 a.m. Billets. Resting.		
"	10	Resting.		
"	11	" A Coy to Canal Bank in sup. to Batts. Lancashire Fusrs. B.C. front line. 8th RR on own right.		
"	12	L.Ts. twenty R.B on own right. My Lt.		bind lancashire Fn C.14. S.D.2.
C.14.C. Trenches	13	No 5196 O/[] Rfr BRYANT. H. B.Coy Killed Bullet	Kd	
		10332 " WILLIAMS.J. A " " "		Ennin Fn
		317 " FORSHAM. A " " " on [being?] hit in [illeg]		C. 25. a. 4. 8.
		525 " WARBOYS. A " " " dug out		
		4873 " CLARKE .W - wounded "		" No 17 C.C.S.[illeg]
		10727 " RUDKIN " died of wounds 13 Jan at No 17 C.C.S.		

Army Form C. 2118.

WAR DIARY
or
INTELLIGENCE SUMMARY.
(Erase heading not required.)

Instructions regarding War Diaries and Intelligence Summaries are contained in F.S. Regs., Part II. and the Staff Manual respectively. Title pages will be prepared in manuscript.

(37)

Hour, Date, Place 1916	Summary of Events and Information	Remarks and references to Appendices
C.14.C. trenches Jan. 14th	No 12748 Rfn JAMES. V. B.Coy. Killed	Buried Brandhoek F. C.14.C. 0.2.
	7327 " YOUNG. H. " " wounded	
	12762 " STOWE. A. " "	
	12657 " HAZZARD. R. " "	
	5104 O/c STANLEY. A. D.Coy.	
	13303 Rfn BRYANT. E. B.Coy. wounded	
	838 " PATTISON. P. " "	
" 15	8812 " FROST. E. C.Coy "	
	Battalion relieved by 8th K.R.R.C.	
" 16	Battalion arrived at Huts A.16.d. arrived 10 p.m.	
Camp A.16.d. " 17	Batt. at rest. (Battalion)	
" 18	Lost 20 other ranks from Battalion. An accident occurred at bombing instruction	
	following Casualties. Lieut BROWN R.C. D.Coy wounded	
	No 2418 a/cpl MACHIN. W. " " "	
	8777 Rfn MANN. J. " " "	
	549 " WESTALL. S. " " "	
	6062 " MARVEL. J. " " "	
	5982 " WHARTON. W. " " "	
	154 " SHANNON. W. " " "	
	7021 Sgt SCOTT. A.J. " " "	
	5840 A/cpl STODDART. F. " " killed	
" 19	Batt. Resting. No 9640 Rfn JONES. A. A.Coy. wounded buried	
	4416 " COUSINS. P. " " at night working parties	Buried from Mil. Cemetery, POPERINGHE Row. D. Grave 15.
" 20	C. Coy to Convert Bacon into trenches in advance of B. Battalion	
	A and D Coys into front line Relieved 8th K.R.R.C.	
C.14.C. Trenches " 21	No 1935 Sgt MILLS. W. B.Coy. wounded buried	
	230 Rfn HALFORD. H. A.Coy " "	

Army Form C. 2118.

WAR DIARY
or
INTELLIGENCE SUMMARY.
(Erase heading not required.)

Place	Hour, Date	Summary of Events and Information	Remarks and references to Appendices
C.II, C. (Sheet 28) Trenches.	1916 Jan. 22	9190 13031. Rfn. JOHNSON. G. A (wounded). Shell. died 23rd h.10 C.C.St. Lieut. WINTER. C.E. wounded. Bullet. whilst transport at 7th dump wounded. Shell. 9190 289 C/Sgt WICKER. W. A Coy " 1853 Rfn. KASS. A " " 13182 " MOGFORD. E " " 2797 " DAWSON. J " " 31 " MILLER. W " " 309 " SEARLE. W " " 1582 A/C DUTTON. H bullet. died 24th MRs 572 Rfn. MACK. T accidentally by discharge of 12070 " MATHER. S.A. B.Cn. a rifle.	9190 3608 Cpl. MURPHY. J. died of wounds on 5 Jan. buried 26 Cem. Hosp. 9190 2569. Cpl. HOARE. C. died of wounds on 7 Jan. buried 11 Gen. Hosp.
"	23 Sunday	1908 C/Q.M.S. PRICE. A. A Coy " Shell " 757 Rfn. DUDLEY. J. B " bullet " 10268 " SPEARING. V. B " Shell "	Buried Jno 10 Gen. Cl. St.
"	24	2516 " JONES. W. C " bullet " 760A " SMITH. E. D " Shell " 3482 A/C. JONES. E.T. C " Shock " B.Jen retired by 8 K.R.R.C. B.Jen billets in POPERINGHE in Bn. arrived at 5 a.m. dug out billets by a Sudan in B.Jen Rest Camp.	MRs MRs MRs
POPERINGHE	25		MRs
"	26	" " "	MRs
"	27	" " "	MRs
"	28	" " " dropt of 30 Sounds Butter	MRs
"	29	" " "	MRs
"	30 Sunday	" " "	MRs
"	31	" " " D. Coy & Comm. Book in attendance	Fighting Strength 25 Ofk 855 O.R.

CONFIDENTIAL

WAR DIARY

OF

7TH BATTN. RIFLE BRIGADE

FROM. 1st ~~February~~ Jan 1916   To 29TH FEBRUARY 1916.

(VOLUME X)

LT COL.

Army Form C. 2118.

WAR DIARY
7th Bn. Rifle Brigade
or
INTELLIGENCE SUMMARY.
(Erase heading not required.)

Hour, Date, Place	1916.	Summary of Events and Information	Remarks and references to Appendices
POPERINGHE	1 Feb.	In trenches C.14.C. Lancashire Fm.	
Trenches Lancashire Fm	2 Feb.	B+C Coy in front. A+D in Support. Relieved 8 KRRC.	Relieve C.14.C.+ Lancashire Fm
		No B. 3331 Rfn GREATOREX. J. C. Cy. No 11262 Rfn FOSTER. J. A Cy wounded. Bullet shell [?]	D.22 Trench impossible to man—drains full.
		1516 " GRANSBY. F. B " killed "	
		7316 " FRANKS. E.S. B " "	
		12075 " HODGES. C. B " "	
		1524 Rfn MOORE. A. C " "	
		At 11.30 a.m the Germans delivered a slight attack against MORTALDJE and the Trenches on our right. Our own men kept up from the...[?] and opened rapid fire. The enemy's attack [?] failed.	
	3 Feb.	Quiet day. One casualty	Wd 1
	4 "	"	Wd 2
	5 "	"	Wd 3
	6 "		Wd 4
	Sunday	No 2896 Rfn WILKINSON. J. C Coy shell killed Str YPRES	
		9563 " DEVEY. J. A " " "	
		2014 " ROBERTS. W. A " " "	
		8291 " HILL. F. A " " "	
		8725 Cpl CROCKER. A. A " " "	
		245 Rfn RANDALL. A. A " " "	
		373 " WILLIAMSON. G. A " " "	
	7	Much artillery activity	Wd 5
		No 2112 Rfn SPENCER. C.H. C Coy wounded	
		11695 " WILLY. G. C " "	Bullet Shell
		Relieved by 8 KRRC. Bn moved to Rest Camp A.16.c.	
Camp. A.16.c.	8.	Base Resting.	Wd 6
Sh 28.	9.	"	Wd 7
	10.	"	Wd 8
	11.	Battn marched to billets round WINNIZEELE. In 14th Corps Reserve	Wd 9
WINNIZEELE	12.	Nothing to report. Lt E.W. POPE rejoined Battn from sick	Wd 10
	13.	Sunday Nothing to report	Wd 11

Army Form C. 2118.

WAR DIARY 7th Bn Rifle Brigade.
or
INTELLIGENCE SUMMARY.
(Erase heading not required.)

Hour, Date, Place 1916.	Summary of Events and Information	Remarks and references to Appendices
WINNIZEELE. Feb. 14th	Nothing to report. Lt. A.P.G. MERRIAM Transferred to 41st Siege Battery.	
" 15.	Battalion marched 2 miles to OUDEZEELE and reinflmenced. Nothing to report.	
OUDEZEELE 16.	Nothing to report.	
" 17.	Capt P.A. SCOTT returned from duty as Town Major, YPRES & 2/Lt L.G.N. LANGMEAD rejoined from sick leave in England. Battn inspected by the C in C at WINNIZEELE and was expressed his pleasure.	
" 18	Nothing in town in forenoon. Nothing to report.	
" 19	"	
" 20	Sunday. " "	
" 21	Battn marched at 5 a.m. to CASSEL and entrained for Boulogne to AMIENS. Battn detrained at LONGUEAU at 8.15 p.m. The Coys marched to NAOURS and 2 Coys went in busses - distance about 10 M. (Naours)	
NAOURS 22	Battn arrived in early morning and billeted.	2/Lt Van MILLIGEN joined R.B.
" 23	Nothing to report. Sermon.	
" 24	Paraded at 2 a.m. in order to be ready to move at short notice. Marched at 11 a.m. to DOULLENS and billeted. (fine)	
DOULLENS 25.	Marched to WARLUZEL. Snowed the whole way - the Troop marched splendid. The storm Transport lost their way and did not arrive till own 8 hours after the arrival of Battn in front areas.	
WARLUZEL 26	Resting & Kitting. Cap. Campbell arrived at ARRAS.	Reinforcement of 13 men arrived.
" 27	Sunday. C.O. & 5 others visited ARRAS	Fighting Strength 30 Officers
" 28	2 i.c. & 6 other went to inspect section to be occupied by Battn	869 O.R.
" 29	Cy Comdrs inspected section between RONVILLE ...	[signature] Lt Col commdg 7th ... Rifle Bgde.

Army Form C. 2118.

WAR DIARY
or
INTELLIGENCE SUMMARY.
(Erase heading not required.)

7th S. Bn Rifle Brigade

Hour, Date, Place	Summary of Events and Information	Remarks and references to Appendices
ARRAS. 1st March.	Battalion took over trenches in RONVILLE Section & Right of French Army. Relieved the 3rd Bn 20th Regt of French Army. All 4 Coys in front line.	
" 2nd	The trenches were left in an extraordinarily filthy and insanitary condition.	
" 3rd	A quiet day in trenches.	
" 4th	" " " "	
" 5th	Sunday. Relieved "B" Section Hudson's Bn. 5th R.B. & French L.I. The left Coy of 8th Bn R.B. extended about 8M to SIMENCOURT its right. Snow.	1st Bn. ? to new reinforcement (?)
SIMENCOURT 6th	Resting. Some athletic sports.	
" 7th	" Very cold but sunny.	
" 8th	" Frosty day. Bn at Musketry practice.	
" 9th	" Hot front light night.	
" 10th	" Snow. Very cold & cloudy.	Lt C.E. WINTER rejoined Battn.
" 11th	" Very cold & cloudy.	
" 12th	Sunday. 1st Tranches E of ARRAS relieving 3rd Bn R.B. arr. B.C. & D Coys in front line. A in Reserve.	
Trenches. ARRAS. St SAUVEUR Section. 13th	7th KRR on left 42nd Bn on right.	
" 14th	No 7175 Rifn BISHOP. H. C Coy bullets. Scalp slight.	
" 15th	6125 " TACHE. P. C " during " in excellent " had "	
" 16th	9309 Rifn PARKINSON. A. C " day trenches order arms &	
" 17th	12749 " LANE. C.B. A Coy at operation. ankle bullet wounds.	Draft of 70 joining Battn. now stationed
	Lovely day.	

Army Form C. 2118.

WAR DIARY
or
INTELLIGENCE SUMMARY.
(Erase heading not required.)

7th Bn. Rifle Brigade.

Hour, Date, Place		Summary of Events and Information	Remarks and references to Appendices
Trenches ARRAS St Sauveur Sectr.	1916 March 18	Fine. Quiet in Trenches. Nothing to report.	
"	19. Sunday	" Relieved by 8th Bn. Rif Bde. Battalion moved to billets in ARRAS in Bde Res.	MR.
ARRAS	20	In Bde Reserve. Working parties at night.	MR MR MR
"	21	" " " "	MR
"	22	" " " h1711 8/9/61 BOARDMAN F. B. Coy wounded. bullet.	MR MR
"	23	" " "	MR
"	24	" " "	MR MR
"	25	Relieved 8th Bn Rifle Bde in Trenches St. SAUVEUR Sectr. 7 KRR on A.C.D in front line. B in Bn Reserve.	MR MR MR
Trenches ARRAS St Sauveur Sectr.	26. Sunday	General day in trenches. Nothing unusual.	
"	27	" " " "	MR MR MR
"	28	Draft of 15 men arrived. Enemy opened an ambition lively bombardment from minnies in [area] opposite [L.56.] 2.Lt A.C. LAWSON woundd. (Shell P)	
"	29	" "	
"	30	Nothing unusual	MR
"	31	Relieved by 8th Bn. Rif Bde. Battalion into Bdn. Reserve at SIMENCOURT.	

Fighting Strength
26 Officers
900. O.R.

[signature]
Comm. 7th Bn. Rif Bde.
31 March 1916.

WAR DIARY
INTELLIGENCE SUMMARY

7th Batt. Rifle Brigade

Army Form C. 2118.

Place	Hour, Date	Summary of Events and Information	Remarks and references to Appendices
SIMENCOURT.	April 1st	Battalion at rest in Divl. Reserve.	Draft of 60 O.R. joined
"	2 Sunday	" " " " " "	
"	3	" " " " " "	
"	4	" " " " " "	
"	5	" " " " " "	
"	6	Battalion went into Trenches St SAUVEUR Section. A.B.D. Coys in front line. C. Coy in B3 Reserve. 7th RB. KRRC on our left. 42nd Div B83 on Right.	
Trenches ARRAS St SAUVEUR Sn.	7	Trenches in excellent order, dry, weather fine. Lt W.M. FRASER rejoined from sick	
	8	Nothing to report.	
	9 (Sunday)	No 2829 Sgt J. MURTAGH C. Coy wounded shrapnel, admitted whilst on sentry at night	
		No 1326 Cpl J. MASON B. Coy bullet wound head.	
	10	Nothing to report.	
	11	" " "	
"	12	Relieved by 8th Bn Rifle Bde.	
	13	In Brigade Reserve.	
ARRAS.	14	" " "	
	15	" " "	
	16 Sunday	" " "	
	17	" " "	
	18	Into Trenches St SAUVEUR Section — relieved 8th R.B. Rfle Bgde. Trenches suffered from rain. A.B.C. Coys in front D Coy in B3 Reserve.	
Trenches ARRAS. St SAUVEUR Sn.	19	No 2054 Rfn R. CLARKE. A.Coy " " instantly killed (sniper)	
	20	No 6983 " A. ROGERS. C. " " " " " (on duty)	
	21	No 12741 " A. TAYLOR.	
	22	No 759 Rfn W. IZZARD A.Cy wounded	
WANQUETIN	23	Suspected rapid firing by 89th B3 Rifle B83. To rest at WANQUETIN	
	24	Relieved by 15th Rl Rl R.	
	25	2/Lt ROGERS joined B3 from 15th Rl Rl.	
	26	Capt de Calry from Hospital	
	27		
	28		
	29		
	30 Sunday	Into Trenches. St SAUVEUR Sectn. Relieved 8th Rl Rl. B.	

CONFIDENTIAL

WAR DIARY

OF

7TH BATTN. RIFLE BRIGADE

FROM 1-5-16   TO 31-5-16

(VOLUME XIII)

[signature] Lt Col

Commdg 7TH B^N RIFLE BRIGADE

1-6-16.

WAR DIARY
or
INTELLIGENCE SUMMARY.
(Erase heading not required.)   7th Bn. Rifle Brigade.

Army Form C. 2118.

(44)

Hour, Date, Place 1916	Summary of Events and Information	Remarks and references to Appendices
ARRAS. Thurs. Aug. 1st	Major E.P.A. Riddel carried out an attack when left to join 13 Bn. R.B.	
St. SAUVEUR Sectn. 2nd	No 5/356 Rfn WILLIS. H. C.Coy wounds. bullet. died of wounds at 42nd over	wounds AVESNES at 37th C.C.S.
" 3rd	No S/10568 " MILLER. A. D.C. B/Ser moved to billets at WANQUETIN.	42 Field Amb at ARRAS
" 4th	Relieved by 1st A+ B.C.L.I. about 2.a.m.	
" 5th	Arrived Very much	
WANQUETIN. 6th	Resting	
" 7th	Sunday Resting	
" 8th	Battalion march to CHELERS and billeted there. Attached 17th Corps.	
CHELERS 9th	1 Corps reserve	
" 10th	" " " "	
" 11th	" " " "	
" 12th	" " " "	
" 13th	" " " "	
" 14th	Sunday " " " Very wet	
" 15th	" " " "	
" 16th	" " " "	
NEUVILLE St.VAAST 17th	Battn. moved to trenches near NEUVILLE St VAAST relieved 8th Bn KRR. not in front line but providing working parties to R.E. Mining Corps.	
Sheet 51.C. F. 6 and F12. 18th	Working parties " Artillery very active. 6-7 p.m. Shells.	No 2227 Rfn WILSON. J. B. Coy accidentally wounds. while listening to this a revolver.
" " 19th	" " " No 3015 Rfn ARNOLD W. D Coy " " " 4515 " NICKLIN. A C 1671 " LININGS. J. C. " Shell shock severe shell " 9.15 p.m.	
" " 20th	Ammunition of B Coy dump exploded in France. Troops in own front trenches taken for Germans in P. sector. Working parties. Quite a day.	
" " 21st	Sunday. Situation normal until 3.30 p.m. when our bombardment parties down from front and heavy German commenced. This lasted with a barrage on where our 2 Coys B+D were exception till 9 p.m. during which time the Germans dug in. The 7th and 8th B. moved front line trenches in P+ Q sector, arranged 2 Coys to support + counter attack if necessary. Then at 2.a.m. 22nd. division by Churches Regt. The Germans left alone and a little D. Coy in	
" 22nd	B. Coy were already employed guarding the counter attack but Brigade night bombardment in supporting the counter attack. The 7th B. informed that no longer manufacturing. P. 99. S. at 1.30 p.m. the 7th B. resumes B+D Coys	

Army Form C. 2118.

(45)

WAR DIARY
or
INTELLIGENCE SUMMARY. 7th Bn Rifle Brigade.
(Erase heading not required.)

Instructions regarding War Diaries and Intelligence Summaries are contained in F.S. Regs., Part II and the Staff Manual respectively. Title pages will be prepared in manuscript.

Hour, Date, Place 1916	Summary of Events and Information	Remarks and references to Appendices
NEUVILLE St VAAST May 22nd	(continued) and Germans seen to return to their trenches. This finished the raid.	For casualties to Germans see App. 3. (N.S.V.)
	The casualties at RIETZ Camp were A.I.C. from 3.30 p.m. till 8.p.m.	
	5 killed (incl 1 Cpl. 6th Hunts) 1 officer wounded (Lt CHORENYARD)	
	34 2/R O.R.	
	4 " " missing	
	x 2 "	
	43	
23rd	Germany quiet: at 8.30 p.m. a continuous bombardment with very heavy machine gun fire on 9th & 10th Rif Bde fronts by 7th D! — This battalion was not actually attacked but came under fire on the North flank. Work & relief in the trenches carried out as usual.	
24th	Quiet day. Relieved by 8th Bn Rif Bde Battn moved to huts N of St Eloy and encamping huts.	
25th	Batta resting	
26th	" "	
27th	" " Brigadier inspected Battalion	
28th SUNDAY	" " Battn resting	
29th	" "	
30th	" "	
31st	" "	Fighting Strength 30 off. 824 O.R.

St ELOY
Sheet 51.C. F.14.2.

W Wheatcroft Major
Comg 7th Bn Rif Bde

APPENDIX III. N.&V. — CASUALTIES — 7th B. Rifle Brigade — APP. III N.&V.

Regtl. No.	Rank	Name		Coy.	Remarks
S/11137	Lieut.	Churchyard	O.P.	A	Wounded 22.5.16
12/10	Rfn.	Howard	J.	"	"
—	Sgt.	Wansborough	R.	"	"
B/1972	A/Cpl.	Brindley	J.	"	Since died of wounds at St. John Ambulance Brigade Hospital 23.5.16. Burial:- Military Cemetery, Etaples, Grave No. E.78
B/792	Rfn.	Harris	J.	"	Wounded 22.5.16
S/5495	"	Burke	J.	"	"
B/1993	Corpl.	Sims	E.	C	"
B/720	Rfn.	Bates	N.	B	"
B/3367	"	Bancroft	J.	A	"
S/9511	"	Burbridge	G.	B	"
B/3393	"	Brooker	A.	A	"
B/1926	"	Smith	W.	"	"
A/1975	"	Standing	T.	"	"
S/11066	"	Charman	S.	"	"
S/17142	"	Fowler	A.	"	"
S/5942	"	Attwood	F.	C	"
S/1975	"	Blyde	J.	"	"
S/17217	"	Hemmings	W.	D	"
S/6912	"	Clifford	J.	"	"
A/2593	"	Stewart	A.	"	Missing
A/2077	"	Hogg	G.	"	"
B/28	A/Cpl.	Caygill	A.	A	Accidentally wounded by bomb accident whilst on course of instruction in Bombing 18.5.16.

Regtl. No.	Rank	Name		Coy.	Remarks
S/183	Rfn.	Smedes	C.	B	Wounded 22.5.16
S/12427	"	Eaton	E.	"	"
4-658	"	Day	W.	A	"
S/11263	"	Duck	S.	"	"
A/543	"	Kennett	J.	B	"
S/9336	"	Moore	A.	"	"
B/1590	"	Pinley	T.	B	"
S/7396	"	Napier	W.	"	"
B/1995	"	Jones	G.	A	"
S/12735	"	Carr	J.	"	"
S/7771	"	Clifton	W.	B	"
S/14578	"	Rose	A.	"	Gassed
S/8110	"	Wall	F.	"	"
B/716	"	Ridley	T.	"	"
B/1642	"	Lowell	G.	"	"
S/11266	"	O'Conner	P.	"	"
Z/1447	C.S.M.	Carpenter	L.	A	"
3052	Rfn.	Borne	J.	C	Killed 22.5.16. Burial:- Ecoivres Cemetery, Row A, Grave No. 27.
5945	"	Griffin	W.	C	Killed 22.5.16. Burial:- Ecoivres Cemetery, Row A, Grave No. 15.
5921	"	Edwards	J.	D	Killed 22.5.16. Burial:- Ecoivres Cemetery, Row D, Grave No. 2.6.
S/9929	"	Clarke	A		Killed 22.5.16. Burial in
S/9324	"	Fairman	W.		Killed 22.5.16. Burial:- Ecoivres Cemetery.

J.F. Wheatland Lt.
Comdg. 7th B. Rifle Bde.

14

7th K.R.R.C.
vol: 9

CONFIDENTIAL

WAR DIARY

OF

7TH BATTN RIFLE BRIGADE

FROM 1/6/16 TO 30/6/16

(VOLUME XIV)

[signature] LT COL
COMMDG 7TH BN RIFLE BRIGADE

JUNE 30th 1916.

Army Form C. 2118.

WAR DIARY
or
INTELLIGENCE SUMMARY. 7th & 13th Rifle Brigade.
(Erase heading not required.)

Instructions regarding War Diaries and Intelligence Summaries are contained in F.S. Regs., Part II and the Staff Manual respectively. Title pages will be prepared in manuscript.

Hour, Date, Place	Summary of Events and Information	Remarks and references to Appendices
St ELOY Sheet 51.C. F.142. June 1st	Battalion resting. Reconnoitring for tomorrow relief.	
" 2nd	Battalion took over working parties at mine heads from 8th Bn R.B.	
MAROUEIL 3.	Bn. H.Q. at MAROUEIL and B Coy. A & C at ANZIN and ROCLINCOURT D Coy. near NEUVILLE St VAAST	
" 4.	Working for R.E. at mine heads.	
" 5.	Sunday	
" 6.	" " " "	
" 7.	" " " " No 299 Qft WICKER. W. A Coy wounded, shell.	slight
" 8.	7413 Rfn BOWRAGE. C. " C Coy. wounds, shell.	
	14357 " ELSDON. F. " B. "	
	9228 " JAMES. W. " C. " died same day	
" 9.	Working for R.E. at mine heads.	wounded at 42nd C.C.S. Mil Cem at AUBIGNY.
" 10.	" " " " Relieved by 8th Bn R.B. Battalion moved	2Lt KIRKPATRICK rejoined
ECOIVRES. 11.	to ECOIVRES.	
" 12.	Resting	1st R.H. LAWSON rejoined
" 13.	"	
" 14.	"	
" 15.	" reinforcement of 35 arrived	
" 16.	"	
" 17.	"	
" 18.	Sunday	
" 19.		
" 20.	Bn marched to ARRAS arrived in shelters & practice trenches.	
ARRAS 21.	Took over trenches (K.1.) ROCLINCOURT system to 8th Battalion. 3 Coys in front A.B.C. D Coy in Reserve. 7 KRRs on our left. 43rd Bde on our right. We relieved 2nd Bn K.O.S.B.	

Army Form C. 2118.

WAR DIARY
or
INTELLIGENCE SUMMARY.

(Erase heading not required.)

7th Bn Rifle Brigade

Place	Date	Hour	Summary of Events and Information	Remarks and references to Appendices
Tincques (K.L.)	1916 June			
Roelincourt	22		No 3331 Rfn GREATOREX. J. C Coy. Killed.	Buried Fosseux # Amien Bois (Q-26 c.8.7)
"	23		Heavy thunder storm damaged trenches.	Reference sheet Q 22
"	24		Trench heavily mortared by enemy, but damage except no casualties.	
"			No 17368 Rfn ROWBOTHAM F. D Coy. wounded. Shell	
"			8531 " BLISS. F. C Coy. " T.M.	
"			2570 Cpl CAMPBELL H. " "	free slight Concussion
"			818 Rfn BONHAM. J.W. " " Shell	" shock
"			5991 " STRUDWICK " " "	
"	25		At 11 pm an bombardment with enemy lines used T.M's & Q.F guns - no retaliation - no casualties.	
"	26		No 1986 Rfn JONES. J. A Coy wounded with detail (9 T.M. Battery) Trench Mortar bomb	
"	27		2 Lieut H.J.R. MOSELEY. C. Coy Killed accidentally by premature of TM bomb.	
"			SLI in Trenches at 1.30 a.m.	
"			Relieved by 8th Bn R.B. Batt. to DUISANS. (L.8.c.)	Buried Q.26.0.8.17. Amiens
DUISANS. L.8.c.	28		Arrived about 3.a.m. Resting.	
" "	29		Resting. reinforcement of 49 joined Battalion.	
" "	30		Resting	Fighting Strength 28 off 1026 O.R.

A.H. Maclean Col.
Comdg 7th Bn Rif. Bde.

CONFIDENTIAL

WAR DIARY

OF

7TH BATTN RIFLE BRIGADE

FROM 1-7-16   TO 31-7-16

(VOLUME XIV)

[signature] LT COL

COMMDG 7th BATTN. THE RIFLE BRIGADE

In the Field
31-7-16.

Army Form C. 2118.

WAR DIARY
or
INTELLIGENCE SUMMARY.
(Erase heading not required.)

7th Batt: Rifle Brigade.

Instructions regarding War Diaries and Intelligence Summaries are contained in F.S. Regs., Part II and the Staff Manual respectively. Title pages will be prepared in manuscript.

Hour, Date, Place		Summary of Events and Information	Remarks and references to Appendices
DUISANS L.8.c.	July 1916 1st	Battn resting in Div¹ Reserve.	
"	2nd	Sunday " " " "	
"	3rd	Battn relieved 2nd Bt R.B. in Trenches near ROCLINCOURT. 7 KRR on our left.	
		43rd Bde on our right. A.B.D. Coys in front line. C. Coy in Bt Res.	
ROCLINCOURT. Trenches K.1. S.E.	4th	Very wet	
	5th	Some trench mortaring. Shell.	
		No. C.1689 Rfn S. ROXLEY B Cy wounded	
		3635 Cpl E. SELMAN " slightly wounded at duty	
		B.346 Rfn G. DUNTON A Cy " " "	
		B.169 " F. EDWARDS " killed	
		S.15779 " J. CHITTLEBURGH B Cy "	
		1909 " W. OST B Cy "	
	6th	A very wet day. Enemy's snipers rather active by some	
		No.2/5415 Rfn BOURKE E.D. junior wounded	
		S/6115 " WHYLEY W.D.G "	
	7th	Very wet. Trench mortaring. Enemy snipers active	
		Fine	
	8th	Quiet day	
	9th	Sunday. Quiet day. Relieved by 2nd R⁸ R.B. Battn went into Bde Reserve	
		at Cp in Roclincourt. B Coy & H⁴ Qrs at St Nicholas. C. Coy in	
St NICHOLAS (ARRAS)	10th	annex & old R.E. D Coy in Caves.	
" "	11th	From trenches at 3 am	
" "	12th	Reserve Waiting at front	Bussex Mil Cem Roclincourt A.29. C.15.
" "	13th	" "	
" "	14th	" "	
" "	15th	Relieves 8th Bt R.B. in Trenches K.2. Roclincourt A.&D. Cy front line. B - in res.	
ROCLINCOURT K.1. Trenches	16th	No.7171 Rfn HAINES W. C Cy Shell. Sy slight.	
"	17	L.13701 " GREGSON. A. A Cy Bullet " " alight at duty	
		4159 Sgt BAXTER. C. D Cy " " " " "	
		1533 Rfn NESTLAKE. M. C. " " " " (at duty)	

Army Form C. 2118.

WAR DIARY or INTELLIGENCE SUMMARY.

(Erase heading not required.) 7th Battn. Rifle Brigade.

Instructions regarding War Diaries and Intelligence Summaries are contained in F.S. Regs., Part II. and the Staff Manual respectively. Title pages will be prepared in manuscript.

Place	Hour, Date	Summary of Events and Information	Remarks and references to Appendices
ROCLINCOURT R.I. Rest.	July 1916 18	2nd Lt T.W. KIRKPATRICK. C. Coy wounded. 2665 A/Cpl PERRY. J. C " " } on patrol 9140 " SCOTHERN. H. C " "	
"	19.	2.11.5. J.C. Bulidge. W.L Shew. S. Knowles joined Bn from 5th S.R. Br. Quiet day in trenches. Working unusual.	
"	20.	" " "	
"	21.	From 8 a.m to 9.30 a.m a lively interchange of Trench missiles and artillery took place owing to an enemy assisting attack. 2 Pte A.N. Van MILLINGEN. D. Cy wounded. Bdr from stretch. 90796 Rfn L. DUNN. C. Coy killed. Vicks Bomb. Late a 5.9 fire from Tilloy fired about 130 rounds in 1/2 hr at a spot near B7 B8 Q7 with absolutely no damage done. Relieved by 8th Br Rg B2. Arrived 4.a.m.	
DUISANS. L & C.	22	Sunday. Bn. resting in Div Reserve.	
"	23	" " " "	
"	24	" " " "	
"	25	" " " "	
"	26	" " " "	
"	27	" " " "	
"	28	" " " "	
"	29	Bn. marched to WANQUETIN. Weather than v.hot.	
"	30	Sunday. Bn. marched at 4.30 am to BEUDRICOURT. Weather	
AT	31	Bn. marched to MOUCHY-(?)MEZEROLLES by day very hot.	

41st Brigade.
14th Division.

1/7th BATTALION

RIFLE BRIGADE.

AUGUST 1 9 1 6

Vol 16

41/14

CONFIDENTIAL

WAR DIARY

OF

7th Bn RIFLE BRIGADE

FROM 1-8-16   31-8-16

(VOLUME XVI)

[signature] Lt Col.

Commdg 7th Bn RIFLE BRIGADE

In the Field
31-8-16

WAR DIARY or **INTELLIGENCE SUMMARY.** 7th Btn Rifle Brigade.

Army Form C. 2118.

Hour. Date, Place 1916	Summary of Events and Information	Remarks and references to Appendices
AMETZ-IERS MEZEROLLES GEZAINCOURT Aug. 1	Battalion arrived at GEZAINCOURT (DOULLENS)	MB
" 2	Resting, Re-organising	MB
" 3	"	MB
" 4	S/13182 Rfn MOGFORD. E. Accy. killed accidentally at training for Lieut. M.G. Brink GEZAINCOURT	
" 5	S/15791 " SHEEHAN. S. " do. do. wounded	MB
" 6	Sunday. Transport left by road to DERAINCOURT (ALBERT)	MB
" 7	Batt. entrained at night and moved "	MB
DERAINCOURT (ALBERT) " 8	Buried & new arrivals dispersed	MB
" 9	Co & Coy Comdrs reconnoitred HIGHWOOD and DELVILLE wood	MB
" 10	Coy Officers Do.	MB
" 11	Brigade inspected by Corps Commander	MB
8 am " 12	Batt. marched to Reserve trenches near MONTAUBAN. S.26.d.	
MONTAUBAN S.26.d. 9am	Relieved Yorks in Support trenches at S.16.c.	
9 pm	" D & A Coys in front line at S.11.b. W & B Coys DELVILLE wood	MB
	Relieved 8th Suffolks C in Bn Reserve S.11.b	
W & DELVILLE wood S.11.b	9h0 5/3393 Rfn BROOKER. H. D Coy wounded shell	
	" 9551 " GOOSEY. G. " "	
	" R/3486 " JONES. O.H. " "	
	13 Sunday put at 9.30 p.m enemy shewed to shew he was attacking they burnt enemy flares etc	
	9h0 6865 Rfn STEAD. H. B. Coy. Killed. Shell } S.10.0.0.5. Shots/S.S.W	
	Y/784 " DANIELS. W. " " Burial	
	S/13152 " DEVEY. A. D Coy " " }"	
	R/17489 " GEORGE. R. " " } Buried	
	C/1488 " WILD. R. " " } S.11.C.SS.	
	continued.	

WAR DIARY or INTELLIGENCE SUMMARY

Army Form C. 2118.

(Erase heading not required.) 7th S. Bn Rifle Brigade

(51)

Hour, Date, Place		Summary of Events and Information	Remarks and references to Appendices
W. of DELVILLE WOOD. S. 11.b.	Aug 1916. 13	Cho. S.8509 Rfn BANNISTER. H. B Coy. wounded by Shell	
		S.11349 a/Cpl MOODY H. " " " " " slight	
		S.12068 Rfn SPEARING V. " " " 2.40 pm	
		S.8757 " LIDDIARD W. " " " at Batt. Hd qrs	
		C.1140 Sgt BAKER W. D Coy " " " "	
		S.6643 a/Cpl FROST G. " " " D. Coy " " died 14th Aug	
		B.3079 " McEVOY J. " " " " "	
		B.2925 " GODDARD H. " " " " "	
		231 Rfn PEARSON E. " " " " "	
		S.10178 " PARSONS T. " " " " "	
		R.17330 " NEWEY J. " " " " "	
		R.17366 " MYERS S. " " " " "	
		R.14067 " TAVENOR F. " " " " "	
		B.2649 " DAVIES J. " " slightly " at duty	
		Z.1968 " BAYLISS B. " " " " "	
		C.1489 " WORRALL E. " " " " "	
	8 a.m. 14	Relieved by 8th Bn R.B. returned to MONTAUBAN. S.26.b.	
MONTAUBAN. S.26.b.	15.	Working parties to front line. D.C.	
		S.6983 Rfn ROGERS A. C. Coy. wounded Shell slight Batt. hdqrs	
		B.621 " BLOOMBERG S.A. B. Coy " " " "	
	16	Preparing for coming attack	
		9/6222 Rfn WOOSTER H. B. Coy Shell	
		S/11798 " WISBEY E. " "	
	10 p.m. 17	Into trenches at W. of DELVILLE WOOD. relieve 8th Bn R.B. A+D in front C in immediate support. B in divisional reserve. Bombarded by own artillery went on all day against Trenches selected for attack.	

WAR DIARY or INTELLIGENCE SUMMARY.

(Erase heading not required.) 7th Bn Rifle Bde

Army Form C. 2118.

Place	Hour, Date	Summary of Events and Information	Remarks and references to Appendices
W of DELVILLE WOOD S.11.d.	18th Aug 1916	Capture of ORCHARD trench and portion of WOOD LANE. The Bn Bn on left of 8 Bde. 7 KRR on right. Bombardment all day until Zero = 2.46 p.m. with intense final bombardment commencing 5 min. during which trenches & barrages were established at 2.52 p.m. when A & D Coys (first out) carried forth and 2 machine guns assisted by C Coy (first out) D Coy were not so successful, & was hung up before reaching the nearest etc their 2nd obj of WOOD LANE. was not reached. Their advance was also hindered by the fire etc Bdes on our left were split somewhat & C Coy & A Coy bombed up & cleared 35 y.d. of WOOD LANE when then established a bombing block. D Coy had many casualties carrying up S.A.A. and material Bde had valuable assistance to consolidate. Casualties. 1 Off. (Capt. W.E. POPE: D Coy) Killed. 6 Officers wounded. 82 other ranks killed. 191 O.R. wounded. 11 O.R. missing.	For list of wounded & killed see APPENDIX. W.L.3. No. 5/15236 Rfn. LORD. J. C Coy Killed buried { C.1432 Rfn TURNER. J. A Coy {Z.128 HOLLIS J. C Coy } Beauvel F 8a. About 3 casualties unaccounted for. Thought to be buried in trench line – 7th protection lines from C 6.
"	19th	Still holding captured trenches. Relieved by Glasgow Highlanders at midnight. Relief completed front line carried out in relief Bdes march to MONTAUBAN A.8.a.	
"	20th	Arrived at 3 am and bivouacked	
MONTAUBAN A.8.a.	21st	Resting.	
"	22nd	" Working parties in front line	
"	23rd	" " " "	
"	24th	{Lt R.H. LAWSON. B Coy Killed {5/5571. Rfn MERRY. J. B Coy Killed buried {B.1396 " WALTON. E. " Killed } Skin.	buried in PORMICA Redoubt

Army Form C. 2118.

WAR DIARY
or
INTELLIGENCE SUMMARY.

(Erase heading not required.)

7th S. Bn Rifle Brigade

Place	Hour, Date.	Summary of Events and Information	Remarks and references to Appendices
MONTAUBAN A.8.c.	1916 Aug 25.	1 a.m. Orders to relieve 8th B⁴ R.B. in front line. Bdes in B. Coy in front line S.12. c. 4. Belville Wood. C. in support A + D in reserve. S. 22. D. 9. 4.	
		S/9180 O/Cpt MARTIN. C. C. Coy. wounded bullet arm.	
		S/5166 Rfn ESTELL. T. C. " killed shell	
		B/2905 " SHEPPARD. F. C. " killed "	
		B/2415 " BARNES. N. D. " killed "	
		S/13599. " BALDWIN. D. C. " wounded "	
		B/347 " DUNTON. J. A. " " shell slight	
	26.	11th B⁰ R.W.F. recommenced to relieve tonight	
		B/A36 Rfn PERCIVAL. C. B. Coy } killed shell.	
		7860 " DOYLE P. " }	
		S/17341 " JONES E. " }	
		S/7366 O/Cpl TYRRELL. A. B. Coy } wounded shell	
		B/1352. Rfn BINKS. D. " }	
		S/1476 " DEAN. W. A. Coy }	
		2/2952 Rfn GRINDLEY. J. A. Coy killed shell	
	27	Sunday. At 3 a.m. having been relieved by 11th B⁰ R.W.F. we took 6 horse to relieve. Th Batn collected at DERNANCOURT where a draft of	
	28	200 (sundry) recruits awaited. Resting.	
DERNANCOURT	29	Resting	
"	30	By Train to WARLUS. (AMIENS)	
"	31	Resting in billets.	
WARLUS (AMIENS)			Fighting Strength 22 Officers 858 O.R.

HA Rhodes and Skeet
Comg 7th S.B. Rifle Bde.

APPENDIX. W.L.3.
A 1

Rank	& Name		Casualty	
Capt	POPE	E.W	Killed in Action	18.8.16.
"	CUMBERBATCH	R.C.	Wounded	"
2/Lieut	SHOOBERT	W.H	"	"
"	KNOWLES	J.L	"	"
"	HALL	J.S	"	"
"	BURBIDGE	J.C.	"	"
"	CAWKELL	E	"	"

J.S. Sumerland Lt Col

Comdg 7th Bn Rifle Brigade

In the Field
21/8/16.

CASUALTY REPORT
12th Bn. K.R.R. Corps attached 7th Bn. Rifle Bde.

REGTL. No	RANK & NAME		COY	CASUALTY	DATE
R/17262	Rfn	Burcombe R	C	Wounded	18-8-16
R/17305	"	Bennett J	D	"	"
A/2658	"	Broughton W	"	"	"
R/1480	"	Collins B	C	Killed in Action	"
R/17372	"	Dunstall C	D	Wounded	"
R/17239	"	Fisher R	C	Wounded	"
R/17619	"	Farmer S.C.	C	"	"
R/5357	Cpl	Gething G.J.	A	"	"
R/17429	Rfn	Howard T.A.	B	"	"
R/3352	"	Hitchcon J	D	"	"
R/6294	"	Hames R	"	"	"
R/17270	"	Holding W	C	"	"
R/17273	"	Harwood A.H.	A	"	"
R/8982	"	Hicken W	D	Killed in Action	"
R/1723	"	Lester J	"	Wounded	"
R/16557	"	Merriman J	C	"	"
R/17740	"	Moxon G	A	Killed in Action	"
R/15885	"	Pritchard A	C	" " "	"
R/16034	"	Richards J	D	Wounded	"
R/17368	"	Rowbotham J	"	Killed in Action	"
R/17490	"	Ramsey J	"	" " "	"
R/17277	"	Lasker R	C	" " "	"
R/17211	"	Wilkenson E	A	Wounded	"
R/17246	"	Williams T	B	"	"

30/8/16.

Commdg 7/Bn Rifle Brigade Lt Col

CASUALTY REPORT
16th Bn. K.R.R. Corps attached 7th Bt. Rifle Bde

Regtl. No	Rank & Name	Coy	Casualties	Date
C/1523	Rfn T. Land	B	Wounded	18-8-16
C/1495	" J. Mathews	"	Killed in Action	"
C/1469	" Robinson A	A	Wounded	"
C/1627	" Southwell W. A	"	"	"
C/1453	" Sooley J	"	"	"
C/1482	" Turner G	"	"	"
C/1545	" Walton M	B	"	"
C/1580	A/C Webster J	D	Killed in Action	"

Comdg 7th Bn. Rifle Brigade Lt Col

31/8/16

7th Bn Rifle Brigade

CASUALTY RETURN

Regtl No	Rank & Name		Coy	Casualty	Date
S/2053	A/Cpl Allen	T	B	Wounded	18-8-16
S/880	Rfn Addis	H	A	"	"
R/197	" Axford	L.E	"	"	"
S/15260	" Abrahams	H	D	"	"
B/444	" Bonter	L.E	A	"	"
2/818	" Bonham	J	C	"	"
S/8257	A/Cpl Bennett	J	D	"	"
S/11586	Rfn Burgess	C	C	"	"
S/11264	" Bonner	G	"	" (Shock)	"
S/15782	" Brodbeck		D	" "	"
2682	Cpl Burton	S	B	"	"
S/9538	Rfn Bathgate	J	D	"	"
B/2189	" Bargent	H	"	Died of Wounds 19-8-16	"
S/9963	" Burnett	A	C	Wounded	"
S/11084	" Batt	C	"	"	"
2/1476	" Booth	W	B	"	"
S/7240	" Brown	A	D	"	"
4808	" Batchelor	A	A	"	"
B/267	Cpl Beikens	J	A	"	"
B/8	Rfn Beattie	H	A	"	"
2/2306	" Butler	C	D	"	"
B/1934	A/Cpl Baxter	W	"	"	"
B/1664	Rfn Brown	a	"	"	"
B/755	" Conley	A	B	"	"

- 2 -

Regtl. No.	Rank & Name		Coy	Casualties.	
7/1501	Rfn	Carter W.	A	Wounded	18-8-16
2/1753	L/Cpl	Cowan J.	"	"	"
3/12759	Rfn	Church A.T.	C	"	"
S/3160	"	Chambers R.	"	"	"
7/2990	"	Clarke L.	D	" (Shock)	"
S/12647	"	Clarke F.	C	"	"
S/6160	"	Carter R.	A	"	"
A/706	"	Callis A.	B	"	"
7/15267	"	Clarke F.	C	"	"
C/2576	"	Clarke L.	"	"	"
B/3475	"	Curtis J.	"	"	"
B/2638	"	Cole H.	A	"	"
S/15872	"	Cunnington H.	C	"	"
C/339	"	Copeland A.	A	Died of Wounds 19-8-16	"
S/10258	"	Chinnery G.	"	Wounded	"
B/5003	"	Clarke F.A.	C	"	"
C/2119	"	Dixon J.	"	"	"
S/10038	"	Drummond J.	"	"	"
4891	"	Deacon	A	"	"
S/13482	"	Drake P.	"	"	"
C/244	A/Cpl	Duddridge J.	"	"	"
S/12858	Rfn	Dudley J.	C	"	"
B/9	A/Cpl	Elliott G.	A	"	"
B/1897	Rfn	Eaton T.	D	"	"

- 3 -

Regtl No	Rank	& Name		Coy	CASUALTY	Date
0/58	Rfn	Elmer	W	A	Wounded	18-8-16
8/1190	"	Franklin	J	C	"	"
7/2389	"	Fisher	J	B	"	"
8/3215	A/Cpl	Garner	H	D	"	"
3/8965	Rfn	Gutheil	S	A	"	"
7/9110	"	Gunning	J	A	"	"
5/5642	"	Griffen	A	B	"	"
8/261	"	Gordan	H	A	"	"
8/909	"	Gregory	E	J	"	"
5/7014	"	Gilbert	W	"	"	"
8/2132	A/Cpl	Gregory	J	A	"	"
5/5834	Rfn	Gamble	J	C	" (Shock)	"
5/12874	"	Gillett	R	D	"	"
2/864	"	Goodwin	S	"	"	"
4/11697	"	Howard	J	"	"	"
3/6565	"	Holmes	J	C	"	"
9921	Sgt	Hine	H	"	"	"
4/394	Rfn	Houlston	Q	A	"	"
5/6660	"	Hallett	C	"	"	"
8/740	"	Holloway	S	B	"	"
8/120	Sgt	Herd	J	D	"	"
4/10374	Rfn	Jones	E	C	"	"
2/1931	"	Keefe	W	A	"	"
6/2586	"	Jared	C	D	"	"
8/1642	"	Lowell	C	B	"	"

- 4 -

Regtl. No	Rank	Name		Coy	Casualty	Date
S/10137	Rfn	Lockhart	T	C	Wounded	18-8-16
S/15830	"	Lowe	T.C	A	"	"
2/1836	"	Lea	T	D	"	"
S/10145	"	Lloyd	J	A	"	"
S/6027	"	Lewin	J	D	"	"
S/2331	"	Midway	H	"	"	"
Z/446	"	Montgomery	T.J	"	"	"
B/2117	A/Cpl	Miller		A	"	"
B/6	"	Mansell	J	"	"	"
C/Z/2184	Rfn	Moffatt	G.H	B	"	"
S/9843	"	Middleton	W	"	"	"
S/6289	"	Martin	Q	C	"	"
B/935	"	Messer	H	C	"	"
Z/1571	"	Milley	J	C	"	"
7806	"	McGibbon	J	C	"	"
B/3234	"	Morley	W	D	"	"
Z/582	"	Monk	J	A	"	"
6/323	Sgt	Needham	C.M.	"	"	"
S/10511	Rfn	Nowell	J	C	"	"
S/12458	"	Nicholls	J	A	"	"
6/2998	"	Oldfield	J	C	"	"
4/2347	A/Cpl	Pearce	J	D	Died of Wounds 19-8-16	"
1078	Sgt	Piercy	A	E	Wounded	"
3/961	"	Pope	L	F	"	"
A/2210	Rfn	Payton	T	C	"	"

- 5 -

REGTL No	RANK & NAME		COY	CASUALTY	DATE
7/2042	Rfn	Pausey J	C	Wounded	18-8-16
8/1590	"	Pimley T	D	"	"
2/928	"	Price A.J	D	"	"
8/1981	"	Phillips J	D	"	"
S/6042	"	Perkins G.H	A	"	"
S/6041	"	Postlewaite H	"	"	"
8/1763	"	Petts J	"	"	"
8/263	"	Pussell J.A	A	"	"
2225	Sgt	Riddle J	C	"	"
8/166	Rfn	Ruffell E.R	A	"	"
8/2587	A/Cpl	Richardson J	D	" (Shock)	"
S/10577	"	Scott J	"	"	"
S/10607	Rfn	Shaile J	C	"	"
3205	A/Cpl	Saxby H	"	"	"
S/13154	Rfn	Shaw H	D	"	"
4815	C.S.M.	Spearing J	"	"	"
8/2274	Cpl	Sears J.G	A	"	"
8/157	C.S.M.	Smith A.J	"	"	"
S/10372	Rfn	Singer W	C	"	"
8/1757	"	Such A	"	"	"
8/1296	"	Smith C	B	"	"
S/5927	"	Sargent A	C	"	"
S/11113	"	Simpson T	A	"	"
S/13692	"	Stevens W.H	C	"	"
8/1666	"	Schofield A.J	D	"	"
S/15865	"	Simson J	A	"	"

- 6 -

Regtl. No	Rank & Name		Coy	Casualties	Date
S/15154	Rfn	Spring G.a.	A	Wounded	18-8-16
S/3567	"	Samuels T	A	"	"
~~S/3567~~	~~"~~	~~Samuels T~~			
B/2647	"	Shaw J.S	J	"	"
S/9034	"	Slade S	J	"	"
8592	"	Smith H.W.	B	"	"
B/1750	"	Tristram T	B	"	"
Z/1358	"	Tucker D	B	" (Shock)	"
S/11268	"	Vaughan S	A	"	"
S/8480	"	Vaughan 7	"	"	"
B/3326	"	Underwood A	D	"	"
B/2502	A/Cpl	Watts W	"	"	"
Z/1971	Rfn	Webber H	A	"	"
8253	Sgt	Williams A.S	"	"	"
S/6214	A/Cpl	Williams A.J	B	"	"
B/249	Rfn	Wright E.A	A	"	"
B/3114	"	Weston E.A	"	"	"
B/83	"	Walsh M.J	"	"	"
B/1842	"	Woods M.W	"	"	"
S/11130	"	Windsor 7	"	"	"
B/A7	A/Sgt	Wheeler S.L	C	Died of Wounds 19-8-16	"
S/11768	Rfn	Webb L	A	Wounded	"
B/354	A/Cpl	Winter C	"	Died of Wounds 21-8-16	"
B/2770	Rfn	Woodcock A	D	Wounded	"
B/1676	"	Youlden A.J	A	"	"
Z/1205	"	Young J	A	"	"

- 7 -

REGTL No	RANK & NAME		COY	CASUALTY	DATE
A/2901	Cpl	Young A	A	Wounded	12-8-16
S/6219	Rfn	Collier E	D	"	"
S/12816	"	Culverson A	"	"	"
S/13701	"	Gregson G	A	"	"
P/311	"	Liddle J	C	"	"
S/15234	"	Nay J	A	"	"
4252	A/Cpl	Smith W	C	"	"
B/3457	Rfn	Bissett J	"	"	"
9/2346	Sgt	Anderson S	A	" (slight)	"
S/15721	Rfn	Cutting B	C	"	"
5305	A/Cpl	Austin S	B	Killed in Action	"
B/80	Rfn	Clark J	A	" " "	"
1196	"	Dunham D	D	" " "	"
S/10447	"	Dennett T	C	Wounded	"
S/13956	"	Downs H	"	"	"
Z/2160	"	Pearce A	"	"	"
S/7230	"	Graham Z	D	Killed in Action	"
8/8741	"	Hollington D	A	" " "	"
B/451	"	Harvey H	C	Wounded	"
D/3025	Cpl	Jarvis E	D	Killed in Action	"
S/15236	Rfn	Ford G	C	" " "	"
S/6589	"	McMullen W	D	Wounded	"
9609	Sgt	Vowles J	C	Killed in Action	"
D/3274	Cpl	Berry H	B	" " "	"
S/14295	Rfn	Toll E	"	" " "	"
S/15784	"	Whiting A	"	" " "	"

- 8 -

REGTL No	RANK & NAME		Coy	CASUALTY	DATE
Z/1947	Rfn	McMahon J	B	Killed in Action	18-8-16
B/72	Sgt	Lee T	A	"	"
S/11068	A/Cpl	Walker A	C	"	"
S/17740	Rfn	Moran G	S	"	"
S/12842	"	Pullen S	"	"	"
S/8649	"	Hurley C.E.	"	"	"
B/2797	"	Dawson J	"	"	"
B/3481	Sgt	Whitely F	C	"	"
S/6217	Rfn	Sheil W	"	"	"
S/8472	"	Allison S	"	"	"
S/9576	"	Melling J	"	"	"
B/1368	Sgt	Nash J	"	"	"
B/2643	Rfn	Moran W	"	"	"
S/11240	"	Farmer S	"	"	"
S/14523	"	Gibb J	"	"	"
B/2775	"	Smith R	"	"	"
3481	A/Cpl	Wilson T	E	"	"
S/7790	Rfn	Altham E	"	"	"
8506	"	Holton J	"	"	"
S/10232	"	Hayward A	"	"	"
Z/778	"	Hemming A	"	"	"
843	A/Cpl	O'Brien T	"	"	"
B/1670	Rfn	Hunt P	"	"	"
B/3032	"	Ferris D	"	"	"
4846	A/Sgt	Newman F	D	"	"
S/11199	A/Cpl	Ollerhead R	"	"	"

- 9 -

REGTL. Nº	RANK & NAME		COY	CASUALTY	DATE
S/7249	Rfn	Burroughes A	D	Killed in Action	18.8.16
S/9709	"	Brookes J	"	" " "	"
B/2695	"	Chilton T	"	" " "	"
S/13437	"	Dacey J	"	" " "	"
S/5067	"	Hitchcock W	"	" " "	"
S/9876	"	Holmes H	"	" " "	"
10/2273	"	Leggett G	"	" " "	"
B/1971	"	Slate B	"	" " "	"
B/1903	"	Toms G	"	" " "	"
S/12969	"	Weding J	"	" " "	"
S/9746	"	Yates A	"	" " "	"
10/2772	"	Smith T	"	" " "	"
S/6113	Sgt	Rogers H	A	" " "	"
B/3030	A/C	Chennells G	"	" " "	"
S/6150	Rfn	Wilkinson E	"	" " "	"
S/702	"	Jenkins F	B	" " "	"
S/6044	"	Cox N	D	" " "	"
S/15769	"	Leader S	"	" " "	"
S/1472	"	Pemberton W	"	" " "	"
S/11601	"	Adams J	"	Missing	"
S/5605	"	Andrews W	"	Do	"
S/5364	"	Brown A	"	Do	"
S/4006	A/Cpl	Butterbury E	"	Do	"
S/5419	Rfn	Burke E	"	Do	"
S/7502	A/Cpl	Gurney C	"	Do	"
B/3246	"	Hawkins C	"	Do	"

- 10 -

Regtl No	Rank & Name		Coy	Casualty	Date
S/15083	Rfn	Powell E	D	Missing	18-8-16
S/5038	"	Spiers W	"	"	"
S/12807	"	Wymer J	"	"	"
S/3093	"	Moss E	"	"	"
S/10330	"	Armstead E	"	Wounded	"
S/1595	"	Brookes J	"	"	"
S/13147	"	Best J	A	"	"
S/2649	"	Davis J	A	"	"
S/9824	"	Davies T	A	"	"
S/3078	A/Rfn	Finbow T	D	"	"
S/8196	"	Hultin W	A	"	"
S/7391	"	Harris C	"	"	"
2/128	Rfn	Hollis	C	"	20-8-16
S/10745	"	Jones E	"	"	18-8-16
7/289	"	Murphy C	D	"	"
S/1841	"	Page J	"	"	"
B/1073	"	Parker W	"	"	"
S/2439	"	Powell A	"	"	"
B/3020	A/Cpl	Peach W	A	"	"
S/8382	C/M	Parslow C	C	"	"
S/10274	Rfn	Riley C	"	"	"
S/328	"	Thatcher A	D	"	"
S/242	"	Wallace A	A	"	"
S/84	"	Walsh T.J.	"	"	"
S/1616	"	Youlden A	D	"	"
S/15123	"	Twistle C	"	"	"

11

Regt No	Rank	& Name		Coy	Casualty	Date
11/103	Sgt	Pearce	T.H.	D	Wounded	18.8.16
5/10798	Rfn	Jones	J	A	Died of Wounds	"
4/1897	"	Eaton	T	D	Do	"
8/58	"	Edmer	W	A	Do	"
5/1872	"	Cunnington	H	A	Do	"

3/8/16.

H. Maitland Lt Col
Commdg. 7th Bn Rifle Brigade

― CONFIDENTIAL ―

WAR DIARY

OF

7TH BATTN RIFLE BRIGADE

FROM 1-9-16   TO 30-9-16

(VOLUME XVII)

V A Mr De Carby MAJOR

COMMDG. 7TH BN RIFLE BRIGADE

In the Field
30-9-16.

WAR DIARY or INTELLIGENCE SUMMARY

Army Form C. 2118.

(54)

7th Bn. Rifle Brigade

(Erase heading not required.)

Hour, Date, Place	Summary of Events and Information	Remarks and references to Appendices
1916 Sept.		
WARLUS (AMIENS) 1	Lt. Col. J.D. Heriot-Maitland CMG, D.S.O. gave up command of the Battalion on promotion to Brigadier-General in cmd. of 98th Inf. Bde. 33rd Division.	
2	Bn. resting in Billets WARLUS	Vaudic.
3	" " " "	Vaudic.
4	" " " " Draft 40 O.R. joined from Depot.	Vaudic.
5	" " " "	Vaudic.
6	" " " "	Vaudic.
7	" " " " Draft 72 O.R. under 2nd Lt. J.R. Robertson joined from 5th Batt. Sheerness.	Vaudic.
DERNANCOURT 8	" " Transport left by road for DERNANCOURT. 2nd Lt J.R. McD. Creed joined from 17th Batt.	Vaudic.
BECORDEL 9	Bn. entrained in French Lorry from 2D.H. S.4. West as 2nd Lt MD	Vaudic.
10	Bn. marched to camp 1000 yds. S.W. BECORDEL	Vaudic.
11	Bn. rested in camp	Vaudic.
MONTAUBAN 12	Bn. marched to MONTAUBAN Defences	Vaudic.
13	" rested "	Vaudic.
14	Major J. Maxwell V.C. appointed 2nd i Cmd. Bn. moved to DELVILLE WOOD in the night and deployed for Attack	Vaudic.
In Action 15	Bn. went into action at 6.20 a.m. (zero) 2nd Lt. H.W. Gosney rejoined the Bn.	Vaudic. 2/Lt T.L Knowles reported wounded after action fought 18th aug now reported killed vide page 52 APPENDIX W.4.3.

Army Form C. 2118.

WAR DIARY
or
INTELLIGENCE SUMMARY.
(Erase heading not required.)

7th Bn. The Rifle Brigade

Hour, Date, Place	Summary of Events and Information	Remarks and references to Appendices
1916 SEPT.		
Account of action fought on this date	15th At 6.20 a.m. (zero) The advance began in conjunction with an intense artillery barrage on the enemy's defences – There had been no preliminary bombardment. Operation orders were as follows:– The 8th KRRC & 8th Rifle Bgde in advance were to seize the TEA support Trench (reported obliterated) and the 3rd (Switch) Line, 2nd Wave – 7th KRRC on left and the 7th R.B. on the Rifle Brigade (right) had GAP trench as objective – position 500 x just the N.E. close to village of FLERS. The objective of the 42nd Bde included the capture of GUEDENCOURT – TEA trench – in the capture of which the Battn became involved – was found to be strongly held. It proved a serious obstacle. Both here and before the 1st objective (switch) the Bn. suffered severely. It pushed on in small parties to its final objective (GAP trench) which it captured – here the resistance of the enemy had considerably diminished. He surrendered everywhere in large numbers, shewing little fight. It reached solely on his rife guns. The 42nd Bde. not advanced through them line towards the 3rd objective. About 2 hours after the scheduled time for its capture the Rattn. were firmly established in GAP trench – and its flanks in touch with the Guards on the right and the 7th KRRC on the left. It was relieved at about midnight 15/16 by the 6th. Lt. 42nd Bde. a/Tu 18 hours hard fighting on an advance of 10/14/15 by 1500x. The Tanks used for the first time in this action did not come into much prominence in these areas. Casualties Officers 1 Killed (A. Rogers) 1 missing 7 wounded. O.R. 18 Killed, 77 missing 210 wounded.	1 Officer Killed wounded & missing so APPENDIX WL4

*This was Gen. Wills no doubt for fuller details.

+ Rogers was buried near the switch trench.

Army Form C. 2118.

(5b)

WAR DIARY
or
INTELLIGENCE SUMMARY.
(Erase heading not required.)

7th Bn. The Rifle Brigade.

Instructions regarding War Diaries and Intelligence Summaries are contained in F.S. Regs., Part II. and the Staff Manual respectively. Title pages will be prepared in manuscript.

Hour, Date, Place		Summary of Events and Information	Remarks and references to Appendices
1916 Sept.	16	The Battalion moved back to BROWN trench – about 400 yards to N.E. Edge of Delville Wood – in reserve – it was shelled intermittently during the 36 hours spent here.	
DERNANCOURT	17	at 7 a.m. The Battn. marched back to DERNANCOURT.	
	18	Bn. at rest & reorganising	
	19	" " "	
	20	" " "	
	21	" Transport left for TALMAS en route for LUCHEUX	
LUCHEUX	22	Bn. entrained in French Lorry Train for LUCHEUX	
	23	" resting & reorganising	
	24	" " "	
	25	" " "	
	26	Bn. proceeded by route march to GOUY-EN-ARTOIS	
WAILLY Trenches Fr Sector	27	" went in 15 Rendezd at WAILLY Fr Sector relieving the 6th R.W. Kent Rgt.	Batt = Strength on 30.9.16. Officers 15 O.R. 676
	28	Quiet day, some rifle grenades and m/g fire from our trenches	
	29	Quiet day, rifle grenades and considerable m/g fire all night No B 8330 Rfm E. Parkinson wounded – Buller	
	30	Enemy fired about 30 H.E. shells from 4.6 How Battery during the morning – our Field guns retaliated	

J.A.S. Elvey Major
Cmdg. 7th Bn. The Rifle Brigade

APPENDIX W.L.4.

7th Battn. The Rifle Brigade

LIST OF CASUALTIES WHICH OCCURED ON
15 - 9 - 16.

SUMMARY OF CASUALTIES

	Officers	O. Ranks
Killed	1	26
Died of Wounds.		1
Wounded & Missing	1	1
Missing		68
Wounded.	7	193
Total	9	289

[signed] Major
Commdg 7th Bn. Rifle Brigade

30/9/16

(2)

No.	Rank	NAME		Coy.	CASUALTY
Y/17560	Rfn.	Ayerst	F	A	Wounded
R/2787	"	Atherton	A	A	"
S/2346	Sgt.	Anderson	S	B	"
Z/1198	L/cpl	Attwood	W	B	"
S/10255	Rfn.	Armstrong	E	B	"
S/11361	L/cpl	Adams	C	C	"
B/3096	Rfn.	Arnold	R	D	Killed
R/20028	"	Allen	A	D	Missing
R/20046	"	Agar	W	D	Wounded
S/15794	Rfn.	Batts	W	A	"
S/17344	"	Barker	E	A	"
R/21690	"	Best	C	A	"
R/21767	"	Bridgewood	W	A	"
R/21776	"	Burrows	H	A	"
B/1744	"	Bailey	A	A	"
S/15757	"	Banchini	J	A	Missing
5607	"	Butcher	J	A	"
S/17459	"	Brown	J	A	"
5935	"	Buckle	C	B	"
B/203020	"	Bark	E.H	B	Killed in Action 15/9/16
S/10491	"	Bundock	E	B	Missing
S/17750	"	Bailey	W	B	"
S/8531	L/cpl	Bliss	F	C	Wounded
R/21795	Rfn.	Bowley	D	C	Missing
R/21440	"	Barmby	W	C	"
R/21710	"	Berry	W	C	Killed
R/21465	"	Barker	A	C	Missing
S/11264	"	Bonner	G	C	Wounded
S/17420	"	Bryant	G	C	"
Z/1968	L/cpl	Bayliss	B	D	"
S/16787	Rfn.	Batchelor	W	D	"
S/12785	"	Buckley	C	D	"
B/2771	"	Beeson	H	D	"

No	Rank	NAME		Coy.	CASUALTY
R/19787	Rfn	Brook	A	D	Wounded
R/21733	"	Brown	H	D	"
B/3393	"	Brooker	A	D	"
S/17421	"	Baker	G	A	"
3/7826	Cpl	Canberton	A	A	Killed
3/2164	Sgt	Collis	A	A	Wounded
S/5103	Cpl	Caughlin	W	A	"
R/21684	Rfn	Cockayne	C	A	"
B/203031	"	Cracknell	W	A	"
S/17147	"	Calf	J	A	Missing
S/7220	"	Canterford	W	B	Wounded
7/2365	"	Clougher	J	B	"
2237	"	Cook	A	B	"
R/21805	"	Clifton	A	B	"
S/17297	"	Cooper	S	B	Missing
R/21842	"	Cresswell	A	C	"
		2/Lt. Combe		D	Wounded & Missing
B/3225	a/Cpl	Cole	J	D	Wounded
S/9794	Rfn	Cutmore	W	D	"
1844	"	Curson	J	D	"
S/10956	"	Corner	L	D	Missing
		2/Lt. Child		D	Wounded Missing
R/21729	a/Cpl	Colthurst	J	D	Wounded
S/17341	Rfn	Coller	P	B	"
B/346	Rfn	Dunton	G	A	"
S/17409	"	Davis	G	A	Missing
R/21711	"	Davis	J.T	A	Wounded
R/20191	a/Cpl	Deves	E	B	"
S/7326	Rfn	Deverell	T	B	"
S/15792	"	Davis	R	B	"
S/16865	"	Dickerson	T	B	Missing
S/16025	"	Dodsworth	J.a	B	"
B/203027	"	Dann	A	C	Wounded

(4)

No	Rank	Name		Coy	Casualty
B/21365	Rfn	Darling	M	C	Wounded
R/21830	"	Double	H	C	"
B/203022	"	Downes	H	C	"
2216	A/Cpl	Deadman	H	D	"
S/5036	Rfn	Davy	A	D	"
R/2614	"	Davis	A	D	"
R/20471	"	Dixon	J	D	"
C/3633	"	Dawes	E	D	"
S/16886	"	Driscoll	R	B	Killed
B/203042	"	Davis	B A	B	Wounded
S/17581	"	Daniels	W	A	Missing
S/10862	"	Elms	J	A	Wounded
R/21724	"	Edwards	W	A	"
R/21692	"	Evans	W	A	"
R/21800	"	Ellis	L	C	"
R/21438	"	Edwards	F	C	Missing
S/18658	"	Eldridge	C	C	"
S/11326	A/Cpl	Eltringham	M	B	"
B/456	Sgt	Forbes	H	A	Wounded
B/310	Rfn	Finton	J	A	"
2/2550	"	Foulsham	W	A	"
R/21708	"	Farmer	S	A	"
B/203032	"	Featherstone	A	A	"
B/707	"	Fincham	C	B	"
B/93	"	Fox	C	B	"
S/17404	"	Farmer	J	B	"
B/466	Sgt	Foweraker	A	C	"
R/21804	Rfn	Filby	H	C	"
R/21467	"	Franklin	J	C	"
B/1190	"	Franklin	M	C	"
S/17814	"	Freeman	E	C	Missing
2/1149	"	Gallagher	M	A	Wounded
2/1119	"	Glenn	A	A	"

No	Rank	NAME		Coy	CASUALTY
S/17563	Rfn	Greenwood	C	A	Killed
S/9455	"	Goulding	J	B	Wounded
S/17342	"	Goldberg	H	B	"
B/616	"	Graves	G	C	"
S/18719	"	Goodey	G	C	"
3383	Cpl	Goodwin	C	D	"
3774	A/Cpl	Gale	E	D	Killed
R/20091	"	Goodall	C	D	Wounded
9551	Rfn	Goosey	G	D	Killed
S/7091	"	Goldsborough	A	D	Wounded
S/1514	"	Hanmer	W	A	Killed
B/351	"	Hall	H	A	Wounded
S/5948	"	Higgins	P	A	"
S/17392	"	Hogarth	H	A	"
S/7238	"	Hicknott	C	A	Missing
S/15704	"	Hogg	C	A	"
B/1902	Sgt	Hunt	H W	B	Wounded
S/11184	Rfn	Hilton	F	B	"
S/9986	"	Hubert	E	B	"
S/9608	"	Henley	W	B	"
S/6276	"	Herbert	G	B	Missing
R/21719	"	Hindle	B	B	"
S/17322	"	Halsall	R	B	"
S/17439	"	Hockley	W	B	"
S/17427	"	Hill	H	B	Killed in Action
S/17448	"	Hayes	W	B	Missing
S/7584	Cpl	Holland	N	C	Wounded
2/1665	A/Cpl	Hilton	J	C	"
R/21769	Rfn	Hallett	W	C	Missing
R/21696	"	Hart	D	C	"
R/21447	"	Holmes	B	C	Wounded
S/18747	"	Haskett	H	C	Missing
S/18729	"	Hirst	G	C	Wounded

(6)

No	Rank	Name		Coy	Casualty
S/11697	Rfn	Howard	F	D	Wounded
B/792	"	Harris	J	D	"
B/1709	"	Howard	W	D	"
R/28762	"	Haddock	S	D	Missing
R/20446	"	Hawkeswood	G	D	Wounded
R/20105	"	Hudson	E	D	Missing
R/20444	"	Harris	G	D	Wounded
3623	"	Higgins		D	"
B/461	"	Joseph	A	A	"
R/21752	"	Johnson	J	A	"
R/21802	"	Joyce	J	C	Killed
S/12747	"	Johnson	A	C	Wounded
S/15733	"	Joyce	J	C	Missing
S/6207	"	Jessup	A	C	Wounded
S/16947	"	Jones	J	D	"
		2/Lt Kibby		A	"
B/307	Rfn	King	C	A	"
S/17645	"	Kerridge	F	A	"
S/1622	A/Cpl	Kibbey	J	B	Died of Wounds 21/9/16
R/21846	Rfn	Kirby	F	C	Wounded
R/21842	"	Kemp	A	C	"
		2/Lt Leech	LB	A	"
1892	CSM	Lyall	W	A	" and Missing
S/10959	Rfn	Liddiard	S	A	Wounded
S/11583	"	Levenson	H	A	Missing
S/17555	"	Latchford	P	A	Wounded
B/443	"	List	G	B	"
S/17441	"	Levey	A	B	"
S/5062	A/Cpl	Lyons	H	B	Missing
S/17438	Rfn	Labrum	T	B	"
5534	A/Cpl	Le Cras	R	C	Wounded
R/21854	Rfn	Lamb	H	C	Missing
6277	"	Lensh	W	C	Killed

No	Rank	Name		Coy	Casualty
6240	Rfn	Lucas	C	C	Wounded
R/21716	"	Lawrence	B	C	"
R/21656	"	Long	C	C	Missing
R/2144	"	Livings	C	C	Wounded
S/17455	"	Layton	F	C	Missing
S/16848	"	Ling	H	D	"
B/203037	A/Cpl	Lovell	F	D	Wounded
B/87	Cpl	Leonard	T	A	"
S/12357	Rfn	McGeorge	W	A	"
2681	"	Mummery	G	A	"
S/6105	"	McBain	CB	A	"
R/20820	"	Morley	E	A	Missing
S/9023	Sgt	Martin	JS	B	Wounded
B/8027	"	Munts	AJ	B	"
R/21831	Rfn	Monk	F	B	"
S/12061	"	Matthews	R	B	"
S/16921	"	Manvell	C	B	Killed in action
S/17502	"	Morton	J	B	"
B/203018	"	McDonald	W	B	Missing
B/1585	A/Cpl	Martin	E	C	Wounded
S/5033	Rfn	Money	H	C	"
S/8699	"	Morgan	R	C	"
S/7534	"	Matthews	J	C	"
S/16205	"	Mears	H	C	"
R/21050	A/Cpl	Morgan	F	D	"
S/11939	Rfn	Miller	G	D	"
R/21429	"	Macefield	R	D	Killed
S/11295	"	Mowles	B	D	Wounded
B/203045	"	Nicholson	J	A	Killed
S/7396	"	Napier	W	B	Wounded
S/17497	"	Neal	J	B	"
B/2591	"	Nicholas	A	D	"
S/8685	"	Organ	E	A	"

(8)

No	Rank	NAME		Coy.	CASUALTY
S/9809	Rfn	Oat	W	B	Wounded
R/21862	"	Ockelford	W	C	Killed in Action
S/5123	Cpl	Phillips	P	A	Wounded
R/21688	Rfn	Prince	F.J	A	Missing
Z/1923	"	Pearse	H	B	Wounded
6035	"	Porter	A.V.	B	"
S/16605	"	Pawley	J	B	"
R/21714	"	Palmer	A.J	B	Missing
S/5260	"	Probert	J	B	"
Z/2160	"	Pearce	J	C	Killed
S/1996	"	Plumridge	F	C	Wounded
R/21426	"	Peters	E	C	Killed
Z/247	"	Phelan	J	D	Wounded
S/18613	"	Paddon	H	D	Missing
B/203039	"	Pearce		D	Wounded
S/15875	"	Reynolds	W	A	"
B/352	"	Rogers	H	A	"
R/21774	"	Rixon	F	A	"
R/21788	"	Reed	E	A	Missing
R/21670	"	Richie	F	A	"
R/21697	"	Roberts	G	A	Wounded
S/5163	"	Russell	GA	B	Killed
S/14575	"	Rowe	D	B	Missing
		~~2/Lt. Rogers~~	~~R~~	~~C~~	~~Killed~~
5504	Cpl	Rout	A	C	Wounded
B/203052	Rfn	Robinson	A	C	Killed
S/15768	"	Rankin	R	C	Wounded
S/6983	"	Rogers	A	C	"
		~~2/Lt. Roberson~~		~~D~~	~~"~~
R/20137	Rfn	Ripley	M	D	"
R/20138	"	Rathmell	J	D	Missing
S/10763	"	Revie	J	D	Wounded
R/20558	"	Robson	G	D	Missing

No	Rank	NAME		Coy	CASUALTY
R/20140	Rfn	Robinson	G	D	Missing
C/12281	"	Rogers	T	D	& "
5027	Sgt	Smith	W	A	Wounded
B/2920	"	Stone	E	A	"
S/15993	Rfn	Smith	W	A	"
R/21790	"	Smith	a	A	"
S/16584	"	Stiff	W	A	Missing
S/17542	"	Staples	F	A	"
R/21835	"	Slade	L	A	"
R/21757	"	Sommers	C	A	Wounded
7/1815	"	Stephenson	J	B	"
B/629	"	Silver	L	B	"
B/2984	"	Scading	W	B	"
7/150	"	Sherratt	J	B	"
S/12840	A/Cpl	Spurgeon	S	B	Missing
B/2123	"	Symons	F	C	Wounded
S/6633	Rfn	Shurton	G	C	Missing
S/8608	"	Shrosbree	G	C	Wounded
B/203028	"	Sharman	a	C	"
C/1630	"	Staunton	W	C	Killed
B/203050	"	Savery	G	C	Wounded
B/2398	Sgt.	Smith	R	D	"
R/20549	Rfn	Sedgwick	L	D	Missing
C/12430	"	Simpson	A	D	Wounded
R/20899	"	Sykes	F	D	"
S/17612	"	Scales	H	D	Missing
B/203040	"	Smith	J	D	Wounded
S/12069	"	Thorne	a	A	"
S/11777	"	Tucker	C	A	"
B/203048	"	Turner	G	A	"
B/1509	A/Cpl	Thomas	H	B	"
S/10482	Rfn	Tippett	W	B	"
S/8788	"	Tebble	E	B	"

(10)

No	Rank	NAME		Coy	CASUALTY
S/12627	Rfn	Taylor	W	B	Wounded
S/16547	"	Tomlinson	C	B	"
B/1236	Sgt	Taffenden	H	B	Missing
S/17354	Rfn	Tinney	G	B	Wounded
S/13055	L/Cpl	Thompson	H	C	"
B/392	Sgt	White	A	A	Killed
R/21863	Rfn	Whiteman	C	A	"
B/90	"	Wright		A	"
B/396	"	Wade	W	A	Wounded
B/569	"	Waters	S	A	"
C/7322	"	Woolmer	E	A	Missing
B/299	Cpl	Wicker	W	B	Killed
S/6023	Rfn	Winfield	H	B	Wounded
S/9121	"	Waters	B	B	"
S/9720	"	White	S	B	"
6296	"	White	L	B	"
B/2267	L/Cpl	Wood	W	C	"
B/3033	Rfn	Wroe	H	C	"
S/9495	L/Cpl	Watkins	J	C	"
R/21868	Rfn	Ward	J	C	"
R/2144	"	Weaver	E	C	Missing
R/21448	"	Williams	H	C	"
S/17447	L/Cpl	Walton	R	D	"
S/7244	Rfn	Weare	A	D	Wounded
C/7926	"	Warriner	W	D	"
C/12580	"	Williams	H	D	"
C/9425	"	Woodward	W	D	"
R/20317	"	Wood	M	D	"
S/16028	"	Wheepley	G	D	"
R/2789	"	Yarrington	R	A	"
S/17604	"	Young	R	A	Missing

Casualties – Officers

2nd/Lieut	R. Rogers	Killed
Lieut & Adjt	Hon. R. Gorell Barnes	Wounded
Lieut	S. F. Purdon	do
2nd/Lieut	M.D. Childs	Missing { now believed wounded and in England. Vaudré
"	G.H.R. Combe	Wounded & Missing
"	L.B. Leech	Wounded
"	S.G. West	do
"	F.V. Kibbey	do
"	J.R. Roberson	do

(signature) Major
Commdg 7th Bn. The Rifle Brigade

30/9/16.

VOL 18

CONFIDENTIAL

WAR DIARY

OF

7th BATTN. THE RIFLE BRIGADE

FROM:- 1-10-16   TO:- 31-10-16

(VOLUME XVIII)

J. Maxwell.
Major
COMMDG 7th BATTN. THE RIFLE BRIGADE

31-10-16.

Army Form C. 2118.

WAR DIARY
or
INTELLIGENCE SUMMARY.
(Erase heading not required.)

7th Bn. The Rifle Brigade.

(57)

Hour, Date, Place	Summary of Events and Information	Remarks and references to Appendices
WAILLY Trenches F1 Sector 1916 October		
1	Bn in trenches activity normal	
	No 9179 A/Cpl. A. Radley killed. Name tomb. B. Coy.	Buried Mil. Cemetery N.E. of LA FERMONT on road to WAILLY.
2	Quiet Day. No. B/1854 Rfn. D. Hailes wounded Bullet B. Coy.	Rfn. A/S Wade wounded
	" S/17391 " A Graves " Shell "	Sgt. C. Steele " Military Medal
		Cpl. A. Hicks "
		Rfn. Burgess "
3	Quiet Day — actn'y normal. Capt. L.G.N. Langmead joined Bn.	V.M.
4	2 Lieuts. C.S. Greenleaf & F.D. Aulagnier joined from 4th Essex Bn.	# Simpson "
5	" activity normal	# Finch "
6	2nd Lieut N.S. Thornton joined from 6th Bn. Rifle Bde. Eastbourne	# Tyrrell "
	No R/21693 Rfn. Doran P. wounded Bullet C. coy.	V.M.
7	Very Heavy Trench Mortar action all day on extreme right	L/Cpl. R.C. Brown wounded Military Cross
8	At 8 p.m. the enemy heavily bombarded the front line	V.M.
	Lifting on to support and back trenches - accompanied by rifled	No A. Jacobs wounded D.C.M.
	Musketry and rifle grn fire. It lasted for 20 minutes to ½ hour	V.M.
	The suddenness of this activity led us to suspect an enemy attack.	
	The S.O.S. Signal rockets were fired and our artillery promptly opened	
	the same, unduly immediately after. After 45 minutes the	
	firing on both sides died out. C. Coy front line badly damaged.	
	2nd Lieut. McClure and Rfn. Wounded Stokes Bomb. A. Coy.	
	No 13564 Rfn. Ashford killed Shell C. Coy.	
	" " M. Hooper died of wds. Bullet (9.10.16) C. Coy	Buried at LE FERMONT. Vide above
	" S/7468 " T.W. Jarvis wounded Bullet C. Coy.	" at Mil. Cemetery AVESNES.

Army Form C. 2118.

WAR DIARY
or
INTELLIGENCE SUMMARY.
(Erase heading not required.)

7th Bn The Rifle Brigade (58)

Hour, Date, Place	Summary of Events and Information	Remarks and references to Appendices
WAILLY Trenches F1 Sector. 1916 October 9	At 11 am a raid was carried out by the 7th Sherwood Foresters on our right — for 1½ hours our artillery trenched enemy trap and wire, corner of BLAIRVILLE wood — opposite right Coy. (E) Enemy reply very feeble — no casualties.	
RIVIERE 10	The Bn was relieved by the 8th K.R.R.C. 2nd [unit] R.H. Stoll + W.C. E.818 ft join from 3rd K.N. Lancashire Regt. Bn resting in billets.	VAUDIC
11	"	VAUDIC
12	"	VALRC
13	"	J.M.
14	"	J.M.
T? 2 Scott 15	2 am - relieved the 9th Bn K.R.R.C. in K2 D+B infantry line, C+A in support	J.M.
16	Bn in trenches	J.M.
17	"	J.M.
18	No/B/5120 Cpl A Lawrence awarded Military Medal	J.M.
19	"	J.M.
20	"	J.M.
21	" Capt. C.E. Winda awarded Military Cross	J.M.
22	"	J.M.
23	" Enemy relieved 11th Bavn "A" B'n in the front line	J.M.
24	" relieved by 6th Buffs (right Coy) and Supports 6th R.W. Kents (left Coy and outposts) 6th Queens (visiting Coy) remainder of troops of own	J.M.

Army Form C. 2118.

WAR DIARY
or
INTELLIGENCE SUMMARY.

(Erase heading not required.) 7th (S) Bn The Rifle Brigade.

Instructions regarding War Diaries and Intelligence Summaries are contained in F. S. Regs., Part II. and the Staff Manual respectively. Title pages will be prepared in manuscript.

Place	Hour, Date	Summary of Events and Information	Remarks and references to Appendices
BEAUMETZ	Oct. 25	Bn. on the march via Flank St. & Beaumetz.	J.M.
SOMBRIN	10.15 a.m. 26	Bn. marched to SOMBRIN resting in billets at SOMBRIN	J.M.
	27	"	J.M.
	28	"	J.M.
	29	" Draft of 128 N.C.O.s and men arrived.	J.M.
	30	"	J.M.
	31	"	
		During the period 27/31 intensive training took place for Lewis Gunners and bombers. Men were in trenches while the rest of the Bn. has been engaged in route marching, semaphoring, bayonet training, run & essay drill, attending N.C.O.s and Rfn. were assembled to military funeral & Battalion subjects.	J.M.
		Died 27.10.16 A. Buckingham Mo. S/4409 Rfn. F. Poore	
		" 3/03 C.Q.M.S. 3/510 L.W. Mason	
		" 8/2330 — 11 — Wintle	
		" — 761 — L. Pike	
		" 18/909 — G. Tovey	
		" 2683 — Sgt. J. Smith	
		" 149 — " Bean	
		" 3/1022 Rfn R.Perry	
		" B/2303 A/C H. Mills	
		" 8/2109 " A. Thomas	
		Lectures by Divisional Gas Expert to Officers, C.S.M.s and the N.C.O.s	J.M.

Fighting Strength
Officers 17
O.R. 717
738

J. Minnitt
Major
Comdg 7th (S) Bn. The Rifle Brigade.
31-10-16

(73989) W4141—463. 400,000. 9/14. H.&J. Ltd. Forms/C. 2118/10.

CONFIDENTIAL.

WAR DIARY

of

7th Battalion THE RIFLE BRIGADE.

From. 1.11.16.   To 30.11.16.

(VOLUME XVIII) [XIX]

                                J. Maxwell
                                        Major

            Commdg. 7th Battn. The RIFLE BDE.

30.11.16.

Army Form C. 2118.

WAR DIARY
or
INTELLIGENCE SUMMARY.

(Erase heading not required.) 7th Bn The Rifle Brigade.

Hour, Date, Place 1916	Summary of Events and Information	Remarks and references to Appendices
SOMBRIN. Nov. 1	Battalion & Company training	Vaude
2	– do – – draft of 30 O.R. joined Bn.	Vaude
3	– do –	Vaude
4	– do –	Vaude
5	– do –	Vaude
6	– do –	Vaude
7	– do – draft of 34 O.R. joined Bn.	Vaude
8	– do – 2nd/Lieut G.D. HARLE promoted from) Ink of sergeant and posted to Bn.)	Vaude
9	– do –	Vaude
10	– do –	Vaude
11	– do –	Vaude
12	– do –	Vaude
13	The 3rd Army Commander, Sir Edmund Allenby inspected the companies at training. He highly complimented C coy under 2/Lt. Shaw on their very smart (smart) appearance.	Vaude
14	Battalion & Company training	Vaude
15	– do –	Vaude
16	– do –	Vaude
17	– do –	Vaude
18	– do –	Vaude
19	– do –	Vaude
20	The VI Corps Commander inspected companies at training. Draft 3 O.R. joined Bn.	Vaude

Army Form C. 2118.

WAR DIARY
or
INTELLIGENCE SUMMARY.
(Erase heading not required.)

7th Batt. The Rifle Brigade

Place	Hour, Date	Summary of Events and Information	Remarks and references to Appendices
SOMERIN	November 21	Battalion & Company training	
	22	2nd Lt H. ANSTEY joined from the M.T., A.S.C. " " B. FOSTER " " The R. Canadian Dragoons " " N.T. COSSAR " " 28th Bn London Rgt.	
	23	Battn & Company Training. The Bn Transport won the 1st prize for the "Best turn out" in the Brigade	
	24	Bn + Coy Training	
	25	- do -	
	26	- do -	
	27	- do -	
	28	- do - Battalion Runners won the Brigade competition	
	29	- do -	
	30	Bn in attack on practice trenches. Brigadier present. "Divisional Runners" competition won by Bn Team	Fighting strength on 30-11-16 Officers 21 O.R. 794 ——— 815 J. Ainsworth Major for O.C. 7th (S)Bn The Rifle Brigade

Vol 20

CONFIDENTIAL

WAR DIARY

OF

7th BATTN. THE RIFLE BRIGADE

FROM 1-12-1916   TO 31-12-1916

(VOLUME XX)

31/12/1916

V.A. Fludr Cobry Lt Col
Commdg 7th Bn. The Rifle Brigade

Army Form C. 2118.

WAR DIARY
or
INTELLIGENCE SUMMARY

(Erase heading not required.) 7th Bn The Rifle Brigade — 62

Place	Date 1916	Hour	Summary of Events and Information	Remarks and references to Appendices
SOMBRIN	Dec. 1		Battalion & Company training	VAUDIC
	2		— do —	VAUDIC
	3		— do —	VAUDIC
	4		— do —	VAUDIC
	5		— do —	VAUDIC
	6		— do —	VAUDIC
	7		— do —	Note 24/11/16. Nº S/8550 Rfn C. SMITH 'A' Coy accidentally killed on Railway collision DOULLENS Stn — VAUDIC
	8		— do —	VAUDIC
	9		— do —	VAUDIC
	10		— do —	VAUDIC
	11		— do —	VAUDIC
	12		— do — Draft 90 O.R joined from the Base including 30 volunteers from King Edward's Horse	VAUDIC
	13		— do — Draft 95 O.R joined from the Base	VAUDIC
GOUY	14		The Battn proceeded by route march to GOUY-en-Artois. Nº 20143 C.S.M. A. LOVE } gazetted and Lieuts. " 1935 Sgt W. MILLS } from 7th/13th and posted to this Battn	VAUDIC
RIVIERE	15		The Battn marched to RIVIERE and relieved the 6th Bn R.W.Kent regt	VAUDIC
	16		Bn in Brigade Reserve Support in billets —	VAUDIC
	17		— do —	VAUDIC
	18		— do — Nº S/10705 Rfn E. DOMBARAND 'D' Coy. Wounded — by Reg Shrapnel —	VAUDIC

WAR DIARY or INTELLIGENCE SUMMARY

Army Form C. 2118.

7⁷ᵗʰ Batt. The Rifle Brigade.

Place	Date 1916	Hour	Summary of Events and Information	Remarks and references to Appendices
RIVIERE	Dec.19		Battⁿ in Brigade Reserve -	Vandje
	20		— do —	Vandje
	21		— do —	Vandje
Trenches F2 Sector	22		Battⁿ went into Trenches in F2 Sector relieving 8ᵗʰ Bⁿ The R/B Brigade Major Tennings Res Bⁿ Royal Fusiliers attached -	Vandje
	23		Battⁿ in Trenches - very quiet -	Vandje
	24		— do —	Vandje
	25	Christmas Day	— do — a certain amount of singing xc in enemy lines draft 7 O.R joined from the Base	Vandje
	26		— do — Enemy indications of emitting gas if wind favourable	Vandje
	27		— do — Bombardment by our Heavy Batteries of the Enemy Lines from 2-4 pm	Vandje
	28		Battⁿ relieved by the 8ᵗʰ Bⁿ The R/B Brigade and marched to BEAUMETZ 2ⁿᵈ Lieut. A.T. CASTLE joined from the Yorkshire Regt. 2ⁿᵈ Lieut G.W FLEMMING joined from 5ᵗʰ Rᵉ Bⁿ The R/B Brigade	Vandje
BEAUMETZ	29		in Divnal Reserve. Xmas Dinners 1st 'A' & 'B' Coys	Vandje
	30		— do — " " " 'C' & 'D' ---	Vandje
	31		Bn. resting in Divnal Reserve	Vandje

Battⁿ Strength on 31.12.16. Officers 25
O.R. 955

VA and Calx Lt Col
Cmdg 7ᵗʰ Bⁿ The Rifle Brigade.

CONFIDENTIAL

WAR DIARY

OF

7th BATTN. THE RIFLE BRIGADE

FROM. 1-1-17   TO.   31-1-17

(VOLUME XXI)

J. Maxwell
Major
Lt. Col.

COMMDG. 7TH BN. THE RIFLE BRIGADE

31-1-17

Army Form C. 2118.

(64)

WAR DIARY
or
INTELLIGENCE SUMMARY

(Erase heading not required.) 7th Bn The Rifle Brigade.

Instructions regarding War Diaries and Intelligence Summaries are contained in F. S. Regs., Part II. and the Staff Manual respectively. Title Pages will be prepared in manuscript.

Place	Date	Hour	Summary of Events and Information	Remarks and references to Appendices
BEAUMETZ	Jan. 1 1917		NEW YEAR'S DAY.	
			Batt'n resting in Divisional Reserve. New Years honours List award.	
			Lt & Adj. Hon. R. Gorell-Barnes. Mil. Cross.	
			Maj. J. Maxwell M.C. Mentioned in despatches	
			Lt. S. Purdon — " —	
			Lt (a/Capt.) C.R. Sharp — " —	
			2/Lt. A.B. Love — " —	
			No 7473 C.S.M., A. Charlton — " —	
	2		— do —	
Trenches F2 Sector	3		Bn relieved the 8th Bn The Rifle Brigade in the Trenches —	Vaudc Pardc
	4		In Trenches quiet day.	
	5		— do — — do — 2nd Lieut. W.E. RUSHBROOKE joined from 5th Bn.	Vaudc ordnly Vaudc
	6		— do — — do — No S/26351 Rfn. J. BAYLISS 'C' Coy. Wounded (slight V. bomb)	Vaudc
	7		— do — — do —	Vaudc
	8		— do — — do —	Vaudc Pardc
RIVIERE	9		Bn relieved, in Brigade Reserve at Riviere.	Vaudc Pardc
	10		Bn in Brigade Reserve —	Vaudc
	11		— do — — do —	Vaudc
	12		— do — — do — Capt. P.A. Scott rejoined from sick leave.	Vaudc
	13		— do — — do — Draft 7. O.R. rejoined from Base. —	Vaudc
	14		— do — — do —	Vaudc
Trenches F2 Sector	15		Bn relieved the 8th Bn The Rifle Brigade in the Trenches.	Vaudc

Army Form C. 2118.

65

WAR DIARY
or
INTELLIGENCE SUMMARY

(Erase heading not required.) 7th Bn The Rifle Brigade -

Instructions regarding War Diaries and Intelligence Summaries are contained in F. S. Regs., Part II. and the Staff Manual respectively. Title Pages will be prepared in manuscript.

Place	Date 1917	Hour	Summary of Events and Information	Remarks and references to Appendices
Trenches F2 Sector	Jan. 16		In trenches. Quiet day very cold.	Maude
	17		— Do — — Do — 2 inches of snow. 2/Lt. J.S.B. Gray joined probn from the Middlesex Regt.	Maude
	18		— " — " —	very cold	J.M.
	19		— " — " — 2/Lt. L.C. Pollard joined for duty from R.W.R.	J.M.
	20		— " — " —	J.M.
	21		The Battalion relieved by 8th Bn The Rifle Brigade. A draft of 1 other Battalion personnel to regt'l units	J.M.
SIMENCOURT	22		in SIMENCOURT	J.M.
	23		The Battalion in divisional Reserve in Rear of Ridge 3/Lt. J.A. Sowerbutts joined for duty from 5th Bdo Rgt.	J.M.
	24		" " draft of 80 O.R. arrived	J.M. 5/Lt Z.H Rep
	25		" "	J.M. W. Naylor died in C.C.S
	26		" "	J.M.
	27		The Battalion relieved the 8th Bn. The Rifle Brigade in F2 Sector about 12.30 am - Major L. Maxwell 6 Officers	J.M.
Trenches F2	28		and 190. O.R. wounded by bullets in MONCHIET training for a Raid	J.M.
			In the Trenches	J.M.
	29		— do — Enemy sent over 2 feld trench mortars	J.M.
	30		— " — Enemy trench mortar 140 - 9 old trench mortars friendly bombarding on front line initiation of an expected a Raiding Party opened	J.M.

2449 Wt. W14957/M90 750,000 1/16 J.B.C. & A. Forms/C.2118/12

Army Form C. 2118.

WAR DIARY
or
INTELLIGENCE SUMMARY

(Erase heading not required.) 7th (S) Bn. The Rifle Brigade

Instructions regarding War Diaries and Intelligence Summaries are contained in F. S. Regs., Part II. and the Staff Manual respectively. Title Pages will be prepared in manuscript.

Place	Date	Hour	Summary of Events and Information	Remarks and references to Appendices
Taushez F.3	31		In the trenches. Quiet day. Officers of the West Surrey Rodney Regt. went round the Battalion Front. Battalion Strength on 31-1-19 — Officers 33, O.R. 1003. Commdg: 7th (S) Bn. The Rifle Brigade	J.M.

CONFIDENTIAL.

WAR DIARY
OF
7th BATTN. THE RIFLE BDE.

FROM. 1-2-17   TO. 28-2-17

(VOLUME XXII)

J. Maxwell.
Major
Commdg 7th Bn. The Rifle Brigade

1-3-1917

Army Form C. 2118.

WAR DIARY
or
INTELLIGENCE SUMMARY

(Erase heading not required.) 7 Bn The Rifle Brigade (6?)

Instructions regarding War Diaries and Intelligence Summaries are contained in F.S. Regs., Part II. and the Staff Manual respectively. Title Pages will be prepared in manuscript.

Place	Date	Hour	Summary of Events and Information	Remarks and references to Appendices
Trenches	Feb 1 1917		In trenches. Enemy 90 - 6" French Mortars sent in. Front line badly damaged.	Vandc Vandc
F2 Sector	" 2		"	
	3		The Battalion was relieved by 6th West Riding Regt. and marched to SIMENCOURT	Vandc
SIMENCOURT	4		The Battalion sent off working parties as under HQrs and remainder marched to SOMBRIN. (a) 8 Officers & 345 O.R. to SAULTY } Construction of new Railway under (b) 2 Officers & 115 O.R. to BAVINCOURT } The Anglesey Coy. R.E.	Vandc Vandc Vandc Vandc
SOMBRIN	5		Reorganising and training in rest billets.	Vandc
	6		" "	Vandc
	7		" "	Vandc
	8		" "	Vandc
	9		" " under 2nd Lt Miles	
	10		Working Party at BAVINCOURT rejoined the Battalion. 60 O.R., composed of men of 5 months service & under proceeded to join the Divisional Depot Battalion at GRAND RULLECOURT for training.	Vandc Vandc
	11		Reorganising & training in rest billets. No.3550S R.S.M. C. MORGAN awarded the Croix de Guerre	Vandc Vandc
	12		" "	Vandc
	13		" "	Vandc
	14		" "	Vandc
	15		" "	Vandc
	16		" " 2/Lt C.A.M. VAN MILLINGEN rejoined from 5th Bn.	Vandc
	17		" " Draft 2 D. O.R. joined from England. (incl. 19 Signallers)	Vandc
	18		" "	Vandc

Army Form C. 2118.

WAR DIARY
or
INTELLIGENCE SUMMARY
(Erase heading not required.)

7th Bn. The Rifle Brigade.

Place	Date 1917	Hour	Summary of Events and Information	Remarks and references to Appendices
SOM BRIN.	Feb 19		Bn. reorganising & training in rest-billets.	Vary
	20		Bn. reorganising and training in rest billets	J.M.
	21		" "	J.M.
	22		" "	J.M.
	23		" "	J.M.
	24		" "	J.M.
	25		" "	J.M.
	26		" "	J.M.
	27		" "	J.M.
	28		" "	J.M.

From the period Feb 11 - 28 inclusive the Battalion found a working party of 350 at Saulty. J.M.

Strength.
Officers 31
O.R. 1007.

J. Ainsworth
Major
Commanding 7th Bn. The Rifle Brigade.

Vol 23

CONFIDENTIAL

WAR DIARY

OF

7th BATTN. THE RIFLE BRIGADE

FROM. 1-3-1917   TO 31-3-1917

(VOLUME XXIII)

V A M D Calry LT COL.
COMMDG. 7th Bn THE RIFLE BRIGADE

31-3-1917

Army Form C. 2118.

WAR DIARY
or
INTELLIGENCE SUMMARY

(Erase heading not required.) 7th Bn The Rifle Brigade

(69)

Place	Date	Hour	Summary of Events and Information	Remarks and references to Appendices
SOMERIN	Mar 1		Bn. Training in Rest Billets.	J.M.
	2		" "	J.M.
	3		The Battalion marched to Billets in DAINVILLE	J.M.
DAINVILLE	4		Bn. resided. Coy Cmdrs reconnoitred areas in which their parties would work	J.M.
	5		Bn. out at work in H.1 sector "A" Coy. Hope ST. "B" Coy. HARDING ST. "C" Coy patrol trench "D" Coy. HAVANNAH and Patrol Trench	J.M.
	6		do	J.M. 7.3.17 NPP/255 Rfn F.RIORDAN "B" coy killed 4 wounded (2 killed instant'ly) Military Cemetery ARMY CHATEAU ST.13. M.2.d.
	7		do	J.M.
	8		do	J.M. No. 3/1407 Cpl R DAWSON A Coy wounded (miles) 8.3.17
	9		do	J.M.
	10		do	J.M. No. 3/200733 Rfn F.A.S.BOYD died of wounds in Military Cemetery ARMY CHATEAU ST.13. M.2.d 10.3.17 J.M.

Army Form C. 2118.

WAR DIARY
or
INTELLIGENCE SUMMARY

(Erase heading not required.) 7th Bn. The Rifle Brigade

Place	Date 1917	Hour	Summary of Events and Information	Remarks and references to Appendices
DAINVILLE	March 11		Bn. working in H.T. subsector	VAUDIC
	12		— Do —	VAUDIC
	13		— Do —	VAUDIC
	14		— Do —	VAUDIC
	15		500 men of Bn. buried Cables at ARRAS & near BERNEVILLE	VAUDIC
	16		— Do —	VAUDIC
	17		— Do —	VAUDIC
	18		— Do — In evening the Bn. marched to GOUY	VAUDIC
GOUY	19		Working parties found for Railway – Bn. having ar. 9.30 am. Snow with drawn all night. 22 O.R. rejoined	VAUDIC
	20		— Do —	VAUDIC
	21		— Do —	VAUDIC
DAINEVILLE	22		Bn. marched to DAINÉVILLE	VAUDIC
	23		Trenches reconnoitred	VAUDIC
ARRAS (RONVILLE)	24		Bn. moved to Caves in Faubourg RONVILLE (ARRAS) into Brigade Reserve	
	25		Bn in Bde Reserve Caves. The following O.R. was wounded by shell (B Coy) No. 4291 Cpl. E. COOLEY " S/26306 Rfn. G. BLACKMAN " S/17429 " N. HOEKKLEY " S/19988 " E. HUBERT	VAUDIC
	26		Bn in Bde Reserve	VAUDIC
	27		— Do — — Do —	VAUDIC
In Trenches H2 Sector (old German Line)	28		Bn relieved The 8th Bn. The Rifle Brigade in the line. Heavy bombardment by enemy in left sector (A) 4 auth. squadron on front No. S/18495 Nº. J. BOYLE Ja Coy slightly wounded at duty B. HOSEGOOD SLA	VAUDIC

Army Form C. 2118.

WAR DIARY
or
INTELLIGENCE SUMMARY

(Erase heading not required.) 7th Bn. The Rifle Brigade.

(7)

Place	Date	Hour	Summary of Events and Information	Remarks and references to Appendices
Trenches H/2 Sector od Germain	1917 March 29		Bn in Trenches, bad state of repair, had 15 to 7 hour considerable shelling	VaWD
	" 30		— Do — Intermittent shelling all day & night	VaWD
	" 31		— Do — No 5/20340 Rfn H. Bush (skull)	VaWDC

Fighting Strength
O.R 756

Officers
M.O + 23

VaWD Caley Lt Col.
Cmdg 7th Bn.
The Rifle Brigade

CONFIDENTIAL

WAR DIARY
OF
7th BATTN THE RIFLE BRIGADE

FROM 1-4-17   TO 30-4-17

(VOLUME XXIV)

V A E. de Calry, Lt Col.
Commdg 7th Bn The Rifle Bde.

30-4-17.

Army Form C. 2118.

WAR DIARY
or
INTELLIGENCE SUMMARY

(Erase heading not required.) 7 Bn The Rifle Brigade

Place	Date	Hour	Summary of Events and Information	Remarks and references to Appendices
RONVILLE (ARRAS) CAVES	April 1		Bn in trenches — usual intermittent shelling — in the evening the Bn was relieved by the 8th Rifle Brigade and moved to the RONVILLE CAVES. H2 Sector.	Vardc
	2		Bn resting in the CAVES —	Vardc
	3		— do —	Note: The caves are a chalk excavation of considerable intricacy, covering a large area under the suburbs partly of ARRAS. The depth varies from 30 to 70 feet. Various exits have been cut for military requirements — they are lit by electricity throughout. Although damp & having a heavy atmosphere there was a complete absence of noise from the guns — the men were fairly comfortable & got good rest.	Vardc
	4		— do — 14 O.R. rejoined from base	Vardc
	5		— do —	Vardc
	6		— do — } Preliminary bombardment of the enemy trenches and counter battery work by British Artillery	Vardc
	7		— do —	Vardc
	8		— do — Bn furnished parties to cut our own bed wire & to prepare the country for moving in the open.	Vardc
			During the above days the Bn	
BATTLE of ARRAS	9		Zero was at 5.30 am — the attack of the XIV (Light) Division commenced at 7.30 am. 1st Objective, the HARP defences — 2nd S. of TILLOY — 3rd & final objective the FEUCHY Line running roughly N+S — some 800 yds. E. of WANCOURT — about 5000 yds from the starting line. The 42 & 4 Bde & 43 Inf. Bde attacked — the 111th Inf. Brigade was kept in Divisional Reserve. At 7.30 am the 4 & 21 Bde left the caves & assembled in the original British Line for sector. This Bn on the left the 7 KRRC on the right — & the two 8 Bns in rear. At noon the Brigade moved in the same order into the German lines opposite where it spent the night — very little enemy shelling & by the evening the 43 Bde was reported to be slowly getting a footing in the final objective.	Vardc

Army Form C. 2118.

WAR DIARY
or
INTELLIGENCE SUMMARY

(Erase heading not required.) 7ᵗʰ Bn The Rifle Brigade

73

Place	Date	Hour	Summary of Events and Information	Remarks and references to Appendices
	1917		Battle of ARRAS (cont?)	
	April 10ᵗʰ	11ᵃ	At noon the Brigade moved in the same order towards the FEUCHY line. The Bⁿ in artillery formation. 'D' Coy on the left 'C' on the right — The Bⁿ was in roughly a company frontage. The H.Q. party followed and in rear. 'A' & 'B' Coys. followed in the same formation after a half for a meal. The Bⁿ re-assembled for the final advance — on to the final objection which had not been entirely made good. Its orders were to relieve the 4/3ʳᵈ Bⁿ — and if circumstances favourable — to push on beyond the FEUCHY line. At this time two Cavalry Brigades came up on the left and the final move was made in conjunction with the Cavalry, in a heavy snowstorm — which blew into the face of the enemy and to a certain measure screened our movements — A considerable enemy artillery Barrage and heavy m/c gun fire from WANCOURT & the ridge behind it caused some casualties. The Cav. advance was checked by wire in front of the objective — The 43ʳᵈ / Bde willdnd as the Bⁿ took over their position — The Cavalry did the same.	For list of casualties see Appendix 73 (a)
		12ᵃ	dark — having suffered heavily — and the situation remained stationary in the line. VAD&C	
			At about 3.30 a.m. orders were received to attack at 6.30 a.m. to seize WANCOURT and the high ground in rear. Our artillery barrage entirely failed and the advance was checked from the very first by heavy m/c gun fire from the front and in enfilade from right & rear. After considerable confusion the Companies were reorganised as before and the Lewis guns effectively silenced the heavy m/c & m/c gun fire. In the evening the Bⁿ was relieved by the 8ᵗʰ Bᵀʰ The R/B Bde ⁽?⁾ VAD&C	
		13ᵗʰ	The Enemy evacuated WANCOURT. The two Bᵗʰ Bns occupied the village & the high ground behind. The Bⁿ returned to the FEUCHY line and remained in Bde Reserve. During the night a relieving Brigade arrived (the 151ˢᵗ) + the Bⁿ returned to ARRAS (relieved by the 6ᵗʰ D.L.I.) VAD&C	
			Casualties:— Officers Killed 1 Wnd 2 O.R. Killed 9 (incl. died of wds) Wnd 80 Missing 4	

WAR DIARY or INTELLIGENCE SUMMARY

Army Form C. 2118.

(Erase heading not required.) 7th Bn The Rifle Brigade.

Place	Date 1917	Hour	Summary of Events and Information	Remarks and references to Appendices
MONCHIET	April 14		The Bn. marched to Billets in Monchiet. 2/Lt R.F. WANSBOROUGH & 22 O.R. joined from the Base	Vandc
SOMBRIN	" 15		— do — — do — in SOMBRIN	Vandc
	" 16		Bn. training and reorganizing. 2/Lt M.D. CHILD rejoined & 104 O.Rs. from Base.	Vandc
	" 17		— do — — do — 2nd Lt L.L. GOOCH joined from Base.	Vandc
	" 18		— do — — do — 2nd Lt B. FOSTER rejoined from Base.	Vandc
	" 19		— do —	Vandc
	" 20		— do —	Vandc
	" 21		— do —	Vandc
	" 22		— do —	Vandc
	" 23		Bn. marched to billets in BERLES-AU-BOIS	Vandc
on march to WANCOURT	" 24		Bn. marched at short notice to FICHEUX. Major T. MAXWELL MC took over command of the Bn.	Vandc
	" 25		Bn. marched to Bivouac at MERCATEL	Vandc
WANCOURT	" 26		Bn. moved into Right Reserve in NIGER Trench nr WANCOURT. Transport camp at BONVILLE.	Vandc
			recent Pull near MONCHIET	
	" 27		Bn. in reserve near WANCOURT S.W. about Square N.21. Casualties (sheet) Killed No S/10125 Rfn H. ROBSON) B. Coy. Wounded WANCOURT Cemetery	
			" 11 — 5874 C. MURRELL) B. Coy.	
			Wounded S/23654 Rfn H. Rosen No S/24001 Rfn W. Moody B. Coy.	
			S/17684 R. Young S/29451 CpL E. Williams C. Coy.	
			S/17894 R. FELDERGHILL) A. Coy. S/13741 Rfn H. BUTER B. Coy.) A.L.S.C.
			S/13586 W. Couchman Slight at duty.	

Army Form C. 2118.

WAR DIARY
or
INTELLIGENCE SUMMARY.

(Erase heading not required.)

7th Bn The Rifle Brigade

Place	Date 1917	Hour	Summary of Events and Information	Remarks and references to Appendices
WANCOURT	April 28	2P	Bn in Reserve at WANCOURT about Square N.22. Quiet Day.	WALDC
			—do— —do— Casualties (sheet) Killed N°S/17705 Sgt. C SHIRE	
			Wounded " S/10459 Rfn J. FLINT.	
			" S/14574 " W. Cooper N° B/203114 R/n F. PaTRick D.	
			" B/200638 " E Brazier " S/15195 " G. Goddard	
			" S/23701 " W. Horton " S/11081 " H. Fennessy J	
			right-a-out. 5/4/17.	Vawoc.
	30		Bn in Bde Reserve in Sq. N.22.c. WaNCOURT.	
			fighting Strength Officers 29	
			O.R. 891	
			V.A.C. Elm Wet	
			Cmdg 7th Bn	
			The Rifle Brigade	

APPENDIX 73(a)

7th Battn. The Rifle Brigade.

Casualty Return.

No.	Rank and Name	Coy.	Nature of Casualty.	
	2nd Lt. H. Anstey		Killed in Action	11/4/17
	Lieut. J.E.B. Gray		Wounded	,,
	2nd Lt. L.C. Pollard		,,	,,
S/9692	Rfn. Betts, H.	A	Killed in Action	,,
B/1	Cpl. Whitcher, A.E.	,,	Wounded	10/4/17
S/9713	L/C. Morgan, H.	,,	,,	,,
S/10144	Rfn. Bennett, A.E.	,,	,,	,,
B/203644	,, Curtis, C.	,,	,,	,, → Died of Wounds.
S/16138	,, Rice, E.	,,	,,	,,
B/370	,, Calcott, W.	,,	,,	11/4/17
S/28577	,, Tallett, H.	,,	,,	,,
S/23386	,, Strange, A.	,,	,,	,,
B/2513	,, Field, W.	,,	,,	,,
B/203132	L/C. Fairy, A.	,,	,,	10/4/17
S/13136	Rfn. Day, W.	,,	,,	,,
S/26300	,, Duffy, L.H.	,,	,,	11/4/17
2925	Sgt. Goddard, H.	,,	,,	10/4/17
8685	Rfn. Organ, E.	,,	,,	,,
S/28580	,, Sladen, E.	,,	,,	11/4/17
B/203030	,, Carlyle, A.	,,	,,	10/4/17
S/26261	,, Conlan, B.	,,	,,	11/4/17
S/6178	,, Clarke, J.	,,	,,	10/4/17
S/28584	,, Clegg, F.	,,	,,	11/4/17
S/17747	,, Isaacs, C.	,,	,,	10/4/17
B/203683	,, Norman, A.	,,	,,	,,
B/203638	,, Herepath, L.	,,	,,	,,
B/200658	,, Tyler, A.	,,	,,	,,
S/20543	,, Etherington, F.	,,	,,	,, → Died of Wounds
6478	CSM. Carson, J.H.J.	,,	,,	,,
B/542	Rfn. Hodges, E.	,,	,,	11/4/17
B/200652	,, Mills, H.	,,	,,	,,
B/203663	,, Wild, D.	,,	,,	,,
B/1597	,, Shelley, F.	,,	,,	10/4/17
S/9284	,, Davies, C.	,,	,,	11/4/17
S/21707	,, Crosley, A.	,,	,,	10/4/17
S/16865	,, Jones, J.J.	B	,,	,,
B/200716	,, Biggar, M.	,,	,,	,,
S/12626	,, Ward, H.	,,	,,	,,
B/200742	,, Willis, W.	,,	,,	,,
6033	,, Hanks, A.	,,	,,	,,
S/26302	,, Bartholomew, T.	,,	,,	,,
S/26309	,, P'Shea, P.	,,	,,	11/4/17
S/23928	L/C. Hamberger, T.	,,	,,	12/4/17
8125	Rfn. Saunders, T.	,,	,,	,,
8080	Sgt. King, G.W.	D	Killed in Action	10/4/17
S/27897	Rfn. D'Arcy, G.	,,	,,	,,
S/15766	Cpl. Dellar, J.	,,	Wounded	,,
B/3113	,, Carrs, R.	,,	,,	,,
S/16744	Rfn. Wiseman, W.	,,	,,	,,
B/20341	,, Whatmough, L.	,,	,,	,,
P/516	,, Brook, S.	,,	,,	,,
S/23968	,, Venus, S.	,,	,,	,,
S/23969	,, Miller, J.	,,	,,	,,
B/203699	,, Gill, H.	,,	,,	,,
B/1593	Sgt. Hulton, C.G.	,,	,,	11/4/17
S/11321	Rfn. Webb, C.	,,	,,	10/4/17
B/203725	,, Wicks, J.	,,	,,	,,
S/26550	,, Peach, P.	,,	,,	,,
S/26555	,, Smallbone, S.	,,	,,	,,
P/80	,, Apps, G.	,,	,,	,,
S/19704	,, Jones, A.J.	,,	,,	,,
S/6863	,, Davis, H.	,,	,,	,, — Rejoined

No.	Rank and Name		Coy.	Nature of Casualty.	
B/2363	Rfn.	Schofield, H.	D	Wounded	10/4/17
S/15782	,,	Brodbeck, A.	,,	Shell shock	,, → Rejoined
B/3393	,,	Brooker, A.	,,	Missing Wounded?	,,
S/148	,,	Hughes, W.	,,	Wounded	,,
6709	,,	Smith, E.	,,	,,	,,
B/200721	,,	Banks, E.I.	C	Killed in Action	10/4/17
Z/818	,,	Bonham, J.	,,	,,	10/4/17
S/14871	,,	Cortes, S.	,,	,,	,,
Z/1191	,,	Hall, R.	,,	,,	,, died of Wounds
B/53	CQMS	Beckingham, A.	,,	Wounded	,,
Z/1039	Sgt.	Eyles, W.	,,	,,	,,
6853	,,	Jeffreys, A.	,,	,, (rejoined)	,,
B/203665	L/C.	Banks, B.H.	,,	,,	,,
S/2584	Rfn.	Hazlewood, J.	,,	,,	,,
S/8596	L/C.	Rock, A.	,,	,,	,,
S/26394	Rfn.	Finn, W.	,,	,,	,,
S/26310	,,	Neale, W.J.	,,	,,	,,
B/200737	,,	Brewster, H.W. Brunsden	,,	,,	,, Died of Wounds
S/25055	,,	Bowker, T.	,,	,,	,,
S/25062	,,	Butt, T.	,,	,,	,,
S/16092	,,	Nixon, H.	,,	,,	,,
S/20005	,,	Rawlings, H.W.	,,	,,	,,
S/26380	,,	Garnett, T.	,,	,,	,,
S/24586	,,	Page, G.	,,	,,	,,
S/9522	,,	Bean, W.	,,	,,	,,
S/7166	,,	Steptoe, A.	,,	,,	,,
Z/2113	,,	Williams, C.	,,	,,	,,
S/10764	,,	Green, W.	,,	,,	,,
B/203379	,,	Knight, A.E.	,,	,,	,,
S/9903	L/C.	Bradford, A.	,,	~~Missing~~ Killed in action	,,
B/1681	Rfn.	Beattie, H.	,,	Missing	,,
S/12782	,,	Bradley, A.	,,	,,	,,
~~S/22252 Cpl. Nutty, P.~~					
S/20909	,,	Peel, E.	,,	Wounded	9/4/17
B/140	Sgt.	Herd, I.	D	,,	5/4/17
B/140	,,	Herd, I.	,,	Died of Wounds	7/4/17

CONFIDENTIAL.

WAR DIARY

OF

7th. BATTN. THE RIFLE BRIGADE.

FROM   1st May, 1917

TO   31st May, 1917.

(VOLUME XXIV)

A.J.H. Shoggett Major,
Commdg. 7th Battn. The Rifle Brigade.

WAR DIARY
or
INTELLIGENCE SUMMARY.

Army Form C. 2118.

7th (S) Bn The Rifle Brigade

Place	Date	Hour	Summary of Events and Information	Remarks and references to Appendices
WANCOURT	May 1		At B Coy moved back about 10 p.m. to NEPAL TRENCH. Casualties "A" Coy. S/21767 Rfn. A.J. Brown killed shell. Buried WANCOURT Cemetery N21c 2.6 "B" Coy. 8/77 Cpl. T. Millward, S/26333 Rfn. G.F. Edwards, S/17391 Rfn. A. Innes, S/348 Cpl. G. Cockerell. wounded "A" Coy B/351 Rfn. H. Hale, S/19220 Rfn. A. Jedrade, 8/23647 Rfn. S. Harwood 6180 Rfn. J. Bennett wounded "D" coy. S/10186 Rfn. S. Lloyd, S/14769 Rfn. E. Kilburn, 2/31740 Rfn. J. Barrett, S/23965 Rfn. H. Simmonds wounded "A" Coy. S/31765 Rfn. T. Ewart, S/31763 Rfn. L. Payne S/4118 Rfn. J. Tadd died of wounds. 2/585 Rfn. G. Appleby shell shock "B" Coy. /30529 8 Rfn. S. Esquire wounded. J.M.	
do	2		The Bn moved forward to support the attack, having been of ALBATROS about 11.30 p.m. "A" Coy to GANNETT and FALCON Trenches, "B" Coy to EGRETT Trench "C" and "D" Comps to DUCK Trench.	
do	3		Zero was at 3.45 am. "A" Coy moved forward to HERON Trench, "B" to EGRETT trench. Casualties in Transport lines in RONVILLE. No B/4104 Rfn. G. Fielder, "A" Coy. No S/1045 Rfn. F. Braythorpe D. Coy. The Bn was not called upon to take active part in the operations. The Rifle was to support the attack as when the two reached. The Blue line was attained with little resistance. The Red Line explained F.F. HASRISY. Bombing up to the Sist. Joint attempts failed owing to heavy M.G. fire from TRIANGLE WOOD. A heavy counter attack was made by the enemy and morning of both flanks having started in the air. the brigade had to withdraw. It continued to withdraw. J.M.	

Army Form C. 2118.

WAR DIARY
or
INTELLIGENCE SUMMARY.
(Erase heading not required.) 7th Bn. The Rifle Brigade

Place	Date	Hour	Summary of Events and Information	Remarks and references to Appendices
MARCOURT	May 3		The first symptoms of an enemy intensification of the artillery bombardment by the morning Coy. in HERON trench came from	
			Meanwhile the rebellion was restricted to a violent trench mortar of S.A. shells, shrank trench wire from HERON to EGRETT, afterwards shifting to DUCK trench and the COJEUR valley on the east were symptoms of the enemies attack being intended to remain the lough ground by MARCOURT Tower, our troops was at once places in the BLUE line and all officers sent back to gain the assurance on both Flanks. No hostile IO both their objectives.	
			Casualties. Capt R.C. BURN. A.C. wounded 2/Lt B. FOSTER shell shock 20. O.R. Killed. 27 J.M. 20 wounded, 9 shell shock. See Appendix 77 a for details.	J.M.
ditto	4		The Bn. was still in support. The day was quiet.	J.M.
ditto	5		At 3 a.m. The Bn. was relieved by the D.C.L.I. and withdrew to NEPAL trench leaving the remainder of the day.	J.M. J.M.
ditto	6		The Bn. marched to NEPAL trench. Under the A 3 rm Bn. tactically. The following officers joined the Bn. from 2/Lts C.A. Doubleday, A.E. Newman, G.V. Reeves, A. Hayward, W. Wortham, N.E. Watkinson. Casualty 2/68561 A/L/l. Nugget. "D" Coy sick.	J.M.

Army Form C. 2118.

WAR DIARY
or
INTELLIGENCE SUMMARY.

(Erase heading not required.) 7th (S) Bn. The Rifle Brigade.

Place	Date 1917	Hour	Summary of Events and Information	Remarks and references to Appendices
WANCOURT	May 7th		The Bn. under the 43rd Bde. tactically. Draft of 40 o.R. joined the Transport line.	J.M.
"	8		" " " " working parties provided in the front line	J.M.
"	9		" " " "	J.M.
"	10		" " " "	J.M.
			Casualty Lt. Col. V.A.M.C. de Caley - Instructing Dragoons - Cavalry. The Bat. also killed by enterprise and buried at British Military cemetery at NEUVILLE - VITASSE M.24 b. 7.4	J.M.
"	11		The Bn. under the tactical command of 43rd Bde. provided working parties. Casualties. S/8072 Rfn. B. Whitehouse "B" Coy. } killed and buried at Mancourt cemetery. N.16.C.4.2	
			5235- " V. Eagles " " } Shell fire }	
			13/1525 " J. S. Dun "	
			B/200737 " J.N. Barker }	
			5/24602 " R. Taylor }	
"	12		The Bn under the tactical command of 43rd Bde. provided working parties. 2/Lt. D.C. Vinding joined the Bn. with a draft of 3 o.R.	J.M.
"	13		The Bn. provided working parties to the 43rd. Infty. Bde.	J.M. 3/11290 Rfn. J. Voges "C" Coy. wounded
"	14		The Bn. relieved the 6th. Bn. Somerset Light Infty in the left front of the Brigade. dispositions of platoons in support of "C" Coy. 2 platoons of "A" Coy. 1 platoon of New Coy. supporting "D" Coy. in Bois en Hache. "B" Coy. in Reserve in occupying the effort line platoon of New Coy. supporting "D" Coy. in Bois en Hache. "B" Coy. in Reserve in occupying and other 2 platoons in Frontline D'ouck and 2 in Hun Trenches.	J.M.

WAR DIARY
or
INTELLIGENCE SUMMARY.

(Erase heading not required.) 7th (S) Bn. The Rifle Brigade

Army Form C. 2118.

79

Place	Date	Hour	Summary of Events and Information	Remarks and references to Appendices
WANCOURT Trenches	1917 May 15th		In the trenches:- Reconnoitring patrols gained contact with the enemy.	2/Lt N.T. Cooper "D" Coy killed (bullet). 5/16795 Rfn. J. Boyd "C" Coy wounded (shell).
"	16th.		" :- quiet day but very bad weather.	J.M.
"	17th.		" :- quiet day: heavy shelling about 6 p.m.	5/28693 Cpl E. Autry 5/22855 Rfn F. Hammond 5/20970 Rfn A. Rentise all of "C" Coy wounded (shrapnel?) J.M.
"	18th.		" :- quiet day	J.M.
"	19th.		" :- 2nd Anniversary of the Battalion's arrival in France for active service. At 3am about 3 of the enemy left their wagon and it will be seen looked down which where they apparently saw officers and his orderly. A short fight ensued in which the officer and his orderly were wounded. The enemy showed off at the double sporting number a heavy rifle fire from the foot. On either flank. The enemy left his rifles and hand grenades. There is no apparent of landclords behind, and the right was dark. Anyway his larger. The intends at the effort was presently ly to held blockly, the garrison of L Coy is indicated, which being now forwards for the salutations defences of this portion of the line. The flanks were being strongly held in lookouts and post home.	2/Lt R.F. Wainsforough 5/26320 Rfn F. Stenner "C" Coy were wounded. Rfn Stenner subsequently died of wounds. J.M.

1577 Wt.W10791/1773 500,000 1/15 D. D. & L. A.D.S.S./Forms/C. 2118.

Army Form C. 2118.

WAR DIARY
or
INTELLIGENCE SUMMARY.

(Erase heading not required.) 7th. (S.) Bn. The Rifle Brigade.

Place	Date	Hour	Summary of Events and Information	Remarks and references to Appendices
WANCOURT Trenches	Aug 19		Enemy shelled right coy in the morning. The Bn. was relieved by the 8th Bn. The Rifle Brigade and proceeded to garrison Bluegrand Trench ("A" coy), "B"s and "D" coys. Honeymark in Nepal Trench. H.Q. in Albatros.	wounded (shell) B/202672 Rfn F. Selby and S/30,1689 Rfn F. Cook (since died of wounds) 9th f.C.' Coy. J.M.
WANCOURT	20		In support. Rifle shot "B" coy wounded. "D" coy. to enter trench and "C" coy to further trench. Major A.J.H. Slappet joined to command Bn. patrols.	J.M. 9M
"	21st		Quiet day.	wounded (shell) R/2947 Rfn. R. Willis C. Coy S/7503 Rfn. F. Wales B/20723 Rfn F. Coys A.F.A.66
"	22nd		Quiet day. Killed S/26960 L/Cpl W. Tate "C" Coy (shell) Allison "C" Coy (shell)	
"	23rd		Batt. Head Quarters shelled from 1-2 pm - otherwise quiet day. Killed S/36592 Rfn. W. Knight "B" Coy (shell) - Wounded 2/127 A/L/Sgt F. Howell "B" Coy (Shell) - Died of wounds 24.5.17) - S/26385 Rfn J.W. Randall "A" Coy (Shell) B. relieved by 9th Bn R.B and proceeded to Div: Support in the vicinity of N.20.a.0.15.	9gas
"	24"		Bn. moved to Div. Reserve in N.10.d.	
BEAURAINS	25" 26" 27"		Resting Kit & Inspection. Honours Award 6173 Rfn W. Waymark "A" Coy awarded Military Medal yft. Kit Inspection Bathing. B/205514 Rfn A. Rosen "A" Coy	

Army Form C. 2118.

WAR DIARY
or
INTELLIGENCE SUMMARY.

(Erase heading not required.)

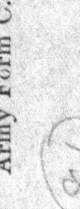

Place	Date	Hour	Summary of Events and Information	Remarks and references to Appendices
BEAURAINS	Aug/17 26th		Company Training - Draft Regard 3f. O.R. - Mentioned in Despatches Supplement L.G. dated 25/5/17 T/Capt: W.T. Shaw. T/Lieut: L.G. Longmead, B/3504 Q.M.S. T. Kuppas, B/1477 Sgt. A. McBurnie, B/104 C/Sgt: G.W. Shields, 1912 Serjt A. Young.	
"	29th		Company Training.	
"	30th		Company Training. Honours award. B/1188 Rfm S. Forman A Coy] Awarded Military Medal B/1589 " H. Godson D " 8061 " E. Woodgate B " 5/2775 " F.H. King A "	
"	31st		Battalion on Range. R.16.c.2.6 Grouping + Application practice.	Fighting Strength Officers 31 - O.R. 838

A.J.H. Mogg H Major
Commdg. 7th A/o Sheffield Bde 31/5/17

"APPENDIX 77a"

7th Battn. The Rifle Brigade.

List of Casualties for Action of 3/4th May.

No.	Rank and Name		Coy.	Nature of Casualty etc.
	Capt.	Brown, R.C., M.C.		Wounded.
	2nd. Lt.	Foster, B.		Shell shock
S/17432	Rfn.	Holland, G.	B	Wounded
S/8652	,,	Maskey, J.	B	,, (Died of Wounds 6-5-17)
B/203652	,,	Popperwell, G.	A	,, (Died of Wounds 9-5-17)
S/14277	,,	Phillips, A.	A	,,
B/1366	L/C.	Devenport, J.	B	,, (Died of Wounds 7-5-17)
S/30599	Rfn.	Plant, E.	B	,, (Died of Wounds 4-5-17)
S/30612	,,	Parton, T.	C	,,
S/24319	,,	Erbe, H.	C	,,
S/11753	,,	Rose, R.	D	,,
B/1296	,,	Smith, C.	B	,,
S/29473	,,	Pearson, E.W.	B	,,
S/17196	,,	McHanwell, J.	C	,,
4735	Sgt.	Key, H.	B	,,
B/3013	,,	Murphy, A.	A	,,
S/24566	Rfn.	Fell, G.	A	,,
B/2590	Sgt.	Hilling, F.	A	,,
S/15527	Rfn.	Simmond, J.	C	,,
S/3659	,,	Elliott, J.	C	,,
S/4976	,,	Dean, W.	A	,,
B/2076	Cpl.	Burke, J.	D	,,
S/12673	Rfn.	Bateman, A.	D	,,
S/10522	L/C.	Parker, J.	B	,,
B/2128	Sgt.	Lawrence, C.	D	Shell shock.
B/203038	L/C.	Newey, J.	D	,,
S/31762	Rfn.	Brown, A.	A	,,
B/203723	,,	Taylor, R.	D	,,
B/203044	,,	Rowley, F.	D	,,
S/30683	,,	Death, H.	D	,,

2.

No.	Rank and Name.		Coy.	Nature of Casualty etc.
B/203708	Rfn.	Lancaster, J.	D	Shell shock
S/10204	L/C.	Rogers, A.	C	,,
S/30616	Rfn.	Trotman, A.	D	Wounded.
S/13761	,,	Rogers, G.	A	,,
B/2514	,,	Gubbins, A.	A	,,
S/15319	,,	Potter, T.	B	,,
S/15272	,,	Heath, H.	B	,,
B/200542	L/C.	Derry, F.	A	,,
6015	Rfn.	McBain, C.	A	Shell shock
B/203735	,,	Redhead, R.	D	Wounded
S/24666	,,	Hanley, J.	C	,,
S/26321	,,	Crickenden, J.	C	,,
S/28963	,,	Smith, F.A.	A	,,
S/6537	,,	Blackwell, W.	D	Killed in Action
S/5331	,,	Chappell, J.	"	,,
S/2557	,,	Buckerfield, W.	"	,,
S/24059	,,	Hunt, H.	"	,,
S/1152	,,	Burke, J.	"	,,
B/1380	Cpl.	Mason, J.	"	,,
S/7839	L/C.	Mottram, J.	"	,,
Z/1688	Rfn.	Pitman, F.	A	,,
S/25224	,,	Wade, W.	"	,,
3899	,,	Brewer, G.	"	,,
B/203642	,,	Biskop, J.	"	,,
S/26325	L/C.	Hardy, W.	B	,,
S/26127	Rfn.	Rowe, J.	"	,,
S/737	,,	Higgins, L.	"	,,
S/26357	,,	Hay, J.	"	,,
8543	,,	Pill, E.	"	,,
S/28593	,,	Rogers, W.	"	,,
B/203056	,,	Pickerell, E.	"	,,
S/20376	,,	Chapman, H.	"	,,
S/26298	,,	Clatworthy, E.	C	,,
B/203734	"	Gouldesborough A	D	"

Summary

Capt R.C. Brown — Wounded
2/Lt B. Foster — Shell Shock
Killed & Died of Wounds — 26 OR
Wounded — 27 "
Shell Shock — 9 "

CONFIDENTIAL

WAR DIARY

OF

7th Battn THE RIFLE BRIGADE

From 1-6-17   To 30-6-17

(VOLUME XXVI)

A.J.H. Sloggett Lt Col
Commdg 7th Bn The Rifle Brigade

In the Field.

Army Form C. 2118.

WAR DIARY
or
INTELLIGENCE SUMMARY.
(Erase heading not required.)

82

Place	Date	Hour	Summary of Events and Information	Remarks and references to Appendices
BEAURAINS M.10.d.	1		Batts inspected by G.O.C. Corps (Lt. Gen. T.D.O. Snow). 2Lt. J.F.H. Jones for duty. Training.	appx
	2		Coy training	appx
	3		Coy training	appx
NEUVILLE VITASSE	4		Batt'n relieved 5th K.S.L.I. in Anzac trenches. Early NEUVILLE VITASSE at 8 p.m.	appx
	5		Coy training	appx
	6		Draft of 3 O.R. joined. Coy training	appx
	7		Range Practices.	appx
	8		Coy training	appx
	9		Batt'n relieved by 10th D.L.I. and proceeded to camp at M.10.d. (BEAURAINS) at 8.30 hm appx	appx
BEAURAINS	10		Batt'n resting, cleaning up + baths.	appx
	11		Batt'n moved to MONCHIET at 5.20 a.m. Heavy Rain. In Nissen Huts	appx
MONCHIET	12		Batt'n moved to SAULTY at 8.30 a.m. In Billets	appx
SAULTY	13		Batt'n moved to BERTRANCOURT at 5.30 a.m. In Nissen Huts + Hutments	appx
BERTRANCOURT	14		Batt'n resting + cleaning up Camp	appx
	15		Batt'n resting + cleaning up camp	appx
	16		"	appx
	17		Coy Training. Manufacture Rifle Range	appx

Army Form C. 2118.

WAR DIARY
or
INTELLIGENCE SUMMARY.
(Erase heading not required.)

Instructions regarding War Diaries and Intelligence Summaries are contained in F. S. Regs., Part II. and the Staff Manual respectively. Title pages will be prepared in manuscript.

Place	Date 19[ ]	Hour	Summary of Events and Information	Remarks and references to Appendices
BERTRANCOURT	June 18		Completion of Range	
	19		Guard of Honour (1 Off. 51 O.R.) from 4 R.H. Duke of Cornwall presented to Santy. Coy training - Musketry, officers of the Guard 2/Lt. G. D. Hoyle.	
	20		Coy training + Musketry	
	21		Draft 2/Lt A. E. Herbert and 102 O.R. joined for duty. 2/Lt R.W.P. Bullin	
	22		" " Battn Sports 1st Day	
	23		" " Battn Sports 1st Day	
	24		" " " " Open Order	
	25		Battn Scheme near AUCHONVILLERS	
	26		Coy Training. Div. Horse Show at MARIEUX. 1/2 hr march by company. E. Heelin Shanks	
	27		" " and musketry. Brigade Sports (Prelim) Events finish 32	
	28		Brigade Scheme cancelled owing to heavy rain. O.R. 9 h. D.	
	29		Coy training + musketry. Brigade Sports (Bayonet fighting + Transport Events)	
	30		Visit by H.R.H. Duke of Connaught (detached) Inspection of Batt, drawn up in Chevron on football ground, 9: Bu. The Rifle Brigade on march in. Parade state O.R. 24. O.R. 650.	

A.T.H. Hoggett Lt. Col.
Comdg. 7th Bn The Rifle Brigade

Vol 27

CONFIDENTIAL

WAR DIARY

OF

7th Battn THE RIFLE BRIGADE

1-7-1917   31-7-1917

(VOLUME XXVII)

A.J.H. Shoggett   LT COL

COMMDG 7th Bn THE RIFLE BRIGADE

In the Field
31-7-1917

WAR DIARY or INTELLIGENCE SUMMARY

Army Form C. 2118.

7th (S) Bn. The Rifle Brigade.

Place	Date	Hour	Summary of Events and Information	Remarks and references to Appendices
BERTRANCOURT	1917 July 1		2/Lt. C. RADBOURNE, 2/Lt. A. GALBRAITH & 2/Lt. J.R. SAUNDERS joined the Battn. C/E parade 9 a.m.	JHR
"	2	Morning	Company training in Physical training & bayonet fighting. Lewis Gun teams fired on the Range.	JHR
"		2-6 p.m.	Heats of Athletic events. Batt Sports.	JHR
"	3		Company training. Finals of Athletic events. Batt Sports. The Batt. received an asgd of 38 points. The Rifle Sports won the Brigadier's prize. The 7" Batt" R.B. were second hand & the 8" were fourth. The 8" R.B. were third with 36 points. The Batt" were first in Rifle Grenade throwing, Lewis Gun competition, Bugle Race, Physical training Running up London, catering competition, Mule race, Filling the bucket & Road Race.	JHR
"	4		Company training.	JHR
"	5		Company shooting competition won by 13 Coy. 2 Squads in final were 10th opd in 1 min & 5 Hrs, entries by target.	JHR
"	6		Batt parade at 8 a.m. for 1st Bde. flag kind which were cancelled owing to inclement weather.	JHR
"	7		Battn training; two companies in trenches in a strong point.	JHR
"	8		2/Lt. T.S. LEA joined the Battn. Church parades for all denominations.	JHR
"	9		R.B.M's parade. Company training in musketry, gun order & arms drill. R.E.s, physical training & bayonet fighting. Officers, revolver practice.	JHR
BERNEVAL	10		The Battn moved to BERNEVAL - about 10 miles.	JHR

WAR DIARY or INTELLIGENCE SUMMARY.

7th 1Bn The Rifle Brigade

Army Form C. 2118.

Place	Date	Hour	Summary of Events and Information	Remarks and references to Appendices
BERWAL	1917 July 11		The Battn. rested at BERWAL.	AJR.
CLARE CAMP C.Roux & Poperinge	12		The Battn. marched to DOULLENS & entrained there at 8 A.M. & detrained at GODESWAERSVELD at 2.15 P.M. & marched thence to CLARE CAMP where it went under canvas.	AJR.
"	13		Companies inspected by O.C. Coys. Officers & N.C.Os. Physical training & bayonet fighting classes.	AJR.
"	14	6-7pm	Coys under C.S.M.S., rifle exercises. Subaltern Officers & N.C.Os. bayonet fighting.	AJR.
"	"	8.30-10	Battn. drill. 10 A.M. matins, training of specialists.	AJR.
"	15.		Parade services for all denominations. Lt.N.S. THORNTON, & 2Lt. I.S. HALL rejoined the Battn. & 2Lt. S.O. COCHRANE joined. "C" Coy received W.P. of 37" Bn. m KEMMEL defences under 89 2d Coy R.E.	AJR.
"	16.		Coy. training & baths. Run with res box respiration parades for gas chamber	AJR.
"	17		Battn. drill. Officers bayonet fighting class. Coy. training in close interval drill, bayonet fighting &	AJR.
"	18.		M.O. commenced monthly inspection of companies. 6-7 A.M. Coys. under C.S.M.s, rifle exercises & rapid loading. Subaltern Officers under R.S.M. 8.30-10 Coy.S. under C.S.M.s; R.S.M. o. Battn drill. Subaltern Officers under R.S.M. 10.30-12 Coys short independent retrench.	AJR.
"	19		Battn. training at BAILLEUL cancelled owing to inclement weather. Coys. carried out some small amount of training between heavy showers.	AJR.
"	20		Early morning parades; R.S.M.'s parade Subaltern officers under Bde. Instructor of Bayonet fighting	AJR.

Army Form C. 2118.

WAR DIARY
or
INTELLIGENCE SUMMARY.
(Erase heading not required.)

17. (S) Bn. The Rifle Brigade.

(86)

Place	Date	Hour	Summary of Events and Information	Remarks and references to Appendices
CLARE CAMP de POPERINGHE contd	July 20 1917	Morning	Coy. training; one hour dummy grenade throwing, one hour short scheme - the Platoon in the attack bringing out the employment of the various arms, one hour bayonet fighting.	OMR
"	21		6-7 R.S.M's parade. Morning Coy. training on similar lines to those of 20th inst.	OMR
"	22		Capt. S.S. JENKYNS joined the Bn. Church of E & R.C. parade services. "A" Coy. relieved "C" Coy for work on KEMMEL defences. 8/3234 Rfn. H.GOODING gassed while with M.P.	OMR
"	23		Selected party from each Coy. Lewis bomb throwing on Corps grenade area. Coy. training (in reminder of h?) Parade under Coy. arrangements. Training of "B att." recruits commenced. 3/30562 Rfn. Hyman gassed.	OMR
"	24		Inclement weather prevented the use of Rifle Range at Mt. CONGREVE. Coy. inspection parades in view of inspection by 2nd Army Commander.	OMR
"	25		Inspection by 2nd Army Commander, General Sir Herbert Plumer at CROIX de POPERINGHE at 11.15 A.M. Strength on parade 21 O. + 95 O.R. (one Coy. being away on W.P.) 4:1" Rif. Bn. Two 8" R.B. formed up in following order; 8" KRRC, 7" KRRC, 7" R.B. 2/c. Coy. Ex. 4 Intelligence Coy. with Lewis & Intelligence Officer's? March Past now held by 19" Bn."	OMR
"	26		6.30 - 7.30 All Coy's Physical training elegant fighting. 9 A.M. C.O.'s parade, Batt" drill. Coy. training. An attack reminder of morning.	OMR
"	27		"B" Coy. relieved "A" Coy. on KEMMEL defences. C. & D. Coy's carried out firing on range at MT. OPRS	OMR
"	28			

Army Form C. 2118.

(87)

WAR DIARY
or
INTELLIGENCE SUMMARY.

7th (S) Bn. The Rifle Brigade.

(Erase heading not required.)

Instructions regarding War Diaries and Intelligence Summaries are contained in F. S. Regs., Part II. and the Staff Manual respectively. Title pages will be prepared in manuscript.

Place	Date	Hour	Summary of Events and Information	Remarks and references to Appendices
CLARE CAMP (Route Poperinghe)	July 1917 (contd) 28		CONSECLEE. Practice fired. 5 rds, rapid & deliberate.	AAH
	29		Church Parades for all denominations.	AAH
FRONTIER CAMP.	30		The Battn moved at 9 p.m. to FRONTIER CAMP & pitched a camp. "B" Coy rejoined from the GHQ.	
"	31		KEMMEL Defences. All Officers & NCOs attended a lecture by the Bde. Sen. Officer 3rd L.T. from the Map. of the Battn. The Batt.n were under 1 hours notice to proceed the time & the day was spent in implementing.	AAH.

A.T.H. Hoggett
Lieut. Colonel.
Comdg. 7."B." The Rifle Brigade.

Fighting Strength
Officers 30
O.R. 801.

July 31st. 1917.

2353 Wt W2344/1454 700,000 5/15 D. D. & L. A.D.S.S./Forms/C. 2118.

CONFIDENTIAL

WAR DIARY

OF

7th Bn. THE RIFLE BRIGADE

FROM 1/8/17.   TO 31/8/17

(VOLUME XXVIII)

A.J.H. Sloggett   LT Col

7th Bn. The Rifle Brigade

31/8/17.

Army Form C. 2118.

82

WAR DIARY
or
INTELLIGENCE SUMMARY. 7th Batt. The Rifle Brigade.
(Erase heading not required.)

Instructions regarding War Diaries and Intelligence Summaries are contained in F.S. Regs., Part II. and the Staff Manual respectively. Title pages will be prepared in manuscript.

Place	Date	Hour	Summary of Events and Information	Remarks and references to Appendices
FRONTIER CAMP.	Aug 1st 1917		The Batt: was still at Havois whilst expecting to move into the line. Bn. reported about one ambulance	
"	Aug. 2.		The Batt: being still under the same arrangements nothing further than the reporting sick &	
"			Short Company marches could be attempted.	
"	Aug.3.		Very bad weather & no training practicable as the Batt: was still under one hours notice	
"	Aug 4		During the morning men went a Batt: route march of about 3 miles as the Batt:	
"			was no longer under one hour's notice.	
"	Aug 5		There were Church Parades during the morning while a Lewis Gun class fired a	
"			course during the afternoon.	
HAZEWIND ST.	Aug 6.		The Batt: marched to HAZEWINDE arriving about 12.30 P.M. a Zepp. overflew over	
"			billets in a scattered area.	
"	Aug 7		Coy training during the morning, two reports about & inspect Lewis & Bombs	
"	Aug. 8.		Similar Coy. training continued, the area being badly selected, it was extremely difficult	
"	Aug. 9.		for one Coy in the morning Coy practiced the attack. The rest of the	
"			remainder of the morning to be informed about transport, fighting	
"			Shere were also two lectures for officers & N.C.Os. during the morning & during the	
"	Aug 10		Very practised trap digging & taking a trench, a complete or compass bearings	

2353 Wt W.2544/1454 700,000 5/15 D.D.& L. A.D.S.S./Forms/C. 2118.

WAR DIARY or INTELLIGENCE SUMMARY

Army Form C. 2118.

7th Batt. Rifle Bde.

(Erase heading not required.)

Place	Date	Hour	Summary of Events and Information	Remarks and references to Appendices
HAZEBROUCK	1917 Aug 11		Officers & JCOs had a further lecture on the system by General in whose scheme Coy training continued.	
"	Aug 12		There were church parades for all denominations. 2/Lt. T.D. Smith joined for duty.	
"	Aug 13		Coys continued the platoon in the advance including deployment & rehearsal over different country.	
"	Aug 14		The Batt. carried out an eight mile route march during the morning.	
"	Aug 15		The Batt. entrained at CAESTRE STN about 10 P.M. & arrived at OUDEZEELE about 11.30 P.M. & marched to camp at DICKEBUSCH	
DICKEBUSCH	Aug 16		At very short notice the Batt. moved up to relieve the 1st line, but was not required immediately & consequently spent the night at CHATEAU SEGARD. The 18th D.L.I. had made an attack that morning & had been heavily counterattacked, the situation was critical.	
CHATEAU SEGARD	Aug 17		The Batt. moved to the Front line with Batt. HQ at Stirling Castle relieving the Bedfords in the front line & a Coy of 12th Middlesex in support.	
FRONT LINE STIRLING CASTLE	Aug 18			
"	19		During this time the Battalion was engaged in considerable strengthening with a sketchy trench system a series of shell hole posts with interconnecting trenches	

Army Form C. 2118.

WAR DIARY
or
INTELLIGENCE SUMMARY.

7th Bn. The Rifle Brigade

(Erase heading not required.)

Place	Date	Hour	Summary of Events and Information	Remarks and references to Appendices
Front Line STIRLING CASTLE	Aug 18 (cont)		more advanced shell-reports. Every effort was made to ascertain by patrolling the position although the enemy position in INVERNESS COPSE; a relief patrol on the right was carried out by Rfn. GASCOIGNE & FARR who penetrated the enemy outer defences. During the four attempts the front line was completely unmolested. The line CLAPHAM JUNCTION – STIRLING CASTLE was continually under a heavy barrage. No more to back areas especially SANCTUARY WOOD & CRAB CRAWL. D Coy was in the front line on the right, C on the left, B in support at JAM SUPPORT / no platoon being in close support at OBSERVATORY POST / A ? Coy being at CRAB CRAWL until brought up also to JAM SUPPORT. The casualties were 4 Officers & 41 O.R. See Appendix A for nominal roll.	
DICKIEBUSCH	Aug 20		The Battn. was relieved by No. 5 Lincolns & returned to camp at DICKIEBUSCH.	
"	Aug 21		The day was spent in re-organization.	
CHATEAUSEGARD	Aug 22		Again at very short notice the Battalion was moved to CHATEAU SEGARD as the toilets in the front line was very anxious and however the Bn. was not immediately required & bivouacked in the field.	
DICKIEBUSCH	Aug 23		After various orders had been received & countermanded the Battalion returned	

WAR DIARY
or
INTELLIGENCE SUMMARY.

(Erase heading not required.) 7th Batt. The Rifle Brigade 85

Army Form C. 2118.

Place	Date	Hour	Summary of Events and Information	Remarks and references to Appendices
DICKEBUSH	May 1917 2,3		to camp about 2 P.M.	
FRONT LINE SHREWSBURY	May 24		The Batt. was again moved at very short notice to an area just E of the MENIN GATE, the move being carried out in buses. The sudden urgence was very precarious in peaceful times owing to enemy counter attacks. At one moment it appeared that the Batt. might be called upon to counter-attack across the open. Eventually at about 6 P.M. the Batt. proceeded to carry out a relief from the remnants of 42nd and 123rd Bdes. Reinforcing the line. The same sector as on the previous tour was taken over, D Coy taking the front line on the right, C the front line on the left, B being in close support to C Coy, & A Coy in support on a new front just E of the STIRLING CASTLE WOOD. A Coy of the 8th Y & L. Regt. was placed at the disposal of O.C. Batt. on 25th inst. & took up a position in WHY SUPPORT with 2 platoons in immediate reserve at OBSERVATORY POST. The position throughout was a very anxious one; the area was extremely shelled for long periods, the position had the conditions in view of expected enemy counter-attacks while two actual operations had to be carried out.	
	25			
	26			

WAR DIARY
INTELLIGENCE SUMMARY.

7th Batt. The Rifle Brigade

Place	Date	Hour	Summary of Events and Information	Remarks and references to Appendices
Front line STIRLING CASTLE	1917 Aug 24 25 26 contd		On 25th inst. orders (B in appendix) were received for the operation, Report of which is given in C. The 21st Rifle Bde Summary of Intelligence for 25th inst. D includes a résumé of the report. The operation was carried out by C Coy. a in the course of it 2nd Lt. W. HOSLER was taken endeavouring to repel the enemy counter attack which immediately developed on the point occupied at 1.45 a.m. He was it is feared killed. On 26th inst. orders were received for operation to be carried out in the morning of 27th Aug. Here orders are given in E, while a further very vital after order E.A. is also included. The operation however was rendered F & F3. The weather turned very wet on the evening of 26th inst, & the station of F & F3. The weather turned very wet on the evening of 26th inst, & the station of Co, which carried out the attack was enormously hampered by the subsidence of the ground in addition to the unreality fact that no tank could not get forward owing to the mud. 2nd Lt. RUSHBROOKE in charge of this attack was wounded. Immediately before the Kenny Batt"- the 8th Y&L. arrived the enemy developed the heavy counter-attack which is reported in G & G*. The latter being the report which the H.Q. Rif. Bde. sent to 41st & 23rd Divisions.	

Army Form C. 2118.

WAR DIARY
or
INTELLIGENCE SUMMARY.

(Erase heading not required.)

7th Batt" The Rifle Bde

(87)

Place	Date	Hour	Summary of Events and Information	Remarks and references to Appendices
FRONT LINE STIRLING CASTLE	1917 Aug 24, 25, 26.		The credit of the successful repulse of this heavy attack belongs to C Coy under Capt. W.I. SHAW & to the platoons of B Coy which were under Capt. HORN at the time. The Casualties during this tour were 3 officers & 131 O.R. See H for Casual Rpt.	
DICKEBUSCH	Aug 27		The relief commenced about 10 P.M. but was not completed until about 8 A.M. on 28" inst. The II CORPS after this period is given in I.	I
DICKEBUSCH	Aug 28		The day was spent in rest & reorganisation.	
METEREN	Aug 29		The Batt. moved about 4 P.M. in Lorries for the METEREN area where it went under Canvas.	
METEREN	Aug 30		The day was spent in reorganisation.	
"	" 31st		" " " "	

A.T.H. Pogge H. Lt Col
Comdg 7th Bn The Rifle Brigade

7th Bn. The Rifle Brigade.

Casualty Return.

No.	Rank.	Name.	Nature of Casualty.	Date.
S/30595	Rfn.	Hunt S.	Wounded	17/8/17.
P/83	"	Murphy E.	Killed	"
S/26218	"	Watson W.	"	"
S/292	"	Davis W.	Wounded	"
Z/84	"	Skinner F.	"	"
S/5648	"	Griffen A.	"	"
S/24002	"	Moody A.	"	"
S/19205	"	Rock A.	"	"
B/200724	"	Harrison A.	"	"
S/16876	"	Pettet C.	"	"
	2/Lt.	Lea T.S.	"	18/8/17
	"	Shoobert W.H.	"	"
	"	Woodhead W.	"	"
S/13512	Rfn.	Williams J.C.	"	"
B/1125	"	Page J.	"	"
S/1164	"	Lorriman J.	"	"
S/17611	"	Keston C.	"	"
S/9497	L/C.	mPye E.	"	"
S/23488	Rfn.	Gavin H.	"	"
S/10212	"	Johnson H.	Killed	"
S/8562	"	Dolphin B.	"	"
B/200642	"	Page C.	Wounded	"
S/25177	"	Reardon C.	"	" (Died of Wds)
B/203126	"	White S.	"	"
S/15080	"	Stone J.	"	"
S/24876	"	Coote P.	"	"
S/14239	"	Gray S.R.	"	"
5571	L/C.	Butterworth J.	"	"
S/28417	Rfn.	Taylor C.	"	"
B/927.	"	Burrell S.	Wounded at Duty.	"
S/38.	"	Knight K.	Wounded.	"
	2/Lt.	Reaval G.N.	"	20/8/17.
S/19586	Rfn.	Faithful R.	"	"
S/12646	"	Wright F.S.	"	"
S/26299	"	Neville W.H.	"	"
S/19707	"	Jones A.G.	"	"
S/25251	"	Watson C.	"	"
B.2587	"	Clarke L.	"	"
S/30660	"	Crosskey E.	"	"
S/30546	"	Steinhart R.	"	"
B.200217	"	Mott W.	"	" (Died of Wds)
B/200653	"	Pyke G.	"	"
S/23740	"	Smith W.J.	"	"
S/11296	"	Price W.	"	"

I. OPERATIONS OF 26th AUGUST, 1917.

SECRET. Bde. No. 322/5.

O.C. 7th Bn. Rifle Brigade.

1. The Corps Commander is very anxious that before the Brigade is relieved the line should be straightened out by the occupation of the trench running from GLENCORSE WOOD about J.14.a.65.55 to INVERNESS COPSE about J.14.c.65.55, portions of which trench at least are occupied by the enemy.

It has been represented that owing to the extension of the front and other movements the occasion is not a convenient one on which to bring on a severe fight.

The Corps Commander will be satisfied therefore if the front is rectified by a chain of posts in accordance with sketch map attached.

At the same time the Corps Commander is anxious that the Brigade should establish itself in portions at least of the trench referred to if such an operation is at all feasible.

2. In the attached map the approximate trench line and posts now held by the Brigade are shown in GREEN, the approximate positions of the posts to be established in BLUE.

3. Posts to be consolidated are allotted to units as follows:-

Nos. 1 & 2 to 8th R.B.
 ,,   3,4,5 & 6 to 7th K.R.R.C.
 ,,   7 to 7th R.B.

4. The garrison of each post is to consist of from one to two sections, one of these sections to be a Lewis Gun section where such can be spared.

5. The posts will be established and consolidated as secretly as possible under cover of standing patrols or other suitable protection.

6. Patrolling and preliminary work to be begun so soon after dusk as is feasible, and the consolidation of the posts to be completed by 2a.m.

7. At any time between 2a.m. and 4.30a.m. units will endeavour to establish posts in the enemy trench already referred to.
The 8th R.B. may be able to advance down the trench from the North and the 7th R.B. up the trench from INVERNESS COPSE with or without a small bombing attack or with the assistance of rifle grenades.

8. There will be no Artillery barrage in connection with these operations but arrangements have been made to place rapidly a barrage on the line J.14.b.0.4 - J.14.d.0.5 - J.14.c.9.1 should the situation demand it.

(Sd.) P.U.B. SKINNER" Brig. Genl.
Commanding 41st Infantry Brigade.

25/8/17.

3.   B.A.T. 352.

H.Q. 41st Inf. Bde.

In conformance with 41st I.B. 385/5 of 25th inst. two sections one of which was a Lewis Gun team, occupied No. 7 Post soon after 1a.m. 26th inst. without opposition.

At the same time patrols were pushed forward to ensure the carrying out of further operations times to commence at 3a.m.

At the latter hour parties moved out to occupy posts at J.14.c.65.55, J.14.c.65.45, J.14.c.55.30 and at J.14.c.52.20.

The information as to what occurred after the occupation of these posts is somewhat obscure. The party who worked down the trench leading out of INVERNESS COPSE found it unoccupied and proceeded to consolidate at J.14.c.65.55, but were after about a quarter of an hour attacked by a superior enemy force with bombs and what were described by men who got back as Flamenwerfer.

It is stated by a reliable officer who witnessed the attack from the Right that the enemy actually employed some form of phosphorous bombs. This attack was delivered about 3.45a.m. and succeeded in driving our post out of the trench with a number of casualties including 2nd Lt. HOSLER reported missing.

A heavy bombardment opened on our front line at about 3.45a.m. while an extremely heavy barrage came down about CLAPHAM JUNCTION and along the STIRLING CASTLE RIDGE. This barrage continued in its greatest intensity until about 4.40a.m.

Under cover of the bombardment the enemy attacked the post at J.4.c.65.45 and succeeded in driving this garrison out also. The posts at J.14.c.55.30 and at J.14.c.52.20 were attacked by weak forces which were successfully driven off.

A further attack was made upon our front line about 4.40a.m. along the N. edge of INVERNESS COPSE and along the MENIN ROAD. A few enemy succeeded in getting into our trench about J.14.c.45.50 but were immediately bombed out.

When it was reported that this attack had penetrated the front line the "S.O.S." was sent up from Battn. H.Q.

Our barrage was very prompt and exceedingly heavy. As soon as it came down the enemy retired and made no further attack.

Additional casualties can be estimated only roughly at present and should not exceed 50 up to 9a.m. 26th inst.

Our present Dispositions are as shown on attached sketch.

(Sd,) A.J.H. SLOGGETT" Lt. Col.
11a.m. 26/8/17.   Comndg. 7th Battn. The Rifle Bde.

CONFIDENTIAL.

41st Infantry Brigade Daily Summary of Information
received to 12 noon 26/8/17.
- - - - - - - - - - - - - - -

OPERATIONS.
Situation. From reports received the situation appears to be as follows :-

During the night the following posts were established:-
J.14.a.75.60 - 75.45 - 70.40 - 69.33 - 45.25 - (through existing post at J.14.a.38.15) - J.14.a.38.05 - (through existing post at J.14.c.35.90) - J.14.c.35.83 - 3370 - 43.60 - 63.55 - 63.45 - 52.26 - 52.18.

At about 4.40a.m. under cover of very heavy barrages of all calibres put down on our front line, on the CLAPHAM JUNCTION - STIRLING CASTLE line, and a line just East of CHATEAU WOOD and through SANCTUARY WOOD, the enemy launched an attack on the above new posts, the Western edge of INVERNESS COPSE, and towards the the strong point at J.14.a.25.25. The attack in the latter area was particularly strong and was supported by parties of the enemy with "FLAMMENWERFER". These parties were dispersed by Lewis Gun fire and the attack was broken up. The garrisons of the posts at J.14.a.69.53, 45.25 and 38.05 are believed to have been all killed and we do not now occupy these three posts. The post at J.14.a.36.15 is believed to be intact.

To the South the enemy drove in the advanced posts at J.14.c. 63.65, 63.45 with superior numbers. At the same time he attacked and entered our position on the Western edge of INVERNESS COPSE, and the remainder of the new posts; by an immediate counter-attack all the enemy were driven out and the line restored with the exception of the two posts at J.14.c.63.65 and 63.45. It is believed that many of the enemy were accounted for in his attack, and our very effective artillery barrage prevented him from being reinforced, or from a renewal of the attack.

- - - - - - - - - - - - -

II. OPERATIONS OF 27th. AUGUST 1917.

S E C R E T.   Copy No. 3.

21st INFANTRY BRIGADE OPERATION ORDER No. 162.
                                            26th August, 1917.

1. The Brigade will tomorrow attack and occupy the enemy trench running from about J.14.a.6.9 to J.14.c.6.6.

2. Four tanks will assist in the operation and there will be two other tanks, either additional or to take the place of tanks knocked out.

3. The tanks will start from an approximate line STRONG POINT at J.14.a.5.8 - J.14.c.9.7 at 4.45a.m. and will operate as follows :-

   No. 1 - Down the MENIN ROAD along the North of INVERNESS COPSE, then Northwards up the German trench.

   No. 2 - Along South side of JAP AVENUE, then turning Southwards along the German trench.

   No. 3 - Along North side of JAP AVENUE, then Northwards along the German trench.

   No. 4 - South of Strong Point along road towards S.W. corner of GLENCORSE WOOD, turning Southwards along German trench.

4. The O.C. 7th R.B. will detail one bombing squad, each to Tanks Nos. 1 & 2, and the O.C. 7th K.R.R.C. one bombing squad each to Tanks Nos. 3 & 4.
   These bombing squads will move close up behind their respective tanks as escorts to these tanks.

5. Each tank will be able to carry 2 boxes S.A.A. and a few stores to assist in consolidation.

6. The average rate of progress of a tank is about 20 yards a minute.

7. Each battalion in front line will detail one strong platoon in addition to any bombing squads furnished as escorts, to attack the trench in conjunction with tanks.

8. The 7th R.B. will attack from INVERNESS COPSE to JAP AVENUE inclusive.
   The 7th K.R.R.C. thence to JARGON DRIVE EXCLUSIVE.
   The 8th R.B. thence to Northern limit of trench held by the enemy.

9. The attack of these platoons will be launched on the iniative of the Officer in command of each when he sees that the tanks attacking his sector are nearing their objective.

10. So soon as the trench has been captured consolidation will be begun and bombing posts pushed out about 40 yards along each of the communication trenches running Eastwards.

11. A barrage will be put down at 5a.m. on a line about J.14.b.2.9 - J.14.b.1.1. - J.14.d. 1.1. and will be continued for so long as required.
   If the wind is favourable there will be some smoke in this barrage.

12. Tanks will remain out to the East of the Enemy trench to cover consolidation.

13. Troops carrying out the attack will light flares if called for by the contact aeroplane.

14. A Tank officer will report at the H.Qs. of the 7th K.R.R.C. and 7th R.B. respectively, and will remain with each of these units during the progress of the attack.

15. There will be some searching fire by our Artillery in GLENCORSE WOOD & INVERNESS COPSE starting at 4.30a.m.

Issued at 7.40p.m.   (Sd.) G.M. LEE, Captain,
                           Brigade Major,
                           41st Infantry Brigade.

- - - - - - - - - - -

LANE.   (Received at 2a.m. 27th).

B.825. AAA.
   By order of G.O.C. should the tanks not arrive the trenches must be carried by a surprise attack at dawn AAA   B.G.C. considers that from 45 to 50 men per Battn. should be sufficient to carry out this attack and this number will not be exceeded AAA B.G.C. will arrange for protective barrage as before but without smoke to come down at 4.45a.m.AAA The assault will be carried out on similar lines to that arranged with Tanks AAA   It is most important to inform B.G.C. as soon as possible whether Tanks will be in time to take part or not.
                           (Sd.) G.M. LEE, Capt.

- - - - - - - - - - -

B.A.T. 363.

H.Q. 41st Inf. Bde.

   In accordance with 41st Inf. Bde. O.O. No. 162 of 26th inst. and with further B 825 of same date this Battn. made an attack upon the enemy running from J. 4.a.8.2 to J.14.c.6.0 at the sector allotted, i.e. from INVERNESS COPSE to JAP AVENUE inclusive.
   After consultation with O.C. Section of 5 tanks which arrived at CLAPHAM JUNCTION at 3a.m. this morning, it was agreed that the tanks could not start until 4.45a.m. owing to there not being sufficient light before that hour.
   O.C. Tanks expected that the tanks would arrive at the objective by 5a.m.
   Consequently as the Protective Barrage was to come down at 5a.m. and in accordance with 41st Inf. Bde. 825 it was agreed by O.C. 7th R.B., 7th K.R.R.C. and 8th R.B. that if the tanks had not then come in sight 5a.m. should be the hour of Zero.
   The Assault Platoon of this Battalion under 2nd Lt. RUSHBROOK formed up on their kicking off line slightly in advance of No. 7 post at 4.30a.m.

5.

n At the hour of Zero not one single tank had come in sight.

The assaulting platoon therefore attacked according to orders at 5a.m.

From the somewhat conflicting statements of the wounded who have come in it appears that in great measure owing to the appaling condition of the ground which hampered all forward movement the attack strung out and consequently arrived very raggedly.

Those who did get into the trench were therefore easily bombed out again.

2nd Lt. RUSHBROOKE went back, formed his men up again and attacked a second time. This attack also failed for similar reasons to those which prevented the success of the former one.

2nd Lt. RUSHBROOKE and a number of his men are missing but from the account of a wounded Cpl. who got back from the second attack it is believed that they may be lying in shell holes close to the objective.

After this second attack the enemy made no attempt to leave his trenches and to attack our line of posts, although he appeared to be in considerable strength in the trench which we attacked.

He replied to the attack and to our Protective Barrage with a general bombardment of this sector commencing about 5.10a.m. and lasting until 6a.m.

At 6.30a.m. he commenced a systematic and very heavy bombardment of our whole area which lasted till 9.30a.m. in its greatest intensity and which has continued spasmodically since.

This latter bombardment consisted of 77mm. 4"9 and 5"9 with a large proportion of the latter and it has put a stop to any movement in this area.

It has therefore been extremely difficult to elicit any further details of this mornings attack.

It is impossible at present to ascertain the casualties suffered either in this attack or during the subsequent bombardment.

10.20a.m.   (Sd.) A.J.H. Sloggett, Lt. Col.
27/8/7.   Commdg. 7th Bn. The Rifle Bde.

III   GERMAN ATTACK OF 27th AUGUST, 1917.

B.A.T. 380

H.Q. 41st Inf. Bde.

At 8p.m. tonight the enemy, following a shower of rifle grenades, attacked the left of our front at the Strong Points J.14.c.45.55 and the post J.14.c.50.45.

They were repulsed and attacked again slightly to the right of the above mentioned posts. They were again repulsed in hand to hand fighting our men meeting them with the bayonet on the parapet.

We claim to have inflicted very heavy casualties upon the enemy, a number of whom were shot down as they advanced.

The Company put up the S.O.S. and it was repeated from Battn. H.Q.

The resulting artillery barrage is reported to have been entirely satisfactory.

At the moment of the enemy attack a very heavy enemy barrage came down along the CLAPHAM JUNCTION - STIRLING CASTLE line and continued till about 9.30p.m.

At 9p.m. runners succeeded in getting through from O.C. Left Coy. with a message to the effect that the situation was well in hand and that all was quiet.

                    (Sd.) A.J.H. SLOGGETT,, Lt. Col.
27/8/17.   Commdg. 7th Battn. The Rifle Brigade.

B.A.T. 395   9A.

Headquarters,
    41st Infantry Brigade.

In continuation of my B.A.T. 380 of 27th inst. the following appears to be the correct account of the enemy attack made on the evening of 27th inst.

"Enemy movement had been noticed during the evening, and it seems clear that his troops had been endeavouring to get into position by creeping from shell hole to shell hole, so that they might advance in the waves in which they actually attacked.

My men were consequently on the alert when the enemy opened a barrage of rifle grenades on my front line at 8p.m. At the same moment his artillery barrage came down as previously reported and the infantry attack developed. The S.O.S. was immediately sent up from the front line and repeated from Battn. H.Q.

The main attack came from the trench running from J.14 a 65.85 to J 14 c 65.55 and was directed against the left flank of my Battn., while a feint attack was made upon the right. Several men carrying Flammenwerfer were noticed, but the strong wind blew the flames towards the enemy. Some four or five waves composed this attack which was met with rifle and lewis gun fire and with bombs, my men using in addition to their own, many German bombs found in our lines. Invaluable assistance was afforded by the garrison of No. 7 Post who enfilades the enemy from the left.

The enemy suffered very heavy casualties, but in some cases succeeded in getting up to our trench where he was met on the parapet in a hand to hand fight with the bayonet.

About 8.10p.m. our barrage opened and at about 8.20p.m. the enemy developed a second attack once more against my left.

This was similarly repulsed, and the enemy in his retirement suffered severely from our artillery barrage. A number of his men came forward with their hands up calling out in English "Dont shoot." One prisoner was taken.

The enemy troops concerned in the attack wore new clean clothing of a smoky grey colour, whereas the men seen holding the line were dressed in a uniform of a light sea green colour. There is every indication that a very strong force of Storm truppen was employed, estimated at between two and three hundred. At dawn a large number of enemy corpses were seen in front of our line.

            (Sd.)   A.J.H. SLOGGETT,   Lieut. Col.
28/8/17.   Commdg. 7th Battn. The Rifle Brigade.

                                    Bde. No. 323/5-1.

14th Division.

Forwarded in continuation of my No. 323/5 of 27th inst. I think this may be considered a very creditable performance on the part of the 7th Rifle Brigade.

            (Sd.) B.C.B. SKINNER,   Brigadier-General.
29th/8/17.   Commanding 41st Infantry Brigade.
(Copy to 23rd Div. for information).

F.A.

CONFIDENTIAL.

41st Infantry Brigade Daily Summary of Information
received up to 12 noon 27/8/17.

OPERATIONS.

The Brigade attacked the enemy front line from J 14 a 65.25 to J.14 c 65.60 this morning at 5a.m. Owing to the rain and condition of the ground, which was extremely bad, 5 tanks which should have assisted in the attack, became ditched after reaching the rendezvous. Consequently at Zero, 5a.m. our three assaulting platoons, (one from each Battn. in the line) attacked with the tanks support the enemy who held the objective very strongly. Owing to losses from hostile shelling while getting into position, by machine gun fire during the assault, and to the state of the ground, very few of our troops reached their objective. Those who did reach it were immediately counter attacked and driven out. The O.C. right Battn. reports that the Officer in charge of the attacking platoon reorganised after the first attack and attacked a second time. This Officer and some of his men are missing; but from the account of a wounded Corporal who got back from the second attack, it is believed that they may be lying in shell holes close to the objective about J.14.c.50.70.

CONFIDENTIAL.

7th Battn. The Rifle Brigade.

Casualty Return.

No.	Rank and Name		Nature of Casualty	Date.
	2nd Lt.	Butler, R.W.P.	Wounded	26/8/17
	,,	Hosler, A.E.	Missing	,,
	,,	Rushbrooke, W.E.	Missing believed Killed	27/8/17.
858	Cpl.	Parker, J.	Killed	27/8/17
S/20017	Rfn.	Bowers, J.	,,	26/8/17
B/241	,,	Harrison, J.	,,	27/8/17
S/17392	,,	Hogarth, H.	,,	,,
B/203663	,,	Wild, D.	,,	26/8/17
S/21745	,,	Wickett, C.	,,	,,
S/12624	L/C.	Short, J.	Wounded	27/8/17
6998	,,	Lemoine, F.	,,	25/8/17
S/14826	,,	Burch, E.	,,	27/8/17
S/3015	,,	Martin, A.	,,	,,
S/13103	,,	Ayton, A.	,,	,,
B/927	Rfn.	Burrell, J.	,,	,,
B/203643	,,	Bennet, A.	,,	26/8/17
S/10131	,,	Bull, W.	,,	25/8/17
S/26392	,,	Calver, R.	Missing	27/8/17
B/200942	,,	Cohen, J.	Wounded	,,
5434	,,	Dolly, W.	,,	,,
B/203645	,,	Dugdale, P.	,,	,,
S/4976	,,	Dean, G.	,,	,,
S/15588	,,	Golden, A.	N.Y.D.	,,
P/4001	,,	Hollingsworth, W.	Wounded	25/8/17
S/13216	,,	Hewitt, G.	,,	,,
B/200645	,,	House, H.	,,	27/8/17
S/25091	,,	Job, F.	,,	,,
S/16947	,,	Jones, J.R.	,,	25/8/17
Z/102	,,	Lafford, G.	,,	27/8/17
S/14284	,,	Longson, S.	,,	,,
S/6191	,,	Mitten, W.	,,	25/8/17
S/9238	,,	Pearce, J.	,,	,,
B/203653	,,	Pitson, H.	,,	,,
B/1893	,,	Payne, A.	,,	27/8/17
S/20755	,,	Seldon, H.	,,	26/8/17
S/23491	,,	Summerell, E.	,,	27/8/17
6173	,,	Waymark, W.V.	,,	26/8/17 Died of Wds
B/203661	,,	Wallis, F.	,,	27/8/17
S/17599	,,	Wareham, F.	,,	,,
S/31757	CSM.	Jackson, R.J.	Wounded at duty	26/8/17
S/23950	Rfn.	Wetherley, W.	,,	,,
S/6222	L/C.	Wooster, H.	,,	,,
S/5901	Rfn.	Rees, L.	,,	,,
S/30479	,,	Anderson, A.	Wounded	25/8/17
B/200042	,,	Avery, L.	,,	,,
S/8438	,,	Annison, A.	,,	,,
S/15106	,,	Brown, H.	,,	,,
S/6616	,,	Brewster, E.	,,	,,
S/24612	,,	Barker, W.	,,	,,
S/31131	,,	Davies, J.T.	,,	26/8/17
S/24643	,,	Ding, A.	,,	,,
S/8935	,,	Hadley, J.	,,	,,
S/16885	,,	Jones, J.J.	,,	,,
S/38	,,	Knight, K	,,	,,
S/9978	,,	Magnus, M.	,,	,, Died of Wds
S/18009	,,	Main, C.S.	,,	,,
5944	,,	Rosser, A.	,,	,,
B/203725	,,	Wicks, J.	,,	,,
3701	L/Sgt.	Dean, G.	,,	,,
B/709	Sgt.	Tovey, G.E.	,,	25/8/17
S/24600	L/C.	Purcell, E.	,,	26/8/17

No.	Rank and Name	Nature of Casualty	Date.
S/8139	L/C. Ellis, T.	Wounded	27/8/17
S/31247	Rfn. Blackley, E.	Missing	,,
S/21573	,, Beness, J.	,,	,,
S/31280	,, Kentish, S.	,,	,,
S/23630	,, Nicholson, A.	,,	,,
S/20681	,, Jones, W.H.	,,	,,
S/19458	Cpl. Bullen, J.	,,	,,
S/24663	Rfn. King, W.	,,	,,
B/203017	Cpl. Golding, A.J.	Killed	,,
5452	,, Divers, J.R.	,,	,,
S/9121	Rfn. Waters, B.	,,	,,
P/1565	,, Mills, G.	,,	,,
B/200374	,, Coombs, E.	,,	,,
B/583	Sgt. Needham, C.R.	,,	25/8/17
S/7584	Cpl. Holland, W.	Missing	26/8/17
S/28957	L/C. White, J.	Wounded	,,
S/13055	Cpl. Thompson, H.	,,	,,
5980	L/C. Royston, C.	,,	,,
S/26323	Rfn. Bryan, E.	,,	,,
S/24660	,, Chapman, S.	,,	,,
B/200941	,, Charity, W.	,,	,,
B/30636	,, Dyason, T.	Killed	25/8/17
5920	,, Durbridge,	N.Y.D.	27/8/17
S/26331	,, Elford, C.	Wounded	25/8/17
S/18643	,, Emmerton, J.	,,	26/8/17
B/200641	,, Goodman, C.	,,	,,
S/25513	,, Humphreys, E.	Missing	,,
S/30477	,, Hilyard, S.	Wounded	,,
S/17183	,, Hutchings, J.	,,	,,
S/30746	,, King, E.	,,	,,
S/24570	,, Prentice, A.	,,	,,
S/15049	,, Pasfield, W.	Killed	,,
S/15602	,, Ryan, C.	Wounded	,,
B/203674	,, Swingler, F.	Killed	25/8/17
S/10339	,, Smith, F.	Wounded	26/8/17
S/9559	,, Watson, S.	Killed	,,
S/25515	,, Sleigh, W.	Wounded	,,
B/203013	L/C. Balmforth, V.	,,	,,
	2nd Lt. Sowerbutts, J.A.	,, at duty	,,
S/10557	Sgt. Scott, G.	,, ,,	,,
B/1585	L/C. Martin, E.	,, ,,	,,
S/26381	Rfn. Grant, A.	,, ,,	,,
1030	Sgt. Thorpe, J.	,,	,,
S/2850	Rfn. Baylis, A.	,,	,,
B/1664	,, Brown, W.	,,	,,
S/12568	,, Bambridge, T.	,,	,,
B/203688	,, Boutell, H.	,,	,,
S/15882	,, Brodbeck, L.	Killed	,,
S/26342	,, Dobinson, J.	Wounded	25/8/17
S/2737	,, Elsom, R.	,,	,,
B/1589	,, Godson, H.	Killed	26/8/17
S/7014	,, Gilbert, H.	Wounded	25/8/17
S/31750	,, Hawker, G.	,,	,,
B/203705	,, Johnson, E.	,,	,,
S/26295	,, Palmer, E.	,,	26/8/17
S/26386	,, Sears, J.	,,	,,
S/26348	,, Salisbury, E.	,,	,,
S/30616	,, Trotman, A.	,,	,,
B/200731	,, Wood, J.	,,	,,
S/13106	,, Whyley, W.	,,	,,
S/30620	,, Williams, S.	,,	,,
S/30603	,, Wood, F.	,,	,,
S/30617	,, Cole, J.	Killed	,,
S/6863	,, Davies, H.	Wounded	25/8/17
S/21521	,, Watson, C.	,,	,,
1533	Cpl. Westlake, M.	Wounded at duty	,,
B/203671	,, Haines, H.	,, ,,	,,
S/7232	,, Warner, J.	,, ,,	26/8/17

3.

No.	Rank and Name	Nature of Casualty	Date
S/15766	Cpl. Dellar, J.	Wounded at duty	26/8/17
B/203730	L/C. Pancke, A.	,,	,,
S/7234	,, Feld, J.	,,	,,
B/203694	Rfn. Eccles, F.	,,	,,
3623	,, Higgins, C.	,,	27/8/17
B/1990	,, Tilbury, H.	,,	,,

W.S. Thornton.
Capt. & Adjt.
7th Battn. The Rifle Brigade.

31/8/17.

Extract from II Corps Summary of Information No. 72

Received up to 6p.m. 28th August, 1917.

Late Information.

It appears from late reports that the enemy attack on our posts in INVERNESS COPSE was a much more determined affair than had been supposed. At 8p.m. a heavy barrage was put down on the CLAPHAM JUNCTION - STRILING CASTLE area simultaneously our posts were attacked by a party - estimated roughly at 150 strong - under cover of a rifle grenade barrage, and supported by Flammenwerfer.

The artillery barrage came down roughly in three lines - one about 200 yards in rear of our posts in INVERNESS COPSE; a second on a N & S line through STRILING CASTLE, and the third from about J 13 central along the Eastern edge of SANCTUARY WOOD. At about 8.30p.m. the front barrage lifted and about the same time a fairly heavy barrage was put down round DORMY HOUSE.

It is not known how far to the North the attack was intended to extend, but the state of the ground round GLENCORSE WOOD is in itself such an obstacle, that it would be very difficult for any attack in this direction to materialise.

Our barrage in reply to the S.O.S. signal came down promptly and is said to have been excellent; but the enemy was actually repulsed by hand to hand fighting and was twice driven back leaving many corpses just in front of our posts.

Although identifications so far made reveal only the presence of the 177th Infantry Regt. (32nd Division) the use of Flamenwerfer and a rifle grenade barrage suggest the presence of a STORM unit also.

CONFIDENTIAL

WAR DIARY

OF

7th BATTALION" THE RIFLE BRIGADE.

FOR

SEPTEMBER, 1917

(VOLUME XXIX).

A.T.H. Sloggett

Lieut. Col.

30/9/17.   Commdg. 7th Bn. The Rifle Brigade.

WAR DIARY
INTELLIGENCE SUMMARY

Army Form C. 2118.

7th Batt. The Rifle Brigade

Place	Date 1917	Hour	Summary of Events and Information	Remarks and references to Appendices
METEREN	Sept 1		Heavy drill, inspection of box respirators etc was carried out	G/R
CELTIC CAMP	2		In the afternoon the Batt. moved to CELTIC CAMP where centres were taken over from 9th R.B.	G/R
	3		The camp had only recently been established & a great deal of work was necessary in order to make the approach at all passable. Owing to enemy a/cs being exceptionally active at night it was found necessary to clear a/cs for the camp inside a wood which meant a great deal of clearing & cutting.	G/R
	4		Work on the camp was continued & a 30yd range was cleared safe for musketry to be started. 2/Lt S.H. BURCH & 2/Lt A.H. HALFORD were posted to Bn. & reported for duty.	G/R
	5		The range was used both morning & afternoon. The Batt. supplied a fatigue party for the funeral of the Colonel & other officers at BAILLEUL Cemetery.	G/R
	6		More work was put in on the camp, while working parties of 20 O.R. were supplied for unloading R.E. material.	G/R
	7		Baths were allotted to the Batt. The range was again used.	G/R
	8		The approach was completed, a road contours road having been constructed.	G/R
SHANNON CAMP NEUVE EGLISE	9		The Batt. moved to SHANNON CAMP, NEUVE EGLISE & came into Divl. Reserve.	G/R

Army Form C. 2118.

WAR DIARY
or
INTELLIGENCE SUMMARY.

(Erase heading not required.) 7th Battn. The Rifle Brigade.

(89)

Place	Date	Hour	Summary of Events and Information	Remarks and references to Appendices
BRISTOL CAMP MESSINES	Sept. 10		The Battn. moved into Brigade Reserve at BRISTOL CAMP, S. MESSINES & occupied part of the old British front line system.	AHS
"	-11 to -16		Fatigue parties up to 180 O.R., were sent nightly into the forward area. Except for a heavy bombardment lasting 2 hours which caused 7 casualties this report was quiet.	AHS
Front line -16			On night of 16th the Battn. moved into the front line, right sector which extended from the HOUVE to the road running E from STEIGNAST FARM. D Coy in preparation for the raid to take place on 20th had gone up on night of 13-14/15th were relieved on night of 16/17. B Coy took over the right front, A the left front & C Coy was in immediate support. B Coy 8"/66th was in support near Batt. H.Q. while	AHS
Right sector	-20th		C Coy 8"/66th were in Reserve in the Cafes Lines. On relief D Coy returned to practice the raid near MEUVE EGLISE & came back to the front line on night of 19"/20".	AHS
			Owing to several practice barrages & to wire cutting operations which necessitated the withdrawal of the front line posts for some 11 hours daily & to the enemy bombardments which followed our activity the Battn. had a very arduous tour. Fortunately the weather was fine except on the evening night of	AHS

WAR DIARY
INTELLIGENCE SUMMARY

(Erase heading not required.) 7th Bn. The Rifle Brigade

Army Form C. 2118.

Place	Date	Hour	Summary of Events and Information	Remarks and references to Appendices
Front Line Right Sector	Sept. 16th to 20th		Nat of 19th/20th. The communication trench was completed only up to NDA FORM. A relief & carrying parties had to proceed over the open. A great deal of work & carrying parties carried out, esp. in the construction of assembly trenches, the laying of existing trenches since the WINDMILL & the clearing of trenches blown in by shell fire. Mine was also put out immediately E & N of the WINDMILL to E end of the ——.	
			APPENDIX. The operation order for the raid is marked "A attached". The account of the raid is marked "B". A list of the casualties list for the Bn is marked "C".	7NB. 7NB. 7NB.
SHANKILL CAMP	Sept 21		The Bn. was relieved on night of 20th/21st. & returned to SHANKILL CAMP.	7NB.
"	" 22		The day was spent in reorganisation & cleaning. The Bn was in Div. Reserve.	7NB.
			Steady drill was carried out & the range used for reregistering SAA rounds a afternoon.	7NB.
"	" 23		Church Parades were held for all denominations and the conclusion of C.of.E. service the R.G.C. thanked the Bn. for their part work on the recent x Battle on April. of NB & omit the names of officers &	ARRAS 7NB.
"	" 24		A Lewis gun class was started. Steady drill was carried out.	7NB.
"	" 25		350 O.R. went on working parties in the forward area. The Lewis Officer	7NB.

Army Form C. 2118.

WAR DIARY
or
INTELLIGENCE SUMMARY.

(Erase heading not required.) 7th Battn The Rifle Brigade

Place	Date	Hour	Summary of Events and Information	Remarks and references to Appendices
SHANKILL CAMP	Sept 25		reconnoitred at ARMENTIERES, the Bde being also in Divl Reserve to 38th Divn.	G.H.S.
"	Sept 26		Further parties reconnoitred at ARMENTIERES. The Rangefinders occupied both morning & afternoon for rapid firing & application practice. Fatigue parties were engaged on new bomb stores and in erecting a concert hall.	G.H.S.
"	Sept 27		Range C was used by D & A Coys in the morning & afternoon respectively with all arms. Gunners of the Battn ran classification on the L.G. range.	G.H.S.
"	Sept 28		350 men were sent on fatigue into the forward area & camp fatigues were also proceeded with.	G.H.S.
"	Sept 29		A gas demonstration was attended by the whole Battn, every man being given an opportunity of smelling mustard gas. 200 men were sent on fatigue into the forward area. 2/Lt. W. ATTENBOROUGH joined the Battn and reported to B Coy.	G.H.S.
"	Sept 30		80 men were sent on working parties. Church Parades were held for all denominations. The honours awarded to the Battn during the last war are given on list marked "D" attached herewith.	G.H.S. Fight Strength 340 Offrs 524 O.R.

A.T.H. Hoggett, Lt Colonel
Comdg. 7th Bn: The Rifle Brigade.

SECRET. A Copy No. 8.

41st INFANTRY BRIGADE OPERATION ORDER No. 169.
18th September, 1917.

Reference Sheet 8150/5 - 1/10,000.

1. In order to assist operations elsewhere, the 7th Rifle Bde, on a date and at a Zero hour to be notified later, will carry out a raid against the enemy opposite their sector.

2. The objectives will consist of the enemy trench U 5 d 70.25 - U 5 d 85.30 - U 5 d 90.80 and the two lines of dugouts or gunpits at right angles to each other on the lines U 5 d 95.35 - U 6 c 15.45. and U 5 d 95.35 - U 6 c 05.15.

3. The operation will be carried out simultaneously with the operations elsewhere referred to above, and in addition to assisting these operations its object is to capture and kill as many of the enemy as possible and secure identifications.

4. O.C. 7th R.B. will detail one Company, strength about 4 Officers and 100 other ranks, under the command of Lieut. C.A.M. Van Millingen 7th R.B., to carry out the raid.

5. By Zero all the garrison of the front line system of the 7th R.B. opposite the objective, including the Raiding Party, will be withdrawn to a distance of 200 yards from the enemy trench U 5 d 85.30 - U 6 c 10.95.

6. At Zero the Artillery 18-pdr. barrage will come down on the enemy trench from U 5 d 85.30 - U 6 c 10.95.
   At zero plus five minutes this barrage will lift off the trench and move back 100 yards.
   At zero plus six minutes this barrage will lift on to the enemy trench on the line U 6 c 40.00 - U 6 c 40.55 - U 6 a 40.00 and will remain on this line till zero plus 40 minutes, when it will cease gradually.

7. Rate of fire of the 18 pdr. barrage will be

   Zero to plus 10 minutes   -   3 rounds per minute
   Plus 10 to plus 20 min.   -   2   ,,   ,,
   Plus 20 min. to plus 30 min.-   3   ,,   ,,
   Plus 30 min. to plus 40 min-   1   ,,   ,,

8. At zero 4.5" Hows. will form a barrage, containing some smoke if the wind suits, on the enemy trench U 12 a 40.65 - U 6 c 40.00 - U 6 c 70.95.
   At zero plus 5 minutes this barrage will lift and form a protective barrage.
   One battery 6" Hows. and one battery 9.2" Hows. will assist.

9. At zero a covering machine gun barrage will open on selected areas, with varying intensity and will continue till zero plus 40 minutes.

10. Tables and map of Artillery barrage and programme of machine gun barrage will be issued separately.

11. At zero, when the Artillery barrage begins, the Raiding Party will leave their trenches and advance as close up to the barrage as possible entering the enemy trench so soon as possible after the barrage has lifted off it.
    The parties detailed to mop up the dugouts referred to in para. 2. will reach these dugouts so soon as they can after the barrage has lifted off them.

12. When the objectives have been reached, a bombing block will be established at about U 5 d 90.80 and Lewis Guns will be installed about U 5 d 90.60 and U 5 d 85.30.
    The dugouts will be rendered untenable by P bombs and Petrol tins with bombs attached, and on leaving the Raiding Party will set the dugouts on fire.

13. The O.C. 41st T.M. Bty. will rstablish two Stokes Mortars to cover the right flank of the Raiding Party and to fire on enemy trenches North of the DOUVE in U 11 b and U 12 a, and two Stokes Mortars to cover the left flank and to fire on the enemy trench from the road exclusive at U 5 c 10.95 - U 6 a 45.00 and trench junctions in this neighbourhood.

    Programme of Stokes Mortar fire will be issued separately.

14. When the Raiding Party has moved off from our trenches the garrisons of the front line system will begin to resume their positions in the front line posts which will be re-occupied at zero plus 5 minutes or as soon after that hour as possible.

15. The garrison of the front line system will render all assistance possible to the Raiding Party, and the enemy trenches U 11 b 80.60 - U 11 b 80.90 and U 6 c 10.95 - U 6 c 30.95 (North and East of the road only) will be kept under Rifle Grenade fire.

16. The Raiding Party will withdraw from the enemy trenches at zero plus twenty minutes, and will be all back in our own trenches by zero plus thirty minutes.

    The signal for withdrawal will be a series of single Green very lights fired by the Raiding Party on the orders of the O.C. the Party.

    The withdrawal will begin at zero plus twenty minutes in no signal has been seen by then.

    The flanks of the portion of the enemy position occupied must be held to the last to enable the parties from the dugouts, and the remainder to get away.

17. Prisoners will be sent back to our own lines as quickly as possible after capture and if the situation permits evacuated at once via Right Battalion and Brigade H.Qs.

    If this is not feasible one or two selected prisoners for interrogation will be sent to Brigade H.Qs. via the front line of the Left Battn. and FANNY communication trench, the remaining prisoners being evacuated after dark.

18. No papers, badges, or means of identification, will be carried or worn by the Raiding Party.

19. An Officer from Brigade H.Qs. will visit all Units to synchronise watches the evening prior to the operation.

(Sd.) G.M. LEE, Captain,
Brigade Major,
41st Infantry Brigade.

Copies to:
```
 1-2   14th Div. "G"
 3-4   7th K.R.R.C.
 5-6   8th K.R.R.C.
 7-8   7th R.B.
 9-10  8th RMB.
11-14  41st M.G. Coy.
15-16  41st T.M. Bty.
17-21  Lt. Can Millingen
   22  D.M.G.O.
   23  25th Inf. Bde.
   24  90th Inf. Bde.
   25  B.G.C.
   26  B.M.
   27  W.D.
28-29  14th D.A.
   30  Liason Officer, R.A.
   31  Right Group, R.A.
```

B.

REPORT ON RAID.

At 5.40a.m. on the 20th the Company left its Assembly Trenches and advanced under cover of the barrage. At Zero - 5, No. 1 Party entered the trench and saw a party of 7 Germans running away to the left. In order to avoid a pursuit which would probably have resulted in our men going too far, O.C. No. 1 Party ordered these Germans to be shot. This was done. Apart from these men there were no more of the enemy in the trench raided by No. 1 Party. The Lewis Gun attached to this party came in action very early and fired 4 drums on several small parties endeavouring to escape from dugouts which were being attacked by No. 3 Party, and inflicted several casualties. On the return journey three of our men came across four of the enemy lying in a shell hole in between the lines. As these showed fight they were killed, except one who made good his escape.

No. 2 Party entered the enemy trench without any opposition and met 7 of the enemy, 4 of whom were killed and 3 taken prisoners. The Lewis Gunners attached to this party fired a couple of drums at escaping Germans.

On leaving the trench No. 3 Party came under heavy M.G. fire from S. of the River and lost their Officer. At the same time a few of the enemy who were at the end of the sap started bombing this party with the result that they were held up for a couple of minutes until the enemy had been killed. Then proceeding to the dugouts they bombed these and killed about 6 men who refused to come out. A party of 4 Germans who tried to escape but 3 were caught and 1 killed. A German officer was shot while trying to pull out his revolver and this and his Field Glasses were brought back.

Casualties inflicted upon enemy by raiding party :-

Killed	Officer	1
	O.R.	21
Prisoners	O.R.	6

besides those inflicted upon the fleeing enemy, by the L.G. the effect of which could not be clearly observed, though several were seen to fall.

Our casualties :-

Killed	Officer	1
	O.R.	1
Died of Wounds	O.R.	1
Wounded	Officer	1
	O.R.	13
Missing	O.R.	1 ∅

∅ this man was seen in our trench but has not returned with the Company.

Enemy Trench	1'6" - 2' deep. All earth piled on our side of trench.
Wire	Concertina - Barbed. No serious obstacle.
Dugouts	1 Concrete pill box. 7 old gun pits and shelters made of corrugated iron and covered over with sods.

All the dugouts were bombed and damaged and one dugout was set on fire.

The Artillery had inflicted a few casualties on the garrison and no hostile machine guns fired except from S. of the River.

That the enemy had repaired his wire as soon as blown in was obvious from the number of coils of barbed wire lying out in front of his trench and from the new wire put up.

Several boxes of enemy bombs were dumped in shell holes full of water and as much damage done as possible.

Though no enemy machine guns were in the line when the raiding party reached the trench there were numerous empty rounds lying about in small heaps and one or two M.G. Belts.

(Sd.) C.A.M. Van Millingen, Capt.

21/9/17.   O.C. "D" Coy. 7th Bn. The Rifle Bde.

C

7th Battn. The Rifle Brigade.

List of Casualties for month of September.

No.	Rank and Name		Coy.	Nature of Casualty.
B/203694	Rfn.	Eccles, F.	D	Wounded 10/9/17
S/26396	L/C.	Plunkett, L.	D	Killed in Action, 11/9/17
S/21968	Rfn.	Pockett, C.	D	,, ,,
B/203719	,,	Smith, W.	D	,, ,,
B/203715	,,	Phipps, E.A.	D	,, ,,
B/200414	L/C.	Butters, A.	D	Wounded 11/9/17
S/31242	Rfn.	Middleton, W.	D	,,
B/203687	,,	Blackburn, W.	D	,,
Z/2540	L/C.	Mannion, J.	A	Wounded 16/9/17
	2nd Lieut.	Berrett, L.G., M.C.		Wounded 18/9/17
S/31248	Rfn.	Allcock, A.	B	,,
5/504	Sgt.	Rout, A.	A	Wounded, 17/9/17
	2nd Lieut.	Cochrane, G.	A	Killed in Action, 19/9/17
B/2083	Sgt.	Allen, J.	B	,, ,,
S/7345	Cpl.	Perkins, J.	B	,, ,,
Z/1892	L/C.	Holden, J.	B	,, ,,
S/8958	Rfn.	McCarthy, J.	B	,, ,,
S/17424	,,	Tobutt, W.	B	,, ,,
S/26309	,,	Ottaway, W.	B	,, ,,
S/6033	,,	Hanks, A.	B	Wounded, 19/9/17
S/25238	,,	Hacknett, R.	B	,, 15/9/17
S/28878	,,	Townley, S.	B	,, ,,
Z/172	L/C.	Cooke, A.	B	,, ,,
S/26338	Rfn.	Robinson, B.	C	,, ,,
B/203381	,,	Masters, W.	C	,, ,,
	2nd Lieut.	Stott, R.H.	D	Killed in Action 20/9/17
	,,	Halford, A.H.	D	Wounded, 20/9/17
	,,	Watkinson, W.E.	C	,, ,,
P/1671	Rfn.	Kealey, E.	A	,, ,,
S/28584	,,	Clegg, J.	A	,, ,,

No.	Rank and Name		Coy.	Nature of Casualty and Date.
S/28584	Rfn.	Hill, J.R.	A	Wounded, 20/9/17.
S/26130	,,	Stevens, S.	B	,, ,,
462	CSM.	Weymont, E.	D	,, ,,
S/10111	Sgt.	Palin, C.	D	,, ,,
B/1789	L/C.	Gale, H.	D	,, ,,
S/28626	,,	Groom, F.	D	,, ,,
B/200663	Rfn.	Butler, A.	D	,, ,,
S/25686	,,	Butt, P.	D	Died of Wounds, 20/9/17.
S/21728	,,	Llanchinski, A	D	Wounded, 20/9/17
Z/797	,,	Lamb, C.	D	,, ,,
S/16355	,,	Moule, A.	D	,, ,,
B/2662	,,	Preston, H.	D	,, ,,
S/8494	,,	Ravenhill, T.	D	,, ,,
B/2664	,,	Stapley, A.	D	,, ,,
5407	,,	Spivey, E.	D	Missing after action 20/9/17.
S/26139	,,	White, J.	D	Killed in Action, 20/9/17
B/1810	,,	Webb, W.	D	Wounded, 20/9/17
S/25248	,,	Crandon, A.	B	,, 18/9/17
Z/125	,,	Pryke, W.	B	,, ,,
S/30593	,,	York, A.	B	,, ,,
S/31220	,,	Skinner, J.	B	,, ,,
B 61	,,	Stonebridge, F.	A	Wounded at duty, 18/9/17
S/31758	CSM.	Young, J.	C	Wounded, 17/9/17
S/19313	Rfn.	Trenwith, E.	C	,, ,,

D

7th Battn. The Rifle Brigade.

List of Honours etc. for September, 1917.

	Captain	C.A.N. Van Millengen	Military Cross
	Captain	W.J. Shaw	Military Cross
	Lieut.	J.A. Sowerbutts	do.
	2nd Lieut.	L.G. Berrett	do.
	,,	T.D. Smith	do.
	,,	F.A. Hawkins	do.
B/1295	Cpl.	G. Jones	Distinguished Conduct Medal
B/1446	,,	J. Townsend	Military Medal.
S/30598	Rfn.	S. Esgrove	do.
S/16294	,,	H. Jones	do.
B/712	Sgt.	A. Bonham	do.
3623	Rfn.	H. Higgins	do.
S/24672	,,	Fullbrook	do.
S/19313	,,	Trenwith	do.
B/635	,,	W. Balderstone	do.
S/3910	L/C.	Gascoigne,	do.
S/7234	,,	W. Feld	do.
S/28647	Rfn.	Rumble,	do.
3650	,,	Elliott,	do.
S/7100	,,	J. Brixey	do.
3331	Sgt.	E. Depper	do. → & DCM
B/1439	,,	F. Robinson	do.
B/203044	L/C.	Rowley,	do.
B/200532	Rfn.	Cowell,	do.
S/11171	,,	E. Mitchell	do.
S/26301	,,	T. Broad	do.
S/10111	Sgt.	C. Palin	do.
B/203704	Cpl.	H. Jowitt	do.
S/31750	L/C.	E. Smart	do.
B/3470	,,	W. Dearman	do.
B/200663	Rfn.	A. Butler	do.
B/2662	,,	H. Preston	do.
S/9909	,,	E. Gregory	do.
S/5033	,,	N. Money	do.
S/8496	,,	T. Ravenhill	do.

WAR DIARY

OF

7th BATTN. THE RIFLE BRIGADE

FOR

OCTOBER 1917.

(VOLUME XXX)

W.J. Shaw Captain,

31/10/17. Commdg. 7th Battn. The Rifle Bde.

Army Form C. 2118.

(78) (Confidential when filled in)

WAR DIARY
or
INTELLIGENCE SUMMARY.
(Erase heading not required.)

7th Batt. The Rifle Brigade

Instructions regarding War Diaries and Intelligence Summaries are contained in F.S. Regs., Part II. and the Staff Manual respectively. Title pages will be prepared in manuscript.

Place	Date	Hour	Summary of Events and Information	Remarks and references to Appendices
SHANKILL CAMP	Oct 1st 1917		As no working parties were supplied training was carried out. Pl. & Coy. carried out Bn grenade throwing while C & D Coy. practised rapid deliberate wiring. Steady drill & fire discipline drill were also carried out. There were football matches in the afternoon.	W/S
"	" 2nd		Working parties of 225 men were supplied for the forward area. Bess Lewis Gun class fired on C Range. Batt. foot training recommenced.	W/S
"	" 3rd		Working parties of 50 men were supplied for the forward area. Lewis bombing & Gassing was carried out. There was a Rifle football match v. 8th/60th.	W/S
"	" 4th		All day course B.V. training for Offr. was commenced. Another Lewis bombing course carried out. There were baths for 150 men. A draft of 16 arrived. An Association football match v. 7th/60th were played. Won by the Batt.	W/S
"	" 5th		B & C Coy. carried out rapid firing on C Range. A & D Coy. practised bombing & wiring. 200 men went to the Baths. The 14th Divn. was transferred to X Corps & the Batt. moved to WOOD CAMP near	W/S
WOOD CAMP	" 6th		RENING HEIST. The Batt. bivouaced under very disagreeable conditions as no tents were available.	W/S

Army Form C. 2118.

WAR DIARY
or
INTELLIGENCE SUMMARY.

(Erase heading not required.) 7th Battn. The Rifle Brigade.

Place	Date	Hour	Summary of Events and Information	Remarks and references to Appendices
WOOD CAMP	1917 Oct. 7		C.O.'s Tennis was cancelled owing to rain. R.E. Tennis was held.	left
	. 8		Tents were pitched in the place of bivouacs but owing to the bad weather the men were far from comfortable.	left
DICKEBUSCH	. 9		The Battn moved to huts at 28 d 31 d 7.5. This was the first occasion where the Battn reached as the rest of Rifle Brign.	left
FRONT LINE	. 10 to . 16		The Battn moved at 7.45 A.M. allotted for 1½ hours at RIDGE WOOD CAMP where details were left behind officers stores. The Battn then moved to B Coy, to MEDFORD HOUSE where battle stores were issued, leaving there at 3.15 P.M. for the front line. The left sector of a Bde. front extending from MENIN RD. to the REUTELBECK was taken over & these were relieved by 13th I.B. of 5th Divn. These consisted of 1st NORFOLKS, 11th WARWICKS & 1.Coy of 14th WARWICKS who had made an unsuccessful attack on the previous day. The relief was carried out though harassing fire on tracks by enemy artillery, about 40 casualties were sustained, Capt. Capt. Van MISSENGEN being wounded. Owing to the shelling, to the indistinct boundaries & the dreadful condition of the tracks guides lost themselves & relief was not completed until 2 A.M. 11 inst.	left

Army Form C. 2118.

WAR DIARY
or
INTELLIGENCE SUMMARY.
(Erase heading not required.)

7th Batt. The Rifle Brigade

Place	Date	Hour	Summary of Events and Information	Remarks and references to Appendices
FRONT LINE	1917 Oct 10th to 16th cont.		D Coy held the right front, C the left front while A & B Coys held the Right & left support positions respectively. When the Batt. took over previously no trenches existed. There were a few pill boxes available otherwise mere shell holes. The town in spite of very bad weather during the first four days a great system was dug. At first a long gap existed between the two front Coys but this was remedied considerably during the town. Both support Coys did a great deal of work in spite of continual shell fire which continued practically without intermission. It was a very trying time for the men such no infantry action at all occurred & they had to sit under this continuous shelling which became violent at times in answer to our practice barrages. The Batt. was relieved on night of 16th Oct by 9th R.B., relief being completed by 7-30 PM. Total casualties were 2 Officers & 17 O.R.;—see Appendix marked A.C. attached herewith.	6A. A.C.
RIDGE WOOD CAMP	Oct 17		The day was spent in reorganization & cleaning	

WAR DIARY
or
INTELLIGENCE SUMMARY.

(Erase heading not required.) 7th Batt. The Buffs (E. Kent Regt)

Army Form C. 2118.

Place	Date	Hour	Summary of Events and Information	Remarks and references to Appendices
RIDGE WOOD CAMP.	1917 Oct 18		Medical Inspection of all Coys were carried out & reorganisation of Coys. proceeded with. Owing to recent casualties throughout the Bn the Coys. were now reorganised on a three platoon basis. Coys. carried out Inspection.	left
"	" 19		The Comd'g Officer inspected Coys & H.Qrs. A.M.C. Coys went to Bath.	left
"	" 20		100 men were sent on fatigue near CAFE BELGE. Improvements necessary were carried out.	left
"	" 21		There were Church Parade for all denominations.	left
MUREUMBRIDGE CAMP	" 22		The Battn moved to Campsite about 4 miles to MUREUMBRIDGE & pitched tents & night in huts.	left
METEREN	" 23		The Battn moved by Companies to METEREN, occupied billets in the village	left
"	" 24		The day was devoted to cleaning. Various comforts for the men were drawn in hand in this area. A field service dinner & Cantalit arranged at the Y.M.C.A.	left
"	" 25		A Range on the training ground & small ground firing were adjusted by Companies all morning. While small arms were carried out.	left
"	" 26		Similar training was carried out. Capt F.E. SPOOLING joined the Battn.	left
"	" 27		Another full morning training was carried out. Lieut MS? Jr was ranked.	left

Army Form C. 2118.

WAR DIARY
or
INTELLIGENCE SUMMARY.

(Erase heading not required.) 7th Batt. The Rifle Brigade (O2)

Instructions regarding War Diaries and Intelligence Summaries are contained in F. S. Regs., Part II. and the Staff Manual respectively. Title pages will be prepared in manuscript.

Place	Date	Hour	Summary of Events and Information	Remarks and references to Appendices
MELZICOURT	1917 Oct 27 with 28		Capt. J.C. Shepherd rejoined Batt. 2nd Lieut. Hollebone joined Bn Batt.	
	29		Tactical exercise for all companies. A Coy find an out post from range. The Bn moving beyond further dummy raid. The Coys were again occupied all the morning beyond further.	
	30		Morning spent doing squad drill were practiced the changes over entered. Afternoon spent digging wire trench.	
	31		Pt C Coy carried out the attack against a line on defense reconnecting which were Bay find out on to enfilade min. Effective strength on 31/10/17 Officers 33 O.R. 782	

W/Shaw. Capt.
Commanding 7th Battn. The Rifle Brigade

7th Battn. The Rifle Brigade.

List of Casualties.

No.	Rank and Name	Nature of Casualty and Date.
	Capt. Van Millingen, C.A.M. M.C.	Wounded 10/10/17
	2nd Lieut. Burch, S.H.	,, 16/10/17
Z/826	Rfn. Pratt, H.	Killed in Action 12/10/16
B/457	Sgt. Forbes, H.	Wounded 15/10/17
S/13386	Rfn. Tyerman, R.	,, 17/10/17
S/6375	,, Bryer, L.	,, 12/10/17 Died of Wds. 13/10/17
S/12624	L/C. Short, J.	,, 15/10/17
S/3161	,, Sabin, C.	,, 11/10/17
S/17335	,, Rawlinson, A.	,, 16/10/17
6015	,, McBain, C.	,, 13/10/17
P/476	Rfn. Gwyer, P.	Killed in Action 13/10/17
B/2514	,, Gubbins, A.	,, ,,
S/28579	,, Fuller, T.H.	,, 15/10/17
B/200013	,, Mynard, H.	,, ,,
B/203195	,, Flackett, S.	,, 10/10/17
S/35229	,, Askew, W.	Wounded 15/10/17
S/26315	,, Breakspeare, J.	,, ,,
S/23942	,, Brown, H.	,, ,,
B/398	,, Unnew, G.	,, 10/10/17
S/13492	,, Cooke, S.	,, 13/10/17
S/20735	,, Claxton, W.	,, 16/10/17
S/31237	,, Desborough, A.	,, 11/10/17
S/23597	,, Endean, A.	,, 13/10/17
S/12794	,, Farley, P.	,, 15/10/17
S/32390	,, Gibson, T.	,, 11/10/17
S/15588	,, Golden, A.	N.Y.D. 10/10/17
S/10642	,, Kavanagh, J.	Wounded ,,
S/31627	,, Meddemmen, J.	,, 11/10/17
S/30799	,, Murray, J.	,, 14/10/17
S/16778	,, Mann, R.	,, 10/10/17
S/32221	,, Relf, R.	,, 16/10/17
S/32617	,, Rule, A.	,, 10/10/17
S/17845	,, Batts, J.	,, ,,
Z/102	,, Lafford, G.	,, ,, Died of Wds. 10/10/17
S/32200	,, Penman, A.	,, 11/10/17
S/26237	,, Grant, G.	,, ,,
B/203596	,, Barker, A.	Missing 16/10/17
S/32223	,, Brooks, W.	,, ,,
S/16857	,, Wilkins, M.	,, ,,
4013	,, Woodhouse, J.	S.W. at duty 16/10/17
B/200942	,, Cohen, J.	,, ,,
S/28725	,, Brett, G.	,, ,,
S/25510	,, Woodman, W.	Killed in Action 10/10/17
S/23410	,, Stilling, G.	,, 11/10/17
S/3549	,, Basghaw, J.	,, ,,
B/1361	L/C. Voice, C.	,, 12/10/17
S/16635	Rfn. Plumpton, C.	,, ,,
S/8154	Sgt. Burns, T.	,, 15/10/17
S/1374	Rfn. Towersey, T.	,, ,,
S/19690	,, Lamey, T.	,, ,,
B/203058	,, Sefton, H.	,, ,,
P/4260	,, Gordon, G.	,, ,,
4051	,, Jones, J.A.	Wounded 10/10/17
B/200741	,, Taylor, F.	,, ,,
Z/1427	,, Carpenter, L.	,, ,,
Z/1851	,, Hailes, D.	,, ,,

No.	Rank and Name	Nature of Casualty and Date.
S/27753	Rfn. Allen, W.	Wounded 10/10/17
S/32151	,, Shean, T.	,, ,,
Z/214	L/C. Murphy, J.	,, ,,
7305	Rfn. Harrison, H.J.	,, 11/10/17
S/31223	,, Appleton, D.	,, ,,
S/30804	,, Price, F.	,, 12/10/17
S/31768	,, Whittingdale, J.	,, ,,
S/30865	,, Shurety, S.	,, 10/10/17
S/10473	L/C. Burke, H.	,, 12/10/17
XZ/364	Rfn. Hall, W.	,, ,,
S/27263	,, Smith, A.J.	,, 15/10/17
S/13639	,, Baxter, J.	,, ,,
B/3103	,, Hawley, T.	,, ,,
4291	Sgt. Cooley, E.	,, 16/10/17
B/172	L/C. Coke, H.	Missing believed killed 10/10/17
S/32216	Rfn. Oliver, W.	,, 10/10/17
S/7326	,, Deverell, T.	Missing believed wounded 16/10/17
S/32245	,, Burgoyne, G.	do. ,,
B/1642	L/C. Lowell, C.	N.Y.D. 15/10/17
S/23497	,, Webster, R.	Wounded ,,
S/9241	Rfn. Richards, R.	Missing believed Killed 16/10/17
S/28951	,, Millingen, H.	,, 16/10/17
S/31240	,, Harris, J.	,, ,,
S/6068	Cpl. Lawrence, A.	Wounded 10/10/17
Z/376	L/C. Barnes, W.	Killed in Action 10/10/17
S/13177	,, Bellamy, S.	Wounded 13/10/17
B/1585	,, Martin, E.	,, 10/10/17
S/28957	,, White, J.	Killed in Action 13/10/17
S/12752	Rfn. Blake, H.	Wounded (N.Y.D.) 10/10/17
S/26320	,, Bennett, E.	,, 10/10/17
S/21456	,, Green, E.	,, ,,
S/32581	,, Hefford, R.	,, ,,
S/26354	,, Hicks, C.	,, ,,
B/3232	,, Noyce, E.	,, ,,
B/203673	,, Nash, W.	,, 16/10/17
Z/1044	,, Panting, J.	,, 10/10/17
S/32602	,, Sheil, W.	,, 16/10/17
Z/2113	,, Williams, C.	,, 10/10/17
S/21822	,, Whiter, H.	,, ,,
367	,, Gibbard, W.	,, 12/10/17
S/30647	,, Clifford, C.	S.W. at duty 10/10/17
B/2128	Sgt. Lawrence, C.	Killed in action 12/10/17
S/5514	,, Saxton, F.	,, ,,
S/8599	Cpl. Bedwell, W.	,, ,,
S/2070	L/C. Keynard, R.	,, 16/10/17
S/32234	Rfn. Coakley, W.	,, 10/10/17
S/32518	,, Jones, B.	,, 12/10/17
S/19881	,, King, A.	,, ,,
S/37968	,, Croxford, C.	,, ,,
S/23797	,, Standing, J.	Missing believed Killed 14/10/17
S/32202	,, Richards, R.	do. ,,
S/5103	Sgt. Caughlan, A.	Wounded 16/10/17
S/15932	L/C. Penfold, C.	,, ,,
B/203044	,, Rowley, F.	,, 13/10/17
S/26654	Rfn. Randall, R.	,, ,,
B/1664	,, Brown, W.	,, ,,
S/26549	,, Oddy, W.	,, ,,
S/31747	,, Farrow, W.	,, 12/10/17
S/15333	,, Bush, W.	,, ,,
S/7186	,, Ripps, L.	,, ,,
S/16585	,, Milanofsky, W.	,, ,,
B/203036	L/C. Hawkins, W.	Missing 16/10/17
5877	Rfn. Shakespeare, H.	,, ,,
S/30683	,, Death, H.	,, ,,

3.

No.	Rank and Name	Nature of Casualty and Date.
S/32259	Rfn. Page, S.	Wounded 16/10/17
S/24638	,, Evan, W.	,, 15/10/17
S/32621	,, Fox, H.	Missing ,,
S/32627	,, Storey, T.	,, 15/10/17
S/14678	,, Godwin, A.	,, ,,

Vol 31

WAR DIARY

OF

7th BATTN. THE RIFLE BRIGADE.

PERIOD

NOVEMBER 1917

(VOLUME XXXI)

30/11/17

A.J.H. Sloggett
Lieut. Col.
Commdg 7th Bn. The Rifle Bde

Army Form C. 2118.

WAR DIARY
or
INTELLIGENCE SUMMARY.
(Erase heading not required.) 7.¹ Batt.ⁿ The Rifle Brigade

Instructions regarding War Diaries and Intelligence Summaries are contained in F. S. Regs., Part II. and the Staff Manual respectively. Title pages will be prepared in manuscript.

103

Place	Date	Hour	Summary of Events and Information	Remarks and references to Appendices
METHUEN	Nov 1st		Coy. training was carried out. Patrols in ... Trumpet ... valley. Work on ... the redoubts ... intestage. ... were ... B.Coy.	appx
"	Nov 2nd		A similar programme was carried out with the addition of wiring to ... on ... The large also being attached to B Coy.	appx
"	Nov 3		Battalion formation went carried out on the training area E of B.O.TTEN. Recce ... an attack sc... an enemy system represented in depth ... was carried out in two stages. The Bat.n was opposed by ... at various ... forces ... the Bat.n itself ... were rested well during ...	appx
	Nov 4		Brit. Formation ... for each D.monstration. The Bat.n ... to be ... The 8th Batt R.B. 325 pt f —	appx
	Nov 5		Baths were allotted to the Batt. ... the men ... specially no Coy. being could be carried out.	appx
	Nov 6		The musketry range was shifted to each Coy in turn during the morning ... General Landon, were the review the ... feature of the afternoon.	appx

2353 Wt. W2544/1454 700,000 5/15 D. D. & L. A.D.S.S./Forms/C. 2118.

WAR DIARY or INTELLIGENCE SUMMARY

Army Form C. 2118.

(Erase heading not required.) 7th Batt. The Rifle Brigade

Place	Date	Hour	Summary of Events and Information	Remarks and references to Appendices
METEREN	Nov 7th		The Platoon shooting competition won on the Bn's Platoon R.O.P. firing drill, signal drill & grenade throwing were carried out by Coy's when not on fatigue.	JMR
"	Nov 8th		The Bn's had a rest unit, men of "A" & "B" Coy were on duty. J. Stuart 4 orders After tea in Officers present.	JMR JMR
"	Nov 9th		Musketry semi drill bayonet fighting & wiring were the order of the day. General programme.	JMR
"	Nov 10th		The troops were allotted to the tasks etc throwing platoons in the shooting competition. Tower Gunners, Scouts & bombers received persistent instruction. 2/Lts Hon'l TOTTENHAM, J.F. THOMPSON, L. MONCOM & J.D. CORBIE joined the Batt.	JMR
ST. MARTIN AU LÆRT	Nov 11th		The Batt. entrained at LYNTRE at 10/17m latving at MEDOCQ at NOON the 10.45 Re for a further period of rest in nears of very comfortable huts. Both HB were at ST. MARTIN. Rocket team & ADS were also billetted there while BHQ was at TATINGHEM 8"0 left	JMR JMR
"	Nov 12th		A march discipline. By boys with field a coy carried out stretcher drill.	JMR JMR
"	Nov 13th		Coys carried out schemes in the attack on prepared works toyed shelter & live grenade throwing was practiced.	JMR

Army Form C. 2118.

WAR DIARY
or
INTELLIGENCE SUMMARY.
(Erase heading not required.) 7th Batt N.Z. Rifle Brigade

Place	Date	Hour	Summary of Events and Information	Remarks and references to Appendices
ST. MARTIN AU LAERT	Nov 14		All H. Coys fired on Charge at 200 & carried out 3 other applications & other rapid at 2 Plan figures	JM
"	Nov 15		All Coys carried out advance in attack on enemy strongpoint. There was also musical training for Lewis Gunners & Sig Sects, while the company H.T. was attached to B Coy.	JM
"	Nov 16		B + C Coys fired at 300 on C Range, 5 rounds application & 5 rounds rapid, while A+D Coys fired & Coys fired in the afternoon at 200 holding guns & Coys carried out advances in attack on enemy strong point, while remainder of Batt'n carried out Squad & Platoon training.	JM JM
"	Nov 17		All Pln Coys carried out Schemes. A+D Coys. Lewis Gunners received detailed training while the remaining fired on SMLE 5 rds rapid. There were Church parades for all denominations.	JM
"	Nov 18 Nov 19		Charge was applied to all Lewis guns who fired 5 rounds rapid & 5 rounds application at 300 while the word SLR & Coy Lewis & Coy Lewis fired at 200 in the afternoon. Lewis Gunner Coy Lewis & Cooks, & Cooks, & Sanitary rec'd & specialist training.	JM JM
"	Nov 20		Baths were allotted to the Battn. & later in the morning the whole Concert	JM JM

WAR DIARY
or
INTELLIGENCE SUMMARY.

(Erase heading not required.) 7th Batt" Rifle Bgde Brigade

Army Form C. 2118.

Place	Date	Hour	Summary of Events and Information	Remarks and references to Appendices
ST MARTIN AU LAERT	Nov 20 cont		1st and 2nd deployed and drill movement with special attention paid to the leadership of the smallest unit.	JM
"	Nov 21/11		B & C Coys fired 10 rounds rapid at 300 x 2 clean from Coy at also had 5 rounds at 200. A & D Coys went out & spent the time were allotted for the march on a portion of a wind of grenade exercise Nipple.	JM
"	Nov 22		All Coys carried out schemes paying particular attention to the stopping of M.G fire by the commander of the smallest unit when an enemy M/G suddenly opened. A & D P.O.10 O.R. teams received instruction in the A.A Lewis employing the R.Engineers. Commander received General Gorringe	JM
"	Nov 23		Bde Route-in-tour. A cross country run of 3½ miles was carried out by 100 men f each Coy in the Bde. Officers moved by the keen displayed for running became of number of the men real was a draw, one tie in each Batt getting a its return in A.G Frank 82 men, J99. C.150, 2D95. The 7th had 4 tie 93 y91.	JM

WAR DIARY
or
INTELLIGENCE SUMMARY

(Erase heading not required.) 7th Batt. Yorkshire Brigade

Army Form C. 2118.

Place	Date	Hour	Summary of Events and Information	Remarks and references to Appendices
ST MARTIN AU LAERT	Nov 24		[illegible handwritten entry]	
"	Nov 25		[illegible handwritten entry]	
"	Nov 26		[illegible handwritten entry]	
"	Nov 27		[illegible handwritten entry]	
"	Nov 28		[illegible handwritten entry]	

WAR DIARY or INTELLIGENCE SUMMARY

Army Form C. 2118.

(Erase heading not required.) 7th Bn. The Rifle Brigade

Place	Date	Hour	Summary of Events and Information	Remarks and references to Appendices
ST MARTIN AU LAERT	2nd 28th Contd.		To first objective, & annulling shelling as an outpost line of rive by Hellfire posts.	
"	29th		A Bde. theoretical day. A Wired Relay Race was won by teams of 3 representing each Batt. The race was won by 8th R.B. 4 p.m. P.G. McCubbin joined the Batt.	Offr
RED ROSE CAMP VLAMERTINGHE	30th 31st		The Batt. entrained at WIZERNES STN. at 7.30 P.M. detrained at BRANDHOEK & went into huts in preparation to moving up into the line.	Offr

To effective Strength — Offrs 34 O.R. 760

A.T.H. Maggott Lt. Colonel
Comdg 7th Bn. The Rifle Brigade.

CONFIDENTIAL

WAR DIARY

OF

7th Battn THE RIFLE BRIGADE

FROM 1/12/17   To 31/12/17

(VOLUME XXXI)

M Thornton. Major
Commdg 7th Bn. The Rifle Brigade

31/12/17

Army Form C. 2118.

WAR DIARY
or
INTELLIGENCE SUMMARY.
(Erase heading not required.)

7th Battn. The Rifle Brigade.

Place	Date	Hour	Summary of Events and Information	Remarks and references to Appendices
RED ROSE CAMP VLAMERTINGHE	Dec. 1st		The day was spent in preparation for moving up into the line.	yes
CAPRICORN CAMP	2nd		The Battn. moved by train from BRANDHOEK to WIELTJE & spent the day at HUSSAR CAMP. In the evening the 41st I.B. relieved 24th I.B. The Battn. went into support at SPREE FARM (CAPRICORN CAMP). A&B Coys however owing to the narrow frontage in the line were sent up in close support at MEETCHEELE.	yes
"	3rd		At night the two Coys returned to camp, fortunately incurring few casualties. Carrying parties were supplied by C & D Coys.	yes
"	4th		C & D Coys supplied carrying parties.	yes
Front line PASSCHENDAELE	5th		The Battn. relieved the 8th KRRC in the front line. All four Coys were in the front line, and furnishing its own supports. The town was overlying on for the men owing to the bitter weather. However it kept dry until the relief & relief. Few cases only of trench feet were evacuated. Casualties are detailed in attached marked A. A great loss to the Bn. was inflicted by the death from wounds of Bn. Qr. Maxwell and Coy. Sjt. K.R.R.C. The town was otherwise without incident.	yes
	- 8th		On the night of 8th the Battn. was relieved by 6th D.C.L.I. & after resting at WIELTJE moved by train to RED ROSE CAMP on morning Sep 9.	yes

Army Form C. 2118.

WAR DIARY
or
INTELLIGENCE SUMMARY.

(Erase heading not required.) 9/4 Batt. The Rifle Brigade.

Instructions regarding War Diaries and Intelligence Summaries are contained in F. S. Regs., Part II. and the Staff Manual respectively. Title pages will be prepared in manuscript.

Place	Date	Hour	Summary of Events and Information	Remarks and references to Appendices
RED ROSE CAMP	Dec 9th to 18th		Lt. E. CHICHESTER & 2nd Lts. F.A. KINGSWELL, C.A. JOHNS, C.R. WELLS, H.W. LETHBRIDGE, W. BAKER joined the Battn. During this period the Battn. found working parties of up to 100 O.R. on alternate days for railway work at WIELTJE. As far as possible training in available portions of their proper curriculum was carried out. The ground was not suitable for training on any comprehensive scale.	nil
HASLER CAMP	19th to 21st		The Battn marched to HASLER CAMP arriving at about 6 P.M. The 4/2/113 came into support. The 4/2/113 going into the line. The Battn. found working parties. It was engaged in preparation for the line.	nil
FRONT LINE PASSCHENDAELE	22nd to 26th		Several attended who paid to the new feet & ears "dry" treatment was given to a certain number. Orders given at the YPRES Batn. In the evening the Battn. relieved the 9/R.B. in the front line H13cD coys. being in the front line & C Coy in support. Said front line Coys found it over supports. The weather was very cold coming fell on 24th Thaw making the conditions exceedingly trying. The moon was nearly full so that movement in the still like outpost line was diff. wit. & dangerous. On the night of relief the incoming Battn was observed by the enemy who put down a heavy barrage. Thanks to the initiative & coolness of the Battn. guides the casualties amongst the relieving Battn – 1st Worcesters	nil

1577 Wt.W10791/1773 500,000 1/15 D.D.&L. A.D.S.S./Forms/C. 2118.

Army Form C. 2118.

WAR DIARY
or
INTELLIGENCE SUMMARY.

(Erase heading not required.) 2nd Batt. The Rifle Brigade

Instructions regarding War Diaries and Intelligence Summaries are contained in F. S. Regs., Part II. and the Staff Manual respectively. Title pages will be prepared in manuscript.

(111)

Place	Date	Hour	Summary of Events and Information	Remarks and references to Appendices
FRONTLINE PASSCHENDAELE	Dec 23rd to 26th Contd.		were comparatively light. Three other ranks for this tour were 62 wounded 15 killed. For this sector they are attacked unusual amounted 13.	
			The enemy showed no intention of attacking on this front every was warned of him except when he was engaged in considerable hi main line of defence. Four cases of trench feet were evacuated.	ref
SETQUES	27th		On coming out of the line the Batt. rested until midday at WEILTJE, moving later by train to SET GUES where billets were taken over.	ref
	28th to 31st		This period was spent in cleaning, reorganising back a time footwear. A continued front sleep was prevented either games or any form of training being carried out.	ref

W. Manden
Major
Comdg 2nd Batt. The Rifle Brigade
31/12/17

Appendix A.

List of Casualties.
1 - 8th Dec. 1917.

No.	Rank	Name	Nature of Casualty and Date.
2682	Sgt.	Burton, S.	Killed in Action 2/12/17.
B/2387	,,	Chatwin, W.	Wounded 2/12/17
S/17439	L/C.	Hockley, W.	,, ,,
S/17431	Rfn.	Collier, P.	,, ,,
S/31215	,,	Hall, G.	,, ,,
S/32543	,,	Levitt, C.	,, ,,
S/32193	,,	Maynard, J.	,, 3/12/17
S/15503	,,	Monk, C.	,, ,,
S/15051	,,	Smith, R.	,, ,,
S/23950	,,	Wetherly, W.	,, ,,
S/26301	,,	Broad, J.	,, 5/12/17.
S/31218	,,	Newbury, C.	,, ,,
	Captain	Spurling, F.E.	,, ,,
	2nd Lieut.	Love, A.B.	,, ,,
	,,	Reavell, G.N.	,, ,,
	Lt. Col.	Maxwell, M.C., J.	,, 4/12/17 Died of Wds. 5/12/17
S/32193	Rfn.	James, F.	,, ,,
S/32260	,,	Geehan, L.	Killed in Action 7/12/17
S/11849	,,	Monks, A.	,, ,,
6/621	,,	Smith, F.	,, ,,
S/30479	,,	Anderson, H.	Missing 8/12/17.
B/200733	,,	Mullins, C.	Wounded 5/12/17
S/12762	L/C.	Stowe, A.	,, ,,
S/32084	Rfn.	Poulter, W.	,, ,,
S/2501	,,	Belfield, C.	,, ,,
B/203650	,,	Larkin, J.	,, ,,
B/188	,,	Forman, S.	,, ,,
B/1230	,,	Hill, E.	,, ,,
P/1671	,,	Kealey, E.	,, at duty 5/12/17.
S/32385	,,	Furze, R.	,, 6/12/17.
S/32402	,,	Marshman, J.	,, at duty, 6/12/17.
S/17604	,,	Young, R.	,, ,, ,,

No.	Rank	and Name	Nature of Casualty and Date.
S/13642	Rfn.	Carter, S.	Killed in Action 6/12/17
S/31744	,,	Edwards, H.	Missing 5/12/17
Z/2336	,,	Muggeridge, F.	,, 7/12/17
6/431	,,	Whitfield, A.	,, 5/12/17
B/200727	,,	Whitehead, J.	Wounded 8/12/17
B/1990	,,	Tilbury, H.	,, 7/12/17
B/203013	Cpl.	Balmforth, V.	,, 5/12/17
S/32666	Rfn.	Stokes, L.	,, 7/12/17
S/24676	,,	Nunan, T.	,, ,,
S/28366	,,	Ayres, G.	,, ,,
S/24650	,,	Cole, L.	,, ,,
S/15768	,,	Rust, W.	,, 8/12/17
S/6408	,,	Valentine, S.	,, ,,

Appendix B.

List of Casualties.
22 - 26/12/1917.

No.	Rank and Name	Nature of Casualty and Date.
	2nd Lieut. H.W.L. Tottenham	Wounded 22/12/17
	,, G.L. Thomson	,, 26/12/17
S/26315	L/C. Morris, A.E.	,, 22/12/17
S/13697	Rfn. Furlonger, G.	Killed in Action 22/12/17
S/32251	,, Merrifield, H.	,, ,,
S/14989	,, Richards, J.	,, ,,
S/34870	,, Plackett, G.	Wounded 23/12/17 Died of Wds. 26th
S/26883	,, Watts W.	Wounded at duty 23/12/17
S/30614	,, Kitcon, L.	Wounded 23/12/17
S/32491	,, Redman, W.	,, ,,
B/200657	L/C. Turner, C.	,, ,,
S/32200	Rfn. Tavender, E.	,, ,,
S/8192	,, Wood, E.	NYD (Shock) 23/12/17
S/15732	,, Joyce, F.	Wounded 24/12/17
S/24372	,, Dye, J.	,, ,,
S/34233	L/C. Wheatcroft, C.	,, 22/12/17
S/32146	Rfn. Emery, A.	Wounded at duty 23/12/17
S/32277	,, Arthurs, J.	,, 22/12/17
S/26393	,, Burbidge, T.	,, ,,
S/15493	,, Hanbury, T.	,, ,,
S/34797	,, Jenkins, H.	,, 26/12/17
S/23982	,, Peacock, J.	,, 22/12/17
S/31590	,, York, A.	Wounded at duty 22/12/17
S/32630	,, Price, G.	,, ,, ,,
S/34894	,, Knight, A.	NYD (Shock) 26/12/17
B/3393	,, Brooker, A.	Wounded ,,
B/203695	,, Eales, F.	,, ,,
S/8494	,, Ravenhill, T.	,, ,,

CONFIDENTIAL

WAR DIARY

OF

7th Bn THE RIFLE BRIGADE

From. 1-1-18   To. 31-1-18

(VOLUME XXXII)

A.T.H. Sloggett Lt Col

Commdg 7th Bn The Rifle Brigade

31-1-18.

Army Form C. 2118.

WAR DIARY
or
INTELLIGENCE SUMMARY. 7th Batt" Rifle Brigade
(Erase heading not required.)

112

Place	Date	Hour	Summary of Events and Information	Remarks and references to Appendices
SETQUES	1915 Jan 1st		Commanding Officers Inspection took place in the morning. Reconnaissance of the road made during morning.	G.M.B
"	2nd		The day was spent in preparation for the move to the reserve on night of 2nd/3rd.	G.M.
CEUSY	3rd		The Batt" marched off at midnight 2nd/3rd. returned at ST. OMER at 2 A.M. detrained at ESQUELBEC at 2 P.M. & arrived after a very exhausting march along slippery roads at CEUSY at 7 P.M. The Batt" transport did not arrive until early in the morning of 4th.	G.M.
"	4th		The day was spent in cleaning up & filling and repaired considerable attention before they could be made habitable.	G.M.
"	5th		Owing to the incessant training as any roads was impossible great care must still be used when attempted.	G.M.
"	6th		There were Church Parades for all denominations including a Jewish parade at VII Corps Convalescent Camp.	G.M.
"	7th		Commanding Officers Inspection took place in the morning, the rainfall still prevents better training.	G.M.

Army Form C. 2118.

(113)

WAR DIARY
or
INTELLIGENCE SUMMARY.

(Erase heading not required.) 7th Batt'n. The Buffs E. Kent Regiment

Place	Date	Hour	Summary of Events and Information	Remarks and references to Appendices
CERISY	Jan. 8th 1918		Commencement was made with training. A model trial system was commenced. Coy drill P.T. a.s.f. were also carried out. Whilst this was specialist training for Lewis Gunners & Coy runs.	GMK.
	" 9th		Heavy rain prevented all training from taking place.	GMK.
	" 10th		Batts. were allotted to the Bn.s. 1st Pte. W.M. McCOFFEY, S. Clerk. 2nd E. GILLESPIE, D.B. MACPHERSON, R. McALISTER, S. HENOD. & GW Eng. Jones the Buffs?	GMK.
	" 11th		There was rifle and clipping & working specialist training for Lewis Gunners & Coy. Works & training for the Platoon shooting Competition.	GMK.
	" 12th		The Batt'n Platoon shooting Competition was won by Plat'n. No. 2. Platoon Commanders were drawn closer together with Batt'n & the Bn. Competition. 5th Army Commander Gen. Sir Hub. de la P. Gough, K.C.B, K.C.V.O attended the Batt'n Ch'ch. Parade at 9 "CoL's arrived & afterwards saw the Batt'n march past in column of route.	GMK.
	" 13th			
	" 14th		There were Bugles, the Batt'n who went through & inspected under the R.C. Gas Officer.	GMK. GMK.

WAR DIARY or INTELLIGENCE SUMMARY

Army Form C. 2118.

(Erase heading not required.) 1" Bn 3" Rifle Brigade (114)

Place	Date	Hour	Summary of Events and Information	Remarks and references to Appendices
CERISY	1918 Jan 15		Trench digging was attempted but the day turned very wet with the result that training was abandoned. In the evening the Pte. Henshaw a dinner to the Offr.s of C.4 Battn. celebrated the unique occasion of a Bn. Offr.s + Division being detailed into a Battery of 8 Leuis our guns. The weather was again very wet and a stand still secured out of CEO Coy lad the attended.	9M 9M
"	16"		The Bn. platoon shooting competition was carried out a very wet weather was won by 13 Coy. Gustav represented the Bn. No.2. Weston represented the Bn. Lewis Gunners Section was no third owing to the inability of Riflemen Lewis Gunners to set upon a Target. Rearick shooting subject work was good tell, but the fewer number of points to had technical faults generally a lack of style about. The competition was nearly at & 300 + 200 yds. while there were if	9M
"	18"		Both intro the 2nd, 3rd, 4th Coys training and Camp fields routes were approximately in 2 cause of a smoke was routed as in a morning. A Coy. + B Coy 2 P.R. amount. A C B Coys. carried out a field attack While C Coy. were on the range 360 carried out coy drill. Pt + 50 a live-shooting.	9M

2353 Wt W2541/1454 700,000 5/15 D. D. & L. A.D.S.S./Forms/C. 2118.

Army Form C. 2118.

WAR DIARY
or
INTELLIGENCE SUMMARY.

(Erase heading not required.) 2'/Batt. Mx Light Brigade

Place	Date	Hour	Summary of Events and Information	Remarks and references to Appendices
CERISY	Jan 19th 1918		C.O. Day. Carried out a trench relief. A Coy were in the Range when B Coy were engaged on the trenches, and two Coys were here.	
"	20th		We were church parade for all denominations including C. of E & R.C. at 3rd Corps Concentrat Camp.	
"	21st		2 Officers & 31 O.R. were inoculated and were inoculated by the Sanit. Sec. Field Coyer Res. Got the Division at 3rd Coy & West there a single instance of sickness from cold. Rats, Rev. & 1st Regts. etc.	
BEAUCOURT	22nd		The Batt: marched from CERISY to BEAUCOURT-EN-SANTERRE a distance of 12 miles.	
LIGNIÈRES	23rd		A further march of 12 miles brought the Batt. to LIGNIÈRES. Rain fell slightly during the march.	
CRISSOLLES	24th		The Batt. marched from LIGNIÈRES to CRISSOLLES a distance of 24 miles, arriving at the destination at 6.30 p.m. The spirit of the troops during this arduous march was fabulous, and they finished this march with half a mile up hill, full of song. Six men only fell out on this march, three of whom continued until they dropped exhausted on the roadside.	
JUSSY	25th		After a very trying march of 14 miles, which was hampered owing to continual	

WAR DIARY or INTELLIGENCE SUMMARY

Army Form C. 2118.

Place	Date	Hour	Summary of Events and Information	Remarks and references to Appendices
Jussy	26.		Stoppages caused by traffic, the Battn arrived at its ultimate destination, JUSSY, at 7 pm.	JMK
"	27.		Coy. commanders and 50% of the Platoon officers and Sergeants reconnoitred the defensive position to be held by the Battn in the event of an enemy attack. Coy/E + R.E. duties were allotted.	JMK
"	28.		The Commanding Officer and Adjutant reconnoitred the front line system held by right of 7th Battn of 7th Brigade. Coy training was carried out.	JMK
"	29.		The Commanding Officer inspected the Battn in the morning. In the afternoon A + B Coys moved to CLASTRES taking over the billets of two Coys of the 7/60 who had moved forward into Brigade support.	JMK
"	30.		Coy training was carried out during the morning. Coy Commanders reconnoitred the front line system held by the right Battn of 1st Bde.	JMK
"	31.		The Commanding Officer inspected B + D Coys. A + C Coys were inspected by the O.C. detachment.	40 strong 1700 OR
				JMK

A.T.H. Nugget H. Lt Colonel
Comdg 7th Bn 7th Rifle Brigade

Confidential 4/14

WAR DIARY
OF
7th Bn THE RIFLE BDE

From 1/2/18 to 28/2/18

(VOLUME XXXIII)

M. Thornton
Major
Commdg 7th Bn The Rifle Bde

28/2/18

Army Form C. 2118.

WAR DIARY
or
INTELLIGENCE SUMMARY.
(Erase heading not required.)

4/13th The Rifle Bde (117)

Place	Date 1918	Hour	Summary of Events and Information	Remarks and references to Appendices
JUSSY	1st		Cleaning & preparation for going into the line occupied the day.	
CLASTRES	2nd		H.Q. moved to CLASTRES. MCD & 2 Lts. to the Rly cutting at ESSIGNY & C Coy to LA MOTTIERE. A Coy being relief at JUSSY. The Battn then came into support of 3rd Bde. 2/Lt "B" Coy.	M
"	3rd		Enemy aeroplanes dropped bombs about 7 P.M. inflicting the following casualties — 3/1393 Sgt. J. McCARTHY, B/3421 Rfn. C. MATTHEWS & S/6120 Rfn. J. UPTON killed. 2/810 Rfn. F. BUNDY, S/2516 Rfn. C.A. MOORE, B/9351 Rfn. J. IOGDEN & S/4358 Rfn. S. TOWNLEY wounded & 3/290 Rfn. J. SHARPLES died of wounds. The Battn relieved the 8th R.B. in the line, A Coy left front, C Coy right front, B Coy Support & D Coy in reserve. The 8th/60th held the left sector of the Bde front & 4/2nd R.B. were on the right.	M M
Int line VRAILLERS	4th		Northern shelled during morning. Many shots in front of our line. Encountered no enemy.	
"	5th		Intermittent shelling of VRAILLERS uncovered Ridge & Line. Patrols went out again & encountered no enemy on our front.	M
"	6th		Enemy patrols. Aeroplanes on front of 9 D.R. joined. Patrols again saw no enemy in their front.	M

2353 Wt W.2544/1454 700,000 5/15 D.D.&L. A.D.S.S./Forms/C. 2118.

WAR DIARY or INTELLIGENCE SUMMARY

Army Form C. 2118.

(Erase heading not required.) 7th Batt. The Rifle Brigade

Place	Date	Hour	Summary of Events and Information	Remarks and references to Appendices
Front line ORVILLERS	Feb 7th		Support line shelled intermittently between 12 & 3 P.M. Patrol from right Coy. raided enemy's wire but observed no movement	
"	8th		Enemy patrol raided SOMME POST at 3.30 A.M. wounding 8/9258 Pte W. HOLLAND & 3/28750 Rfn. W. BOROUGH. The latter is missing we believe to have been taken prisoner. Patrol from right front Coy inspected tracks in "No Man's Land" but encountered no signs of enemy patrol. 9/13 & 1 Rfn. A. WEBB was wounded.	20
"	9th		Shelling of OVILLERS at intervals from ZOLLERN. D Coy relieved A in L.F. & B Coy relieved C in R.F. Explosions occurred in enemy's wire in front of 150 yds at B24c. 8.5 apparently bombs thrown by the enemy.	24
"	10th		Fighting patrol at source M.O.D. 020 saw no enemy.	
"	11th		Again a patrol saw no enemy. Draft of 60 O.R. joined.	24
"	12th		Enemy report seen approaching CASTLE but were driven off by L.S. front. A party followed them up but owing to thick mist no retaliation taken.	209
"	13th		90th front. Right shelling of OVILLERS & SUPPORT LINE. Patrol again at BOTH Coy fronts	

WAR DIARY
or
INTELLIGENCE SUMMARY.

(Erase heading not required.) 7th Batt. The Rifle Brigade

Place	Date	Hour	Summary of Events and Information	Remarks and references to Appendices
Front line VERMELLES District	1916 13th/14th		Saw no enemy.	
"	14th		VERMELLES shelled at intervals. Inspected enemy night post. were examined by patrol which found a river of our wire artificially made & ready to be cut. There were no signs of recent occupation. 2/Lt Rfn. F. COLLINS was accidentally wounded.	
"	15th		The enemy party of 5 men approached SOMME post. They were fired upon & H ran off. One was captured feebly hit & unable to supply information. He showed signs of having the previous identification of the unit against us 2 8th Bn Bowerman S/9525 Rfn. 7. Thake 1320 Rfn. J.Foley & S/3242 Rfn. W. Seed. were found and a recent photo showing the reserve area. The Batt" was relieved by 8th/60th & proceeded to Bde Support. HQ. A & C Coy. at CENTRES Old at LA SABLIERE. B & D Coy in the Rly Cutting.	
			The tour was very quiet & the weather was good. The condition of the line in front of stony Pride & front line is very bad owing to constant nightly wiring on a large scale. Dying stores were established on the front support line. Owing	

WAR DIARY
or
INTELLIGENCE SUMMARY.

(Erase heading not required.)

Army Form C. 2118.

(120)

Place	Date	Hour	Summary of Events and Information	Remarks and references to Appendices
Front line VRUILLERS	1918 Feb 15th contd.		The difficult nature of the ground & the great distance between the enemy patrols experienced great difficulty in locating any enemy patrols. Gone here previously been allowed to seize the mastery of No Mans Land.	
CAESTRES VRUILLERS	16th 17th 18th -20th		The day was spent in cleaning. Draft of 7 OR. joined. Batt. HQ. moved to No rly. cutting at VRUILLERS. The Batt was inspected by Coy. for tomorrow and any difficulty the Battn gave definite at VRUILLERS. Cpl. C.F. GOODYEAR was accidentally wounded. 4/1 & 2/Lt B. E. BRYANT & 2/Lt S. S. F. VENNINGS were wounded.	
Front line VRUILLERS	21st 22nd -26th		The Battn. relieved the 8th RB in the left sector. Pt. Spt. Dn. Sypoet. Bn. Reserve. The weather was extremely good with moonlight nights. Agreed deal of wiring in the VRUILLERS system in front of MAES & of the advanced pts. was carried out. Indian artillery activity. Patrols went out every night & no intelligence about the enemy.	
" "	27th 28th		Relieved A.S.C. 6th.G.G. relieved C. There were no casualties up to this date. The enemy appears to be carrying out more registration bursts on his dist.	

28/2/18

14th Division.
41st Brigade.

7th BATTALION

THE RIFLE BRIGADE

MARCH 1918

41/14

CONFIDENTIAL

WAR DIARY

OF

7th Bn THE RIFLE BRIGADE

FROM 1-3-18   TO 31-3-18

(VOLUME XXXIV)

P. A. Scott Major
Commdg 7th Bn The Rifle Bde

2-5-18.

Army Form C. 2118.

WAR DIARY
or
INTELLIGENCE SUMMARY.
(Erase heading not required.)

Place	Date	Hour	Summary of Events and Information	Remarks and references to Appendices
	1918			
# Front Line URVILLERS	4/18 March 13th		Extension of Front taken over. Dispositions of Coys altered in consequence. Evening of 4th and Strong Points. Batln. H.Q defence strengthened by Garrisons. a S.O.S signal was sent up from CALVAIRE by F.O.O. At 8.30 pm which was repeated by O.C. Right Front Coy. Our artillery but furiously opened fire at 8.20 p.m. Causing a patrol under 2/Lt FLEMMING to return to our line. Immediately after S.O.S. was sent up, enemy laid down a barrage on Support line and Route 44. Causing following casualties:- 9/34367 Rfn. R. SMITH, 9/31340 Rfn. W. SHELSHER, 9/31435. Rfn. J. SIMMONDS and 9/265 Rfn. T. HAZELL Killed; 9/30207 Rfn. H. HOLMES, 9/31484 Rfn. A. BONNER and 9/2415 C/L. KIMBER wounded. No enemy infantry action followed. Capt. C. R. Stuart to England.	P.W.
	2nd to 5th March		A considerable amount of wiring was done on posts and Strong points, trenches deepened in places. Bombing posts and firesteps constructed and new trenches dug as arranged by B.I.C. Patrols were out every night, but failed to come in contact with any enemy patrols. Enemy shelling was of a spasmodic nature and mainly confined to Support line, Route 44 and URVILLERS.	
	5/6/4		Batts were relieved by 8/R.B. and proceeded to CLASTRES, Draft of 33 O.Rs. joined 5th.	P.M.S P.M.S
	6th		Medical inspection of "C" & "D" Coy.	B.O.S
	7th to 12th		Coy by bringing cable. 2 Coys working on Reserve line and one Coy training at CLASTRES daily. Coys on work carried out at various forms of training and musketry. Small schemes. Show programme was in execution during the period. Capt W. T. Shaw to England 8th. Bn. Works Platoon relieved.	P.C.A P.M.S

Army Form C. 2118.

WAR DIARY
or
INTELLIGENCE SUMMARY.

(Erase heading not required.)

122

Place	Date	Hour	Summary of Events and Information	Remarks and references to Appendices
CLASTRES	1918 Mar. 12th		Bath. relieved 8th R.B. in Support. Hd Qrs and 2 Coys in Rly. cutting, one Coy at ESSIGNY and one Coy at LA SABLIERE.	P.M.S.
RLY. CUTTING ESSIGNY & LA SABLIERE	13th to 19th		Battalion engaged on work on defences in vicinity of ESSIGNY and in BATTLE ZONE. Drawing whole parading to and from work.	P.M.S.
"	20th		Batn. engaged on burying cable. Battalion occupied Battle position during night.	P.M.S.
"	21st		Enemy opened a heavy drum fire bombardment at about 4 a.m. A considerable amount of gas shells being used. From this time onwards no communication could be established with the Battalion, despite repeated efforts by the 9th R.B. Runners, who were prevented by a new heavy barrage from achieving their object. Owing to the fact that no one who was present in the Battle Zone with the Battalion succeeded in establishing that sent the Transport, it is impossible to attempt to give any lucid account of what happened on the Forward Zone. It is believed that the enemy penetrated the front at LE PIRE ALLER on the left of the Divisional front and worked his way down to LA MANUFACTURE FARM while on the right of the Divisional front he penetrated as far as LA SABLIERE, subsequently encircling ESSIGNY and later in the day establishing himself South of ESSIGNY, midway between that village and LE PAY FARM. The Transport received a sudden order at about 1 p.m. to move forthwith West of TUGNY CANAL and proceeded to BEAUMONT-EN-BEINE.	P.M.S. P.M.S.

7th Rifle Brigade

Diary March 1918 p. 123.

The action described as being on the 22nd March must have been that of the 23rd March.
            H R Davies
5.1.25.

WAR DIARY
or
INTELLIGENCE SUMMARY.

Army Form C. 2118.

Place	Date	Hour	Summary of Events and Information	Remarks and references to Appendices
CLASTRES JUSSY CANAL	1918 March 21		Meanwhile, Major N.S. THORNTON collected all the 7th R.B. details, and explained it to be proposed to take up a suitable position in the vicinity and dig in as long as possible. A hasty reconnaissance revealed that no suitable position could be defended except on the West side of JUSSY CANAL. The details therefore took up position and commenced to strengthen the defences. Small bridges were demolished and No 1 Bridge was prepared for destruction by the R.E. when occasion should arise. Astride of the 42nd Brigade were established on the right of Bridge 1 at approx. M.8. c. 7.5 whilst the details 7R.B. details - augmented by a number of stragglers, held the canal from left of Bridge 1 to approx. M.8. a. 0.5. Ammunition and tools were sent for when duly arrived at about 6 p.m. The details manned the line until relieved the following morning by the 8 R.B. They thereupon marched to BEAUMONT-EN-BEINE at 8 a.m. —	P.W.A. Casualties 1 officer 20 officers 525 Other Ranks missing
BEAUMONT-EN-BEINE.	March 22.	X	The Details of the Battalion, numbering 4 Officers and 100 other ranks, proceeded to PETIT DETROIT Cheermakers, Gunlen, Pioneers, Storemen and remnants of the Battalion, at 3 a.m., and remained there until 10 a.m., when a position in rear of FLAVY LE MARTEL was occupied. Some heavy fighting took place in the vicinity, and after holding the position for some hours, the enemy compelled a withdrawal, owing to his having almost encircled the village of FLAVY ==LE MARTEL and the position occupied by the 7th R.B.	P.M.A.

WAR DIARY
or
INTELLIGENCE SUMMARY.
(Erase heading not required.)

Army Form C. 2118.

(124)

Place	Date	Hour	Summary of Events and Information	Remarks and references to Appendices
FLAVY LE MARTEL	1918 March 23rd		Details. A hazardous withdrawal was carried out in the direction of CUGNY, during which time the enemy employed a considerable number of machine guns assisted by GRANATENWERFERS. Enemy fire was coming from three sides during the withdrawal and he followed quickly on the heels of the retiring elements. A further stand was made near CUGNY but owing to the small number of troops in comparison with the enemy's overwhelming forces, a further withdrawal was necessitated after a couple of hours standing in new	
	23/24th		position was taken up in front of BEAUMONT-EN-BEINE, where a number of French troops were already digging in. The enemy attacked at midnight but was completely repulsed by fire from French 75's assisted by machine gun and rifle fire. His attack was accompanied by the blowing of bugles evidently to spur his men on; but he sustained heavy losses. (It is reported by several N.C.O.s and men that during the fighting round FLAVY LE MARTEL & CUGNY the enemy fired soft nosed bullets from his machine guns, which caused nasty jagged wounds). The remainder of the night passed quietly.	P.W.
	24th		In conjunction with the French, and owing to enemy pressure on the flanks, a withdrawal was effected to a position in the vicinity of BEINES, where a	P.O.L.

Army Form C. 2118.

WAR DIARY
or
INTELLIGENCE SUMMARY.
(Erase heading not required.)

Instructions regarding War Diaries and Intelligence Summaries are contained in F.S. Regs., Part II. and the Staff Manual respectively. Title pages will be prepared in manuscript.

Place	Date	Hour	Summary of Events and Information	Remarks and references to Appendices
BEINES	1918 Mch 24		Hasty line was dug. Orders were then received to withdraw to BUCHOIRE and from here the details proceeded to CUSSOLES, arriving here at about 11 pm. After	P.A.P.
PORQUERICOURT	25th		a 2 hours rest a further move was ordered to PORQUERICOURT and a line was dug in the vicinity of the village. This line was occupied at 10 am. and manned throughout the day. The French were to relieve the Division elements at 6.30 pm and occupy a line a short distance in front of the line held by the elements. An attack developed against the French some distance in front of the line held by the elements, and French troops were seen to be pressed back. This took place late in the evening. At 7.30 pm during actual stand to the French had retired up to a position in rear, a 'retirement was ordered. This was by sections without too, small parties under an officer concentrating at a point some 500 yards in rear and at 8.30 pm the whole party marched to THIESCOURT, where they spent the night.	P.O.P.
THIESCOURT	26th		A draft of 1 S.O. 80 other ranks joined the Battalion at the village. The whole detail then proceeded to a wood N.E. of ELINCOURT and remained there throughout the day, ready to take up position, but this was not necessary. The French detained	

WAR DIARY or INTELLIGENCE SUMMARY

Army Form C. 2118.

126

Place	Date	Hour	Summary of Events and Information	Remarks and references to Appendices
THIESCOURT ELINCOURT	1917 Nov 26		where the Battalion, which had proceeded to ELINCOURT and were billeted there during the night.	P.W.S
ROUVILLERS	27th		The Bath. marched to ROUVILLERS, arriving there in the afternoon and billeted for the night.	P.W.S
"	28th		The Battalion was ordered to take up a position outside the village during the morning and occupied same until 1p.m. when they marched to CINQUEUX and billeted the night.	P.A.S P.W.S
CINQUEUX	29th		The Battalion left CINQUEUX in the morning and marched to NOGENT-SUR-L'OISE, where they camped in a field on arrival and entrained at about 9pm for EBBICOURT	P.W.S P.A.S
NOGENT-SUR-L'OISE EBBICOURT	30th		arriving there at 5 a.m. The Bath marched from EBBICOURT and arrived at BACOUEL at 11am, billeting there for the night.	P.W.S
BACOUEL	31st		Draft of 7 Officers and 330 Other Ranks joined Battalion from No. 14 Entrenching Battalion. (K.O.Y.L.I.) The time table of the Bath transport during the above transition was:- 21st CLASTRES,, 22nd BEAUMONT-EN-BEINE 23rd MUIRANCOURT 24th LAGNY, 25th PESSONS-SUR-MATZ 26th BIENVILLE 27th ROUVILLERS 28th CINQUEUX 29th NOGENT-SUR-L'OISE 30th ST REMY-EN-L'EAU 31st HAUDIVILLERS.	P.W.S

Army Form C. 2118.

WAR DIARY
or
INTELLIGENCE SUMMARY.
(Erase heading not required.)

Instructions regarding War Diaries and Intelligence Summaries are contained in F.S. Regs., Part II. and the Staff Manual respectively. Title pages will be prepared in manuscript.

(127)

Place	Date	Hour	Summary of Events and Information	Remarks and references to Appendices
BACOUEL	1918 Mch 31st		SUMMARY of Casualties during period 21st to 31st March 1918. Mch 21st 20 Officers and 525 other Ranks MISSING 23rd/31st 10 Officers and 17 O.R. Wounded 5 O.R. Killed	

P.W.Nott Major
Commanding, 16th H.B.P. Bde.

41st Inf.Bde.
14th Div.

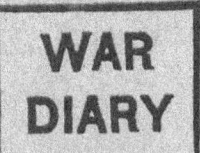

7th BATTN. THE RIFLE BRIGADE.

A P R I L

1 9 1 8

CONFIDENTIAL 4/14

WAR DIARY OF

7th Battn. The Rifle Brigade

FROM 1-4-18 TO 30-4-18

(VOLUME XXXV)

P.N. Scott MAJOR

Commdg 7th Bn. The Rifle Bde

FIELD

16-5-18.

WAR DIARY
INTELLIGENCE SUMMARY

Army Form C. 2118.

(129)

Place	Date 1918	Hour	Summary of Events and Information	Remarks and references to Appendices
BACOUEL	Apl 1st	8.30am	Proceeded to Boves in Buses, arriving about midday, then marched to Divisional Reserve in T.22.d Sheet 62D. Remaining here until 8pm when the Battalion moved forward to DORMART Sector and relieved a portion of General SEELY'S Cavalry detachment. Situation was quiet throughout the night and remained so	P.W.J
DORMART Sub Sect	Apl 2nd		until 5.30pm, when a heavy enemy barrage caused several casualties. The Battalion was relieved by Units of the 141st Regt (French) during the night and marched to BLANGY WOOD N.36 (Sheet 62D) where the Division was concentrating in Reserve.	P.W.J
	Apl 3rd		Major Thornton proceeded to Lt Col WHITMORE'S HdQrs in VAIRE Wood, and arranged details of relief, and Reconnoitred position to be held in the afternoon.	P.W.J
		8pm	Battalion marched to Bois de VAIRE, where guides failed to present, causing some confusion owing to troops occupying wrong positions. Adjustment had not been completed when the Enemy attacked the following morning. Some digging was done throughout the night. Situation was fairly quiet.	
	Apl 4th	6.20am	The enemy opened a heavy bombardment on the Battalion front and in rear, which continued in intensity for 2 hours. The enemy commenced an attack at about 7.15am Observation was bad owing to rain and mist. From the fire on the right flank it was apparent that he had broken through, but the Battalion line remained intact until 9.30am when the enemy had broken through on the right flank. It became so serious that a withdrawal to a position 500 yards in	P.W.J

Place	Date	Hour	Summary of Events and Information	Remarks and references to Appendices
VAIRE WOOD Vicinity.	Apl 4th		rear had to be effected to avoid an encircling move, which appeared to be imminent owing to the left flank having also been pressed back. The new position was held for about 2 hours, during which time the Battalion suffered heavy casualties owing to an intense bombardment of positions held. In the meantime the Enemy had continued to press his advance on the flanks, more especially the right and this necessitated a further withdrawal in order to secure touch with the flanks. A new position was taken up on ridge in P.8 and 13 (Sheet 62 D). During this withdrawal Coys became split up into small parties, emergent upon heavy enemy artillery and machine gun fire, and a considerable portion of Battalion occupied a line in rear of HAMEL. These positions were held until the night	P.W.S
	Apl 5th		of 5th April, when the Battalion details were relieved by Australian troops.	P.W.S
	Apl 6th		The Battalion took up a position in Army Reserve line from O.27a to O.21a (Sheet 62 D) and were engaged in strengthening the line, and constructing Centres of resistance capable of bringing flanking fire on the line, on each flank, until relieved	
	Apl 7th		about 7.30 pm. by the 30th Australian Battalion. Battalion proceeded to ST. FUSCIEN	P.W.S
	" 8th		arriving there in the early hours of the morning. The remainder of the day was	P.W.S
	" 9th		spent in resting, reorganising and cleaning up.	P.W.S

Army Form C. 2118.

WAR DIARY
or
INTELLIGENCE SUMMARY.
(Erase heading not required.)

Place	Date	Hour	Summary of Events and Information	Remarks and references to Appendices
	1918			
ST. FUSCIEN	Apr 10th	4.30am	The Battalion marched to SALEUX and entrained for GAMACHES, detraining at latter place at 3pm and marched to EMBREVILLE where the Battalion billeted.	P.M.S
	" 11th		Resting and cleaning up. Battalion marched to EU at 11pm and entrained there	P.M.S
	" 12th		at 3am for HESDIN, arriving at latter place at about 9am. The Battalion marched to COUPELLE VIEILLE, arriving there about 6.30pm and billeted the night.	P.M.S
	" 13th		at COUPELLE VIEILLE	P.M.S
	" 14th		Moved to LISBOURG about midday.	P.M.S
	" 15th		Battalion received drafts from 8th & 9th R.B and formed into Composite Battalion (7th 8th & 9th Btns D'Battn.) for tactical purposes as a temporary measure and marched to MOLINGHEM. Lt.Col Hon N.G.Blyth C.O., Major Young 2nd i/c and Lt Crowther Adjutant. Strength 30 Officers. 1030 other Ranks. Battalion moved to GUARBEP/S 21st	
	16/26		Work on G.H.Q. Defence line between AIRE and LILLERS. Major M.Sen rejoined 19th.	P.M.S
	27th		2 officers and 382 other Ranks of 7th R.B. proceeded to ETAP/S Base. Remainder of Battalion, consisting of Bnth. Training Staff, remained at GUARBEQUE and	P.M.S
	28th		moved the following day to LISBOURG.	P.M.S

Army Form C. 2118.

WAR DIARY
or
INTELLIGENCE SUMMARY.
(Erase heading not required.)

(132)

Place	Date	Hour	Summary of Events and Information	Remarks and references to Appendices
	1918			
LISBOURG	19th		Moved to FRESSIN. Major P.A. Scott assumes Command of Bn Training Staff, 2Lt S.James Asst.	P.M. P.M.
FRESSIN	30th		FRESSIN. Battn. Training staff undergoing specialist training.	
			SUMMARY OF CASUALTIES during month.	
			Officers. 6 Wounded (Major N.S. Thornton Bm chief of wounds 10/4/18)	P.M.
			Other Ranks. 21 Killed	
			91 Missing (since reduced to 67)	
			63 Wounded (since increased to 84)	

P.A. Scott
Major
Commdg. 9th The Rifle Brigade

CONFIDENTIAL

WAR DIARY

OF

7th Bn. THE RIFLE BRIGADE

FROM. 1-5-18   To 31-5-18

(VOLUME XXXVI)

P.N. Scott Major
Commdg 7th Bn. The Rifle Bde.

31/5/18

Army Form C. 2118.

WAR DIARY
or
INTELLIGENCE SUMMARY.
(Erase heading not required.)

Instructions regarding War Diaries and Intelligence Summaries are contained in F. S. Regs., Part II. and the Staff Manual respectively. Title pages will be prepared in manuscript.

(133)

Place	Date	Hour	Summary of Events and Information	Remarks and references to Appendices
FRESSIN	May 1st 1918		FRESSIN. Training Staff undergoing specialist Training	
EMBRY	2nd		Moved to Embry.	
-do-	3rd		Specialist Training. Transport inspected by the Commanding Officer	
-do-	4th		-do-	
-do-	5th		Divine Service. Recreational Training	
-do-	6th		Transport provided on Route March. Route. EMBRY – LEBIEZ – HESMOND – BIMBERS – to billets Specialist + Recreational Training	
-do-	7th		-Ditto-	
-do-	8th		-do- Capt A N Warren proceeds to Base E/able Awards for gallantry in the field during recent operations	
-do-	9th		Major N S Thornton (Scinde) M.C.; 2/Lt S James and O A Johns M.C., 2/Lt H Spencer M.M. and 234490 Sgt. 2/J Pugh, 2/Lt H J Roe and 25283 Pte H Spencer M.M. Both Specialist and recreational Training	
-do-	10th		Specialist + Recreational Training. 2/Lt C R Wills and 7/2nd T/- J D Athan (K.O.Y.L.I.) attached 7th R.I.R) awarded M.M.E. for gallantry in the field during recent Operations	
-do-	11th		Both. Specialist and recreational Training Transport personnel less Establishment for Battn Training Staff proceeded to C.U.C.O.	
-do-	12			

WAR DIARY
or
INTELLIGENCE SUMMARY.

(Erase heading not required.)

Army Form C. 2118.

Instructions regarding War Diaries and Intelligence Summaries are contained in F. S. Regs., Part II. and the Staff Manual respectively. Title pages will be prepared in manuscript.

(134)

Place	Date	Hour	Summary of Events and Information	Remarks and references to Appendices
EMBRY	1918 13th		Capt C.A.M. Van Millingen M.C. joined. Specialist & Recreational Training.	P.M.P
-do-	14th		Batln Training Staff carried out an outpost scheme as a Brigade.	P.M.P
-do-	15th		Entrained for BOESEGHEM.	P.M.P
BOESEGHEM	16th		Specialist & Recreational Training	P.M.P
do	17th		Commanding Officer Inspection.	P.M.P
do	18th		Specialist and recreational training. Officers reconnoitred route to Les Ciseaux area and sort that was engaged upon.	P.M.P
LES CISEAUX	19th		3rd Anniversary of Battalions arrival in France. Specialist & recreational training.	P.M.P
-do-	20th/25th		Reconnaissance of Sub Sector, and guide posts and routes. Defensive scheme compiled for STEENBECQUE area.	P.M.P
-do-	26th		75th day in commemoration of Rhine advancement held. Sports, dinner and concert.	P.M.P
-do-	27th		Specialist & Recreational Training	P.M.P
-do-	28th		ditto	P.M.P
-do-	29th		ditto	P.M.P
-do-	30th		ditto	P.M.P
-do-	31st		ditto Officers Physical Training Class.	P.M.P

P. W. Mark Major
Commanding 17th Royal Rifles

www.ingramcontent.com/pod-product-compliance
Lightning Source LLC
Chambersburg PA
CBHW080858230426
43663CB00013B/2572